A Theory of Political Decision Modes

A Theory of Political Decision Modes

Intraparty Decision Making in Switzerland

by Jürg Steiner
and Robert H. Dorff

The University of North Carolina Press

Chapel Hill

© 1980 The University of North Carolina Press

All rights reserved
Manufactured in the United States of America
Library of Congress Catalog Card Number 79-16390
ISBN 0-8078-1406-7

Library of Congress Cataloging in Publication Data

Steiner, Jürg
    A theory of political decision modes.

    Bibliography: p.
    Includes index.
    1. Freisinnig-demokratische Partei der Schweiz. 2.
Bern (Canton)—Politics and government. 3. Political
science—Decision making. I. Dorff, Robert H.,
1951– joint author. II. Title.
JN9219.A55S73   301.15'54   79-16390
ISBN 0-8078-1406-7

To Rudolf Wildenmann
teacher and friend

Contents

115619

Tables

Chart

Preface

This book is based on a study of decision making in the Free Democratic party in the canton of Bern, Switzerland, in 1969–70. Using the methods of participant observation, interview, and analysis of documents, we studied 111 meetings of the various party committees and identified 466 conflicts in those meetings. Analyzing these conflicts, we tried to discover with what modes they were decided. We distinguished the following four decision modes: majority decision (employed in 12 percent of the cases), decision by amicable agreement (21 percent), nondecision (30 percent), and decision by interpretation (37 percent). To explain this variation among these four decision modes, we assumed that political decision makers try to optimize the following four values: power, solidarity, rectitude, and time.

Although this project grew out of an interest in the literature on consociational theory, it is not just another version of the consociational theory. Our critique of the consociational literature (see chapter 1) led us to an attempt to develop a more general theory of political decision modes. Chapter 2 presents the framework within which we tried to develop this theory, a framework that can be applied to any face-to-face group. In chapter 3 we describe why we used decisions in intraparty conflicts as our data base. Chapter 4 shows how the typology of the four decision modes was developed from the data base. Chapters 5 through 8 present a discussion of the statistical methods that we used to explain the variation among the four decision modes, including a bivariate analysis (chapter 6), a discriminant analysis (chapter 7), and a simulation (chapter 8). Finally, in the last two chapters we offer some comments concerning strategies for further research and the normative implications of our research.

We must thank the members of the Free Democratic party of the canton of Bern and in particular the party president Arthur Hänsenberger and the party secretary Urs Kunz for their generous granting of access to their meetings and documents and for their willingness to be interviewed. We are also grateful to the Swiss National Science Foundation for the financial support of the project. Furthermore, we should acknowledge the free access to computer time at the Institute for Research in Social Science at The University of North Carolina at Chapel Hill.

During the ten years that we have been working on this project, many friends and colleagues have given us valuable advice and encouragement. We should like to thank in particular William Keech, Duncan MacRae, Jeffrey Obler, George Rabinowitz, Donald Searing, Alan Stern, James White, Martin Zechman (all at The University of North Carolina at Chapel Hill), Franz Lehner (University of Mannheim), and Arend Lijphart (University of California at San Diego). Mr. and Mrs. Philip H. Dorff and Mr. and Mrs. Willi Hüske also deserve special recognition. Finally, Pamela DeLargy provided helpful assistance in the preparation of the final manuscript.

Chapel Hill   Jürg Steiner
and East Lansing   Robert H. Dorff
January 1979

PART I

The Problem

CHAPTER 1

A Critique of the Literature on Consociational Theory

Consociational theory was first presented to a broad audience at the World Congress of the International Political Science Association in 1967.[1] At that time, the most innovative aspect of the theory was that the mode of decision making was treated in a systematic way as a theoretical variable. In the 1950s and 1960s, mainstream theory building had tended to neglect the mode of decision making, often treating it as a "black box." Heavy emphasis had been placed on variables of the environment such as economic development, urbanization, education, relative deprivation of the population, and so on. One of the main champions of that orientation has been Gabriel A. Almond, but in a recent book Almond himself recognizes the need for opening the "black box" of political decision making, arguing that "human choice, bargaining, risk-taking, skill, and chance must be thrown in to explain the actual outcome."[2]

With its emphasis on decision modes, the current literature on consociational theory is a good starting point for the presentation of our research project. First, we will briefly summarize the theory. Then we will criticize it on three grounds, and on the basis of the critique we will say how our project attempts to look beyond current consociational theory to a more general theory of decision modes.

Consociational Theory

Consociational theory can best be tested in countries that have strongly developed cultural groups. The crux of the theory is that the decision-making behavior of the political elites affects the level of violence among such groups. Two main types of political decision making have been identified. In the words of Gerhard Lehm-bruch, they are:

a. the competitive pattern of conflict management (the fundamental de-vice of which is the majority principle);
b. the noncompetitive, "cartelized" pluralist pattern (which works by *amicabilis compositio*, "amicable agreement").[3]

Instead of amicable agreement, Arend Lijphart uses the term *con-sociational decision making*, which we will use, too. As Brian Barry has correctly pointed out, there is some confusion in the literature about the terms *consociationalism* and *consociational democracy*.[4] These terms are used interchangeably in a descriptive and in a theoretical sense: descriptively, they designate a particular type of decision making whereas theoretically they refer to a complex theory stipulating the pattern of decision making as a key variable. We will speak of *consociational decision making* if we mean the descriptive term and of *consociational theory* if we are referring to the theoretical meaning of the term.

Consociational theory postulates that in countries that are sub-culturally strongly segmented consociational decision making is more likely to lead to peaceful relations among the subcultures than is competitive decision making. Lijphart has embedded this central hypothesis into various other propositions. He suggests that the following four facilitating conditions must be present if con-sociational decision making is to be implemented:

1. the elites [must] have the ability to accommodate the divergent inter-ests and demands of the subcultures;
2. this requires that [the elites] have the ability to transcend cleavages and to join in a common effort with the elites of rival subcultures;
3. this in turn depends on [the elites'] commitment to the maintenance of the system and to the improvement of its cohesion and stability;
4. finally, all of the above requirements are based on the assumption that the elites understand the perils of political fragmentation.[5]

In a further step, Lijphart indicates preconditions under which the above four requirements are most likely to be fulfilled. These preconditions can be summarized in three main categories. The first category relates to intersubcultural relations among elites. Lijphart argues that the following preconditions are conducive to consociational decision making: (a) the existence of external threats to the country; (b) a multiple balance of power among the subcultures instead of either a dual balance or a clear hegemony by one subculture; (c) a relatively low total load on the decision-making apparatus. The second category concerns intersubcultural relations at the mass level; here the crucial precondition for consociational decision making consists of distinct lines of cleavage among the subcultures. The third category involves the elite-mass relationships within the individual subcultures for which Lijphart enumerates the following favorable preconditions for consociational decision making: (a) a high degree of internal political cohesion of the subcultures; (b) an adequate articulation of the interests of the subcultures; (c) a widespread approval of the principle of government by elite cartel. In addition to these preconditions for consociational decision making, Lijphart's theory includes a side effect or consequence of this particular mode of decision making, namely, "a certain degree of immobilism."

Lehmbruch does not spell out consociational theory in the same detail. His major contribution, which goes beyond Lijphart's, is his strong emphasis on the historical dimension. He gives great weight to the argument that consociational decision making can be understood only if it is viewed in its historical context. For example, Lehmbruch argues that, in Austria,

political parties continue to manage their conflicts according to those rules of the parliamentary game which (as for example the *Junktim*) were used in the Hapsburg Empire to establish the fragile modus vivendi of the different nations of the monarchy, and the political usages of the Republic still bear the impact of the politics of *Ausgleich*, that is, the settlement of ethnic antagonisms by institutional devices such as patronage, committees representing the different groups, demarcation of autonomous spheres of influence, and so on.[6]

Our critique identifies three ambiguities in current consociational theory:

1. It is unclear to what universe of cases the theory applies because the concept of subcultural segmentation is not clearly defined.
2. It is unclear precisely how the predominant decision-making pattern of a country can be classified as either competitive or consociational.

3. It is unclear precisely how the variables of the theory are causally related.

The Theoretical Universe:
Subculturally Segmented Countries

To help define the nature of subculturally segmented countries, we offer Switzerland as a case in point. The authors writing about consociational theory assume that Switzerland is subculturally segmented. Recently, however, scholars like Raimund Germann and Brian Barry have raised some questions with regard to this assumption.[7]

At first glance the question whether Switzerland is subculturally strongly segmented may seem rhetorical, for the Swiss speak four different languages and practice two major religions. It would appear that this diversity alone should qualify Switzerland a priori for membership in the universe of consociational theory. But the matter is not so simple, for it seems important to differentiate conceptually between *cultural diversity* and *subcultural segmentation*. By cultural diversity we mean simply that the members of a political system differ with regard to cultural attributes, such as language and religion. The people sharing the same cultural attributes may or may not develop a sense of identity that distinguishes them from other members of the system. We speak of subcultural segmentation only if such feelings of self-identification exist. Responses to attitudinal survey questions, frequency of interactions among the members of a subculture, and organizational ties within a subculture can be used as indicators of the differences between cultural diversity and subcultural segmentation. The concept of cultural diversity is often poorly distinguished from the concept of subcultural segmentation and we agree with Hans Daalder who notes cogently that "demographic variables are often assumed to be of attitudinal importance, with little investigation of the degree to which this is actually true."[8] Switzerland, of course, has strong cultural diversity with regard to languages and religions and we might employ the formula of Douglas W. Rae and Michael Taylor to compute the degree of that cultural diversity in an elegant and formal way.[9] However, we are interested not in the level of cultural diversity, but in the level of subcultural segmentation, and it is that emphasis that makes it difficult to arrive at accurate data for Switzerland.

The Department of Political Science at the University of Geneva has conducted a broad, systematic analysis of Swiss political cleavages, based on a national survey sample of the Swiss electorate in 1972.[10] These data reveal interesting political differences among the groups formed by Swiss linguistic, religious, and class cleavages. For example, 30 percent of the French-speaking and 16 percent of the German-speaking Swiss consider themselves primarily members of their linguistic group rather than members of their canton or nation.[11] Although there are no linguistic parties, language differences, as demonstrated by Henry H. Kerr, have a bearing on voters' preferences; controlling for religion and class, Kerr found that French-speaking Swiss are more sympathetic to the parties of the left than are the German-speaking Swiss.[12]

The survey did not establish the degree to which the Swiss consider themselves members of their religious group. However, clear differences in partisan choice were revealed: practicing Catholics tend to support the Christian-Democrats, while nonpracticing Catholics and Protestants are more likely to vote for the other major parties—the Free Democrats, the Social Democrats and the Swiss People's party. A link between social class and partisan choice was also established; not surprisingly, manual workers vote most often for the Social Democratic party.

The three cleavages cross-cut one another. The relative importance of the cleavages as well as their cross-cutting structure vary considerably from one canton to another. For many issues the cleavages are politically salient at the cantonal rather than at the national level. There are many impressionistic studies of Swiss subcultures,[13] but nobody has as yet undertaken a systematic study to determine the precise number and relative strengths of the subcultures at the cantonal and national levels. At present, we can only state that the Swiss subcultural structure is extremely complex; a great number of actors engage in subcultural confrontation in the cantonal and national arenas.

The Geneva survey also offers age-cohort data, which provide a means to assess how group identities and partisan choices have varied over time. These data suggest that the ties between the individual and his linguistic and religious group may have declined and this, in turn, may indicate a more general decline in the degree of subcultural segmentation. Among younger voters, and especially among Catholic voters, religion and religiosity are less salient considerations than they have been in the past. Language differences, which were particularly important for the generation that reached political maturity during World War I, are likewise a less prominent determinant of political choice. The impact of class differences, on the other hand, has remained fairly constant over several generations. The survey also revealed that the sense of national identity among the Swiss has become more prevalent. Among the French-speaking Swiss, for example, only 31 percent of the older age-cohort, but 55 percent of the youngest, think of themselves primarily as Swiss.

Is Switzerland still subculturally segmented or has it become a relatively homogeneous country? There is no easy answer because no yardsticks exist; no simple computation formula is available for subcultural segmentation similar to the one Rae and Taylor have developed for cultural diversity. Switzerland illustrates nicely the difficulties of delimiting the universe of cases to which consociational theory should apply. If we classify Switzerland as subculturally segmented, what other European countries can still be considered homogeneous? Denmark and Sweden would most likely be two cases. But how about France, Italy, and Great Britain for example? Do these countries not have subcultures that are equally strong as those in Switzerland? Perhaps. Another example: If the Austria of today is subculturally segmented, would West Germany not also fall into this category? But perhaps the Austria of the 1970s, unlike the Austria of the 1950s, is no longer subculturally segmented. If the Netherlands was subculturally segmented in the 1950s, is it still so today?[14] The literature on consociational theory offers no clear answers to such questions and so it remains somewhat ambiguous to what universe of cases the theory should apply.

Consociational Decision Making versus
Competitive Decision Making

A debate has also developed about whether several countries have been properly classified as either consociational or competitive. The debate shows that the two modes of decision making are not sufficiently clearly defined. On one hand, doubts have arisen whether countries that have traditionally been classified as consociational, such as Switzerland, Austria, Belgium, and the Netherlands, really have more competitive elements than is commonly assumed. On the other hand, the argument is made that countries like Sweden, Norway, and even Great Britain are more consociational than is generally assumed.[15]

Lijphart states that "the grand coalition is the most typical and obvious, but not the only possible consociational solution." Advisory committees may be of great importance in a consociational society, and Lijphart considers the "powerful Social and Economic Council of the Netherlands a perfect example of a cartel of economic elites." These committees may also be "ad hoc bodies, such as the cartels of top party leaders that negotiated the 'school pacts' in Holland in 1917 and in Belgium in 1958." According to Lijphart, "the degree of competitive or cooperative behavior by elites must . . . be seen as a continuum," so that most countries would have "some consociational features." As examples Lijphart mentions the grand coalition in West Germany from 1966 to 1969 and "a consociational arrangement" in the United States after the Civil War "that gave to the Southern leaders—by such means as chairmanships of key Congressional committees and the filibuster—a crucial position in federal decision making."[16]

Lijphart's efforts seem to establish a good sense of what is meant by consociational decision making, but a closer look at individual countries reveals a number of ambiguities. Switzerland is again a good case to help define the problem. For some time Switzerland has been treated in the literature as one of the clearest models of consociational decision making. However, Barry has recently expressed doubts about whether Switzerland is "preponderantly" consociational.[17] An analysis of decision making in Switzerland indicates how difficult it is to classify the predominant decision-making pattern of a country.

The most obvious sign of elite accommodation in Switzerland is the composition of the collegial Swiss executive, the Federal Council, which is elected for the full legislative period of four years and is not subject to a vote of no-confidence.[18] The Federal Council includes members of the four major political parties. The Christian Democrats, the Free Democrats, and the Social Democrats each have two representatives on the Council, and the Swiss People's party has one representative. This allocation of positions on the Council is roughly proportional to the parties' share of the popular vote. Given the size of the Federal Council, no other party is entitled to a seat based on its share of the popular vote. The practice of having all or most major parties represented in the Council has a long tradition in Swiss political history. The last step in the equitable distribution of executive power was taken in 1959 when the Social Democrats were accorded a proportionate share of seats. Efforts are also taken to have the "appropriate" mix of linguistic, religious, and cantonal representatives.

This spirit of accommodation, mirrored in the distribution of seats on the Federal Council, may spill over into the formulation of public policy. Indeed, numerous studies of Swiss decision making underline the willingness of Swiss political leaders to compromise in order to avoid conflict.[19] But compromises are common also in political systems that are not normally considered consociational. Moreover, there are several features of the Swiss decision-making process that do not conform to the consociational model of decision making.

First, the Swiss parties that are partners in the Federal Council do not formally agree to support an articulated set of policies. Until 1967, policy issues were never formally discussed by the Swiss coalition partners. For the legislative period 1967 to 1971, the Federal Council, for the first time, formulated a paper containing "guidelines" for governmental activities. These guidelines were not nearly as formal as platforms developed in other political settings. They were negotiated, not by the government parties but by the federal councilors after they had been elected for a four-year term. The guidelines were not binding; after four years the legislature discussed a report issued by the Federal Council on the ful-fillment of the guidelines, but the legislature had no sanctions to indicate their dissatisfaction with the report. After the 1971 election, the government parties themselves agreed on a set of policies to be implemented in the coming session, but these policies were formulated in such a general and vague way that their actual significance was minimal. After the 1975 election, the government parties gave up the idea of formally recording an agreement on policy goals. The Federal Council, however, again formulated guidelines for its governmental activities. The point here is that no specially articulated consensus on Swiss public policy exists among the major national political parties. Any agreement that emerges takes place on a largely ad hoc basis.

Second, although there is agreement concerning the party distribution in the Federal Council, there is no agreement among the major parties concerning the particular individuals who should be elected to the Federal Council. The candidates are presented to the Federal Assembly (both houses of the parliament meeting in a joint session) by the individual parties and not by the government coalition as a whole. Occasionally, a candidate who is supported by a particular party will *not* be elected by the Federal Assembly. This usually happens when a party nominates a candidate from one of its extreme factions and, as a consequence, the other parties do not find the nominee acceptable.

Third, just as the Swiss political leaders avoid conflict through compromise, there are instances when compromises are not reached and decisions are either made through nonconsociational means or are not made at all.[20] Disagreement among Swiss political leaders is not uncommon. Since the deliberations and votes in the Federal Council are secret, it is not possible to ascertain the actual degree of consensus among the councilors. But parliamentary sessions are open and therefore the disagreement within and among parties as well as the conflicts between the parliament and the Federal Council are visible.[21]

Fourth, the existence of a referendum procedure also weakens the consociational character of the decision-making process. Many key policy issues in Switzerland are decided through the referendum, and by its very character, the referendum is an institution that permits a majority to impose its solution on the minority. It should be noted, however, that the referendum is essentially a process of mass decision making and not of elite decision making, and consociational theory is explicitly concerned with elite decision making and not with mass decision making. Yet it is also true that the referendum is important for the resolution of conflicts among the government parties: if no solution can be found in the Federal Council or in the parliament, the conflict is often settled through the referendum.

The preceding discussion suggests that since the Swiss decision-making process includes consociational as well as nonconsociational elements, it is not a simple matter to classify the Swiss system. Neither the consociational nor the competitive elements are so dominant that Switzerland could be neatly classified as one of the two types. It also seems difficult to classify Switzerland on a continuum from consociational to competitive since the major problem would be to determine what weight to give to the different elements of the decision-making process. How important is the federal level as opposed to the cantonal and the communal levels? Should decisions in the Federal Council be weighted more than those of the parliament? Although it might not be impossible to solve these problems of weighting in a satisfactory way, it would certainly be quite difficult.

Austria, the Netherlands, and Belgium are the three other countries that are traditionally classified as consociational. For these countries, too, a closer look at the decision-making process raises doubts about whether the traditional classification is appropriate. Having described the problems of classification in some detail for Switzerland, we can be briefer with these other countries.[22] In Austria, from 1945 to 1966 the two largest parties—the Austrian People's party (OeVP) and the Socialist Party of Austria (SPOe)—which together have never won less than 83 percent of the vote in any postwar parliamentary election, formed one great coalition after another. In 1966, the OeVP formed Austria's first postwar one-party government and since 1970 the SPOe has led successive one-party governments. Can we conclude from this that decision making in Austria was consociational from 1945 until 1966 and then turned competitive after 1966? Students of Austrian politics do not concur on whether the 1966 demise of the great coalition was simply a change in political form or whether it represented a substantial alteration in the distribution of political authority and the decision-making process. On one hand, Rodney Stiefbold claims that the "dissolution of the Great Coalition in 1966 amounted to a change not merely of governments but, to a great extent, also of regimes."[23] Kurt Steiner, on the other hand, supports the view that although the Austrian elite has evolved toward more competitive relations, the 1966 shift "did not involve an abrupt change in elite behavior." He further quotes approvingly a high-ranking Socialist politician who commented in a 1968 interview that "only the shape of the top of the iceberg—the composition of the cabinet—had been altered."[24] Along this line, Gerhard Lehmbruch notes that the spirit of accommodation between the coalition partners had begun to erode in the early 1960s and he observes that prior to 1966, the OeVP and SPOe often practiced "Bereichsopposition" whereas since 1966 they have frequently engaged in "Bereichskoalition."[25] That elite cooperation has survived one-party cabinets is suggested by Heinz Fischer who has demonstrated that between 1966 and 1973 about 80 percent of all parliamentary votes, including many on key foreign policy and economic issues, were unanimous.[26]

Several other indicators suggest the persistence of consociationalism: great coalitions are still common among the Länder (state) governments; the major economic interest groups continue to display a remarkable consensus and willingness to compromise;[27] and one-party governments have not markedly departed from the application of the proportionality principle in the bureaucracies.[28] Manfried Welan perceptively describes how elite behavior differs in the public and the nonpublic arenas. He argues that although cooperation between the leaders of the two large parties has continued after 1966 in the nonpublic arena, a change to a more competitive behavior pattern has taken place in the public arena.[29]

In order to test consociational theory it would be important to determine how the predominant mode of decision making in a country has developed over time. Such longitudinal data would indicate whether the level of hostility among the subcultures of a country could indeed be explained by the predominant mode of decision making. The Austrian example shows how difficult it is to say whether and at what point in time a change took place from consociational to competitive decision making. Similar difficulties emerge in the case of the Netherlands. Lijphart argues that the 1950s were the "heyday" of consociational decision making; he sees a much more competitive pattern in the 1970s.[30] The literature does not clarify how strong this change was and at what points in time it has taken place. Was the change in the Netherlands stronger or weaker, earlier or later than in Austria? The conceptual ambiguity in the distinction between consociational and competitive decision making does not provide an answer to this question.

The conceptual problem of distinguishing between consociational and competitive decision making is perhaps most apparent in the linguistic conflict in Belgium. Observers disagree over exactly how the Belgian elites have reacted to the linguistic conflict. James Dunn points to the erosion of elite accommodation since the early 1960s,[31] while Eric Nordlinger stresses how through cooperation the elites have played a positive role in regulating the conflict.[32] That Dunn and Nordlinger offer these conflicting views is due, we would argue, to a conceptual confusion: depending on what criteria one applies, elite relations during the linguistic crisis could be categorized as conciliatory or competitive, as conforming to or departing from the consociational pattern. If we take as our yardstick countries like Northern Ireland or Cyprus, Belgium certainly appears to be relatively consociational. But compared with Switzerland, Belgium seems quite competitive. Belgium also seems at least as competitive as Norway or Sweden, countries that are usually not classified as consociational. The overall conclusion of this section is that it is difficult to classify countries as predominantly consociational or competitive. The reason for this difficulty lies not only in the lack of sufficient empirical data but also, and even more so, in the conceptual ambiguity of the distinction between consociational and competitive decision making.

Recently this conceptual confusion has even been increased by the fact that the term *corporatism* is again becoming widely used in the social science literature. Martin Heisler, for example, speaks of neocorporatism, using the concept more or less as a synonym for consociationalism. In a neocorporate system "spokesmen of voluntary associations, religious denomination-based groups, agencies of socioeconomic representation, governmental bodies, mixed or quasi-governmental agencies, and expressly political entities (such as parties) participate in the decision-making process on a continuing basis. Access is established and structured. The consequent decision-making structure has been described by Lijphart as a 'cartel of elites.'"[33] Leo Panitch objects to the conflation of "consociationalism and corporatism" and warns against "utter confusion between the two." For Panitch the concept of corporatism stresses "the centrality of functional representation in socioeconomic policy-making. . . . The corporatist paradigm [is] understood to connote a political structure within advanced capitalism which integrates organized socioeconomic producer groups through a system of representation and cooperative mutual interaction at the leadership level and of mobilization and social control at the mass level."[34] Philippe C. Schmitter and Gerhard Lehmbruch also employ the term corporatism as distinct from consociationalism, with Schmitter further differentiating between state and societal corporatism and Lehmbruch differentiating between authoritarian and liberal corporatism.[35] It is not necessary in the present context to go further into the various definitions of corporatism. The main point is that the reappearance of the term corporatism and its unclear distinction from consociationalism have not made it easier to classify a country according to its predominant decision-making pattern.

Problems of Causality

A test of consociational theory must also solve the problem of how to measure the level of hostility among the subcultures of a country. This does not seem to be a particularly difficult task since publications like the *World Handbook of Political and Social Indicators* contain quite a few indicators for domestic violence.[36] But there are more problems involved with such indicators than one might at first expect. One difficulty is that hostility among subcultures is often not distinguished from other kinds of domestic violence. Thus, if the *World Handbook* indicates that in Belgium domestic violence produced ten deaths from 1948 to 1967, it remains unclear how many of these deaths were linked with conflicts among subcultures. Another difficulty is that the literature on consociational theory is somewhat vague about the exact meaning of the term *hostility*. It often remains unclear whether only physical or also psychological hostility should be included. In Austria, for example, a 1967 survey asked whether a government controlled by the other "Lager" would ever seriously endanger the welfare of the country.[37] An affirmative answer to this question certainly indicates feelings of psychological hostility between the two major Austrian subcultures, but it is not clear to what extent such psychological hostility is relevant for a test of consociational theory. Sometimes, the term *hostility* is replaced with the term *instability*, which is even more vague and consequently still more difficult to use.[38]

Until now we have only raised questions of measurement. Let us now assume that all these questions could be resolved so that we could determine the countries with subcultural segmentation and for each of these countries the predominant mode of decision making and the level of hostility among its subcultures. Let us further assume a tendency for consociational systems to have a low level of hostility among their subcultures. Would this necessarily be a positive test for consociational theory? Such a result would certainly lend some support to the theory and one could try to argue that consociational decision making is indeed the cause of low levels of hostility. But it would also be possible to reverse the causal relationship and make the argument that consociational decision making is not the cause but the consequence of low levels of hostility. Such an argument would make it necessary to search for other explanations of low levels of hostility. Since Switzerland, Austria, and the Netherlands are most often mentioned in support of consociational theory, we shall turn to them once again for illustrations. It is possible to find plausible explanations for the low level of hostility in each of these countries without referring to the predominant mode of decision making as an explanatory variable.

In Switzerland the high economic development may satisfy the demands of the various subcultures to such an extent that no strong feelings of relative deprivation arise.[39] It may also be important that the three major languages have about the same international prestige. This is not the case, for example, in Belgium, where the uneven international prestige of the two major languages is said to have contributed to many of the current problems. A third cause of the low level of hostility in Switzerland may be that the load on the central system is not very heavy. Because of the federal structure, many tricky problems are dealt with primarily at the cantonal and even at the local level. Switzerland's neutrality, too, reduces the load of problems that has to be handled by the central political arena. This brief discussion points out that there are other plausible explanations besides consociational decision making for the low level of hostility in Switzerland.

William Bluhm asserts that in Austria consociationalism has helped to create peaceful relations between the subcultures. He indicates that although "Lager" hostility was still pronounced in 1945, relations among political leaders were far more conciliatory than they had been during the First Republic. Stressing the significance of traumatic adult socialization, he ascribes this change to the fact that many postwar Austrian leaders had "suffered a common persecution under the Nazis, either in their persons or in the persons of close friends and party comrades, and this counted for a great deal in promoting mutual tolerance, respect and even affection."[40] While recognizing their basic differences in political values, the leaders of the rival "Lager," according to Bluhm, were still willing to resolve pressing issues through compromise; he names this spirit of cooperation "pragmatism of dissensus." Elite accommodation so effectively fostered social integration, he contends, that by the mid-1960s Austrian society had become subculturally relatively homogeneous.

However, Bluhm's interpretation raises several difficulties. First, the existence of subcultural enmity in 1945 is assumed but never convincingly documented. Perhaps the common wartime suffering had salutary effects on subcultural relations at the mass as well as at the elite levels. Perhaps most Austrian people shared the leaders' conviction that given the imperative of economic reconstruction, as well as the country's precarious international position, internal solidarity was essential. Second, that subcultural hostility has been so much more limited in the Second Austrian Republic than in the First may be attributed to changes other than those in the style of decision making. Thus Bluhm recognizes the contribution that postwar economic development made in establishing the necessary social and psychological bases for stable liberal democracy. But although he argues further that consociationalism facilitated the economic miracle, he cannot really demonstrate that the Austrian economic recovery would not have occurred in the absence of consociationalism. After all, the postwar economic boom took place in other European countries, such as France and West Germany, where majoritarian practices prevail. Furthermore, a decline in religiosity may explain why the traditional conflict between Catholics and anticlerics is no longer a pressing political issue.[41] In addition, in Austria, as in other highly industrialized societies, a more complex social stratification system, highlighted by a growing, diversified middle class as well as by a more heterogeneous working class, has developed over the past generations. The simple class dichotomy mirrored in the traditional "Lager" has become less relevant to Austrian politics;[42] consequently, many contemporary social issues cut across rather than between the "Lager." These considerations suggest that perhaps too much stress has been placed on the role of consociational decision making in establishing the political calm in postwar Austria.

According to Lijphart, the Netherlands in the 1950s was a strongly consociational society.[43] During this time, and up until the mid-1960s, an association did seem to exist between consociational decision making and low levels of subcultural hostility. But as with Switzerland and Austria, there is another plausible explanation for this low hostility, namely, that in the two decades following World War II perceived deprivation among the subcultures was not pronounced. No subculture was compelled to resort to violence in order to alleviate or escape subordination. By the late 1940s the Dutch subcultures had realized their emancipation. They had achieved the goals—state support for religious schools, universal suffrage, and a comprehensive social welfare program— that originally had spurred the organization of the blocs. Yet the pillars lingered, perhaps because the bloc leaders wanted them to. The leaders realized that their authority rested on the willingness of Dutch citizens to remain loyal to their respective subcultures.

This discussion of Switzerland, Austria, and the Netherlands indicates that variation in hostility can be accounted for in plausible ways without referring to the mode of decision making as an explanatory variable. To be sure, it is plausible to argue that the level of hostility depends on the mode of decision making, but it may also be that the mode of decision making depends on the level of hostility or that both these variables depend on a third variable such as economic development. The crucial point is that the simultaneous appearance of consociational decision making and a low level of hostility does not necessarily mean that the former is a cause of the latter.

A recent development in the debate about consociational theory has further complicated the question of causality. Several authors claim that in the long run consociational decision making may contribute to malaise and even to hostility. Raimund Germann uses Switzerland as a case in point to argue that consociational decision making is very damaging to the innovation capacity of a political system, since the process is very slow and the most conservative group always has a veto power. Germann also complains that elite cooperation prohibits the citizens from casting instrumental votes, for they are unable to replace one set of leaders with another. The lack of innovation and of meaningful political participation causes, following the analysis of Germann, frustrations on the part of the citizens. These frustrations may ultimately lead to the outbreak of violence.[44]

There are some empirical data that can be used in support of Germann's thesis. In a recent national survey, Ronald Inglehart and Dusan Sidjanski have found a diffuse sense of frustration among the Swiss population.[45] This frustration was recently expressed in some referenda in which proposals supported by all major parties were defeated or only barely accepted. Max Imboden, too, has noticed growing frustration in Switzerland; as early as 1964 he spoke of a "Malaise Helvetique," an expression that has been widely used since then.[46] An obvious argument against linking the Malaise Helvetique with consociational decision making is that in countries without consociationalism, like France and Italy, frustration may be even greater. However, in comparisons such as these, many variables do not remain constant. Thus it may be that the level of frustration in France and Italy might be far greater if these countries had practiced consociational decision making for a long period of time.

Germann's thesis is strongly supported by data from Austria. During the great coalition from 1945 to 1966, the population increasingly complained that the system was not innovative enough and that the citizens did not have sufficient means for effective political participation. In Austria, too, there was more and more talk of a developing malaise. Since the dissolution of the great coalition in 1966 and the change to one-party governments, the level of frustration seems to have decreased in Austria.[47]

Conclusion

Our critical observations about consociational theory should not obscure the view expressed at the beginning of this chapter that the theory is innovative in the sense that it uses the mode of decision making as a theoretical variable. The theory has raised significant questions about the decision-making strategies of politicians. The literature on consociational theory has been very stimulating in the development of our research. Having worked for some time within the consociational-theory framework, we now plan to move in the direction of a more general theory of political decision modes. The major change in our research strategy is that we will take as units of analysis not political systems but individual conflicts. Thus we will reduce the conflicts of a political system to their individual elements. One may call this a change from a macro-theoretical to a micro-theoretical level. In our view, working at the micro-level of individual conflicts has at least three advantages.

First, it is certainly easier to classify decision modes for individual conflicts than for aggregates of conflicts. By examining the subtleties of how individual conflicts are decided, we should be able to construct a more satisfactory typology than is currently used in consociational theory. If we develop a good typology of decision modes at the micro-level, we should be able to approach the question at the macro-level in a new and more meaningful way. In chapter 9 we will return to the issue of how to transfer the typology of decision modes from the micro-level to the macro-level.

Second, by changing the level of analysis, we should be able to grasp better the causal relationships among the theoretically interesting variables. Working with individual conflicts will allow us to increase the number of cases so greatly that it will become feasible to apply more sophisticated statistical methods to the detection of causal flows. It will also become possible to observe more carefully in what time sequences the variables change so that it will be easier to identify cause and effect.

A third advantage of working at the micro-level is that we will be able to compare different kinds of conflicts. Thus we will be able to study not only conflicts *between* linguistic and religious groups but also conflicts *within* each of these groups. Furthermore, conflicts that have no direct reference to cultural groups can be included in the analysis, which will enable us to aim at a general theory of decision modes. We hope to take some steps in that direction in the following chapters.

CHAPTER 2

The Theoretical Framework

As we elaborated in the first chapter, our units of analysis are individual conflicts. Our research attempts to describe and explain the decision modes with which these conflicts are resolved. In this chapter, we will outline the framework within which we wish to construct our theory. But first we need to make some additional comments concerning the units of analysis. This study will concentrate on a subset of all conflicts, namely, on manifest conflicts among individual actors meeting face to face in a group situation. Thus, the actors are individuals and are not aggregates of individuals in the sense of organizations; moreover, conflicts that do not involve actors meeting in face-to-face group situations, for example, conflicts handled by correspondence, are excluded. Although groups meeting face to face may have both manifest and latent conflicts, our theory will deal only with manifest conflicts, that is situations in which a disagreement is orally expressed in the formal setting of a meeting. In chapter 3 we will describe the operational means by which we have identified manifest conflicts. In our research, we also tried to investigate latent conflicts—that is, disagreements between the actors of a group that do not appear on the formal agenda of a meeting—by observing interactions outside the formal meetings. However, the results of these observations were not very satisfactory, and consequently, we have deferred them to a brief section in the appendix.

Manifest conflicts among physically assembled actors can take place in many different settings. For example, they can take place in parliaments, cabinets, courts, political parties, interest groups, bureaucracies, or international conferences. Thus, our theory aims at a broad range of applications. Having defined the units of analysis, the next task is to develop a typology of the mechanisms by which these manifest conflicts are resolved. This typology is constructed along the three dimensions that are presented in table 2.1.

Table 2.1   *Typology of Decision Modes for Manifest Conflicts in Face-to-Face Groups*

	Substance of conflict is		
	Resolved		Not resolved
	Decision formalized	Decision not formalized	
Dissent persists	MAJORITY DECISION	DECISION BY INTERPRE- TATION	NONDECISION
Dissent vanishes	AMICABLE AGREE- MENT		

If a disagreement is openly articulated in a group, the first question is whether the substance of the conflict is resolved or not. If it is unresolved, we can still speak of a decision, but this decision is limited to the procedural matter of leaving the conflict unresolved. For this situation, which we define as a *nondecision*, there is no need to differentiate further along the two remaining dimensions. The concept of nondecision as we employ it is used in a much narrower sense than the concept originally developed by Peter Bachrach and Morton S. Baratz.[1] We address this question of terminology in an appendix devoted to a consideration of latent conflicts.

If, in contrast, the substance of a conflict is resolved, a distinction can be made along the second dimension, *formalization of the decision*. A decision is made in a formalized way if at the end of the discussion all actors who have expressed an opinion explicitly state their final positions. A decision is not formalized if one of the actors simply interprets what he or she considers to be the essence of the discussion and this interpretation is then tacitly accepted by the other actors. We refer to such nonformalized decisions as *decisions by interpretation*. For this mode, a further differentiation along our third dimension is not feasible, because it is precisely a property of decision by interpretation that it remains uncertain whether the dissent in the group has vanished or whether it persists.

This uncertainty does not exist for formalized decisions, and here we can also apply our third dimension. If the dissent in the group persists, we speak of a *majority decision*. There are different formal rules for defining a winning majority: a simple majority in the sense of a plurality, an absolute majority, or a qualified majority (for example, of two-thirds). In contrast, if the dissent vanishes at the end of the discussion, we have a decision by *amicable agreement*. Consensus may be expressed through a unanimous vote, a verbal statement, or an approving gesture. Amicable agreement does not necessarily mean that the latent conflicts have also disappeared from the group; it means only that there are no more manifest disagreements in the group concerning that particular conflict. If an actor with a dissenting opinion has never spoken up, a decision may still be made by amicable agreement, because his dissenting voice has not become manifest in the group discussion.

This classification gives us a typology of four decision modes. Three of these modes (majority decision, amicable agreement, and nondecision) are discussed relatively often in the literature, although not always under the same labels. The concept of decision by interpretation is our own. It refers to a decision mode that seems to be used quite frequently in a variety of decision situations; however, this decision mode has not as yet been clearly conceptualized. There are clear references to decisions by interpretation in the British Cabinet. Richard Crossman, who was himself a member of the Cabinet, considers one of the chief jobs of the prime minister "to decide when the time has come in a Cabinet meeting to formulate the decisions. Then he sums up in two parts, stating first the conclusions reached, and second the decision on the course of action to be taken."[2] It is interesting in the present context that Crossman refers explicitly to "the Prime Minister's right to *interpret* the consensus of the Cabinet" (our emphasis).[3] Patrick Gordon Walker, another insider of the British Cabinet, describes an imaginary Cabinet meeting.[4] After a lengthy discussion the prime minister sums up and concludes as follows: "Is the Cabinet agreed with my summing up and the additional points made by the Chancellor? (Silence, with a few muttered 'agreeds.')" We found a second clear occurrence of decisions by interpretation in Quaker meetings. As described by Gary B. Nash, someone with high status "would gently urge disquieted souls to moderation, [he] would be universally accepted as a kind of final arbiter due to his wisdom and strength of character."[5] At the end of a debate, in other words, this arbiter expresses the sense of the meeting.

The closest to a conceptualization of decisions by interpretation we found in the literature is a study by Sherif El-Hakim about a village in the Sudan.[6] El-Hakim distinguishes a strict form of consensual decision making requiring explicit unanimity, which corresponds to our concept of amicable agreement, from a looser form that corresponds closely to our decision by interpretation, although El-Hakim does not use the concept. The villagers debate first in small groups, and then the discussion extends slowly to all of the people assembled. "After a time . . . the group focuses on a single spokesman invariably different from the one who opened the meeting. This spokesman presents what he feels is the general consensus of the meeting, laying out a course of action or decision for the group to ratify."[7] If no opposition is voiced, "the meeting comes to an end, the proposition presented being the collective decision. If, on the other hand, complications arise, the meeting swings back to its noisy state until a new proposition emerges or until so much time passes that the meeting breaks up without a positive decision."[8] The crucial characteristic of this decision mode is that no explicit unanimity is reached. The silence of the villagers may very well indicate that they agree with the proposed conclusion. But the silence may also hide persisting dissent.

The examples of the British Cabinet, the Quaker meetings, and the Sudan village indicate that decisions by interpretation are indeed used in a large variety of decision situations. We have evidence that this decision mode is also widely used by the Wisconsin Winnebago Indians,[9] in many parts of the political system of Japan,[10] in the Rally for the Republic of France,[11] and in many political science departments.[12]

In chapter 4, we will describe how the concept of decision by interpretation has grown out of our research project. There, we will also describe how we have operationalized all four decision modes for our data.

Political Values

Having conceptualized our dependent variable, we must now search for independent variables that can explain variation among the four decision modes. This search must be guided by some basic assumptions about the motivations and the behavior of political decision makers. These assumptions must be neither too complex nor too simple because, in the words of George Rabinowitz, "the purpose of modeling is to simplify real world processes enough to give us a handle on them, without so over-simplifying them that we greatly distort the process that we are trying to understand."[13] We assume first that the choice of a decision mode by a group depends on the values that the members of the group want to maximize. However, we do not expect that politicians always try to maximize the same values. We agree with Franz Lehner and Hans Gerd Schütte who argue for a "theory of behaviour that takes into account changes of goals and preferences."[14] The same point is made by Kenneth R. MacCrimmon and David M. Messick, who expect motives that are "situational and influenced by a variety of aspects of the interpersonal relationship."[15]

In attempting to simplify the real world without grossly distorting it, we assume that the following four values are important for actors in a political decision-making situation: (1) power, (2) group solidarity, (3) rectitude, (4) time. Whereas power, group solidarity, and rectitude are positive values that politicians strive for, time can be conceptualized as an opportunity cost. Moreover, the weights of the individual values may vary from actor to actor and, for each actor, from situation to situation. For the derivation of these values, we profited greatly not only from the literature on consociational theory discussed in chapter 1, but also from the work of Mancur Olson and James Q. Wilson.[16]

Concerning the first value, *power*, we can say that for centuries most political thinkers have assumed that striving for power is an important incentive for political decision makers.[17] In the context of a decision group, power is the capacity of an actor to make other group members do things that they would not have done otherwise.[18] According to Olson, political decision makers want to have a "perceptible effect," and the motivation to have such an effect may or may not be selfish. Even an unselfish person, who is only interested in helping others, must rationally pursue "means that are efficient and effective for achieving these objectives." Olson recognizes, however, that in political decision-making situations a "self-interested behavior" may be much more common.[19] This self-interest may stem from a desire for the material wealth that one expects to obtain by exercising political power. As examples of such material incentives, Wilson mentions "wages and salaries, fringe benefits, reductions in taxes, changes in tariff levels, improvements in property values, discounts on various commodities and services, and personal services and gifts for which one would otherwise have to pay."[20] Another selfish motivation underlying the pursuit of power may be a desire for the prestige and status that one expects to obtain by exercising power. Olson speaks of "a desire to win prestige [and] respect," and Wilson of "specific solidary incentives," which are intangible rewards including "offices, honors, and deference."[21] Finally, the exercise of power may be enjoyed for its own sake: for some persons it may be rewarding to have a perceptible effect on others.

Some scholars assume that the reasons for seeking power are so manifold and compelling that they neglect all other values, treating the search for power as the sole incentive in political decision situations. This is the position, for example, of William H. Riker, who, according to the summary of Steven J. Brams, "simplifies the goal of political man to one that involves achievement of a specifiable outcome—winning—where all power accrues to the victors."[22] In our view, such an assumption oversimplifies and consequently distorts reality. This can be seen in the case of the central hypothesis that Riker derives from this general assumption, namely, that political decision makers tend to form the smallest possible winning coalitions.[23] We do not deny that there may be some decision situations in which all of the actors try to maximize power and nothing else, but it is unrealistic to assume that in all decision situations power will be the sole incentive.

The second value that we postulate is *group solidarity*. One of the major contributions of the literature on consociational theory is its emphasis on the importance of group solidarity as an incentive for political decision makers. As stressed in this literature, group solidarity is important not only for intraorganizational but also for interorganizational decision making. If, for example, representatives of different political parties meet, group solidarity may develop. Wilson has probably developed the most systematic argument for the importance of group solidarity as an incentive for political decision makers. He argues that "organizations tend to persist [and that this] is the most important thing to know about them."[24] According to Wilson, maintenance of an organization "includes not only survival, but also securing essential contributions of effort and resources from members, managing an effective system of communications, and helping formulate purposes: in short, producing and sustaining cooperative effort."[25] Wilson states correctly that intangible rewards result from group solidarity—rewards that "have some of the characteristics of what economists call a 'public good' in that particular individuals within the organization cannot feasibly be excluded from their benefit."[26] Wilson calls these intangible rewards collective solidary incentives, which "involve the fun and conviviality of coming together, the sense of group membership or exclusiveness, and such collective status or esteem as the group as a whole may enjoy."[27] Edward J. Lawler and George A. Youngs also refer to the importance of group solidarity as an incentive when they say that "attitudinal similarity may be an end in itself."[28]

As a third value we postulate *rectitude*. Cynics maintain that politicians are not concerned with the substantive outcomes of their decisions; they are interested merely in their individual power and perhaps in the maintenance of their organizations. Although there are certainly politicians to whom such a cynical view applies, it would be a serious distortion of reality to assume that politicians never care about the "rightness" of their decisions. To give only one example, some politicians fight against the construction of nuclear reactors because such a position is dictated by their moral convictions. Thus, we assume that at least some of the politicians strive at least some of the time for rectitude. Harold D. Lasswell

uses the term rectitude "when the participants are making evalua-
tions of goodness or badness. More generally, a rectitude evaluation is in terms of responsibility or irresponsibility."[29] In the same
vein, Wilson speaks of a "belief in a larger purpose."[30] Instead of
rectitude, Wilson uses the term "purposive incentives," which "are
intangible rewards that derive from the sense of satisfaction of having contributed to the attainment of a worthwhile cause."[31] Wilson
mentions "protests against corruption or injustice, a desire for con-
servation and beautification of the environment, [and] a call for
revolution or patriotism" as examples of such causes.[32] In our
usage, rectitude is a very broad term. It includes all ideological
and policy goals as long as these goals are pursued for their own sake.

For our fourth value we postulate *time*, which we conceptualize
as an opportunity cost. For politicians, time is a relatively scarce
resource. At the beginning of an important decision session, some
actors may think that they have virtually limitless time to participate
in the process. But as the meeting lengthens, many of the participants may begin to wonder whether their time could not be better
invested for other purposes. They begin to perceive time as an
opportunity cost. Of the four postulated values, time is probably the
most dynamic because its importance is most likely to change during
a decision process.

Given the four values that we have postulated, our assumptions
have already attained a high degree of complexity. This is especially true if we consider that the relative weights of the individual
values may change from actor to actor and for each actor over
time. Adding more values would entail a further increase in complexity, resulting in so much confusion that we would not get a
clear and accurate understanding of reality. Consequently, we will
restrict our initial postulates to these four values.[33]

Causality

Moving to a consideration of causality, we begin with the simple
model in figure 2.1. According to this model, the decision mode
depends on the values that the decision makers try to maximize
in a particular decision situation. In the research for this study
the relation between values and decision modes has not been in-

vestigated in an empirical way because we did not collect data for the values of the decision makers. Thus, we have treated the values as inferred variables as shown in figure 2.2. The hypotheses that we will test empirically link the observable preconditions of the values to the decision modes. The inferred values will still be important because they will help us to fill in the logical linkage between the two observed sets of data.

Figure 2.1

Values   Decision Modes

Although it would certainly be preferable to know the values of the decision makers, measuring these values would probably be possible only in a laboratory experiment, not in a real-life situation. Because we assume that the values may change during the decision process itself, it would be necessary to interrupt this process at short intervals in order to measure possible changes in the values. Such interruptions are feasible in the laboratory, but certainly not in real-life situations involving politicians. Moreover, the experimental method is strongly limited in other respects in the study of political decision-making processes. In politics each decision tends to be seen in connection with numerous earlier and later decisions: politicians are engaged in a continuous flow of decision

Figure 2.2

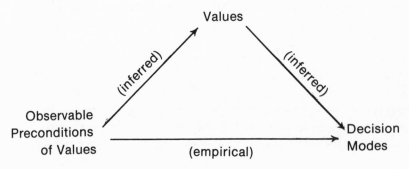

making. Certainly, one can tell the participants in an experiment that they should consider themselves engaged in an endless flow of decision making and that they should take account of this fact when they make a particular decision in the experiment, but we doubt whether such instructions are capable of simulating a real-life setting. Furthermore, most politicians play different roles in political life, and in many decision-making situations several roles are relevant. It hardly seems possible that participants in an experiment can be made aware of the subtleties of such role accumulations. Although we do not deny that such experiments may have some heuristic value, as a general rule they seem of moderate importance for the development of decision-making theories. We agree with Brams who doubts that a theory can gain wide acceptance "unless its abstract concepts can be related to real-world phenomena."[34] However, as we will argue in chapter 9, further development of our theory can be pursued through the use of such experiments.

Although the values of decision makers were not measured in this project, they are still important for the construction of the theory. These values have helped us to make the logical linkage between the observed independent variables and the decision modes. In working out this linkage, we were careful to refer only to the four values that we have postulated and not to introduce in an ad hoc way additional values. Consequently, we can claim a certain rigor and formalization for our theory.

As a first step in developing the theory, we assume situations in which all members of a decision group maximize only one and the same value. In the political world such decision situations probably occur only rarely, if at all, but we find it useful to begin the construction of the theory with such pure or ideal types because the simplicity of the situation allows us to spell out the basic arguments with more clarity.

Power Dominance

First, we assume a condition in which all decision makers are interested in maximizing only their individual power. Considerations of group solidarity, rectitude, and time are so unimportant for the moment that they can be neglected. Which decision mode is most likely to occur under these conditions? If power is the only incentive, decision making tends to become a zero-sum game. As some actors gain power, others must necessarily lose it, because it is not possible for all members of a decision group to be at the top of the power hierarchy. Given these circumstances, majority rule seems the most probable decision mode. Whoever has the necessary votes to form a majority has no incentive to make any concessions to the minority. The majority will take advantage of the voting mechanism to impose its will and thus to increase its power. There may even be a tendency to form a majority of a minimal size, so that the increase in power can be distributed among as few members as possible.[35]

We expect one general exception, which should occur if the most powerful members in a group anticipate that they will be on the losing side of a majority decision. In such a situation these powerful members will try to impose a decision by interpretation on the group. With this decision mode they have the chance of manipulating the decision process in such a way that the decision outcome will be in their favor. Even if they lose with a decision by interpretation, the powerholders can to a certain extent "save face" because a loss is less visible with a decision by interpretation than with a majority decision. This reduced visibility lowers the risk that the powerholders will lose a significant amount of their accumulated power.

A nondecision is another viable strategy for the powerful members of a group if they anticipate that they will lose in a majority decision. A nondecision will certainly not increase their power, but it should not detract from it either. Because powerful actors have more to lose than to gain, a nondecision may be quite appealing to them. There is, of course, the risk that the group members who have the necessary votes to win a majority decision will object to a nondecision, but here again, the powerholders may apply their power with so much skill that they will be able to manipulate the decision process in such a way that it ends without any decision being reached.

Amicable agreement is the least likely decision mode if all actors are maximizing only power. If an explicit agreement among all competing positions has to be reached, all sides must compromise to a certain degree, but there is little incentive to compromise for those actors who have the votes to win a majority decision. The worst that can happen to such a majority is that it might be manipulated into a decision by interpretation or a nondecision. The majority may not have the necessary skills to prevent such a manipulation, but by no means will it voluntarily share victory with the minority by pursuing amicable agreement.

Group Solidarity Dominance

Second, we consider decision situations in which all group members are concerned with maximizing only group solidarity. Here, amicable agreement should be the most likely, and majority rule the least likely, decision mode. If group members must make concessions to reach a final decision that is acceptable to everyone, group solidarity suffers a minimum of strain. If, on the other hand, the majority simply outvotes the minority, frustrations may develop in the losers. Such a risk is particularly great if the same actors are repeatedly on the losing side. These frustrations may become a threat to group solidarity. After a time the frustrated losers may even quit the organization, choosing the "exit-strategy" described by Albert O. Hirschman.[36] If it is not possible for all participants to agree amicably on a common solution, decision by interpretation and nondecision seem the next best options. With both of these decision modes the question of who lost remains somewhat ambiguous; thus, the strain on group solidarity should not be too heavy.

Rectitude Dominance

As a third illustrative case we assume that only rectitude is important for decision makers. In such situations all actors have very strong moral convictions. They are willing to fight for these convictions regardless of what happens to their power base and to group solidarity and with no concern for the time it takes to make a decision. Under these conditions majority rule seems the most probable decision mode. All actors stick to their original positions, and the voting mechanism simply registers which position has a majority. Amicable agreement seems unlikely because no member in the group has an incentive to compromise on a position that he considers morally correct. Decisions by interpretation are also expected to be rare, primarily because they presuppose the presence of some actors who are interested in being "wheelers and dealers." Such actors are more likely to be found in situations in which power and group solidarity are primary considerations. If rectitude is the sole value that counts, the group members will prefer fighting for their positions in a straightforward way to maneuvering for decisions by interpretation. Likewise, nondecision does not appear to be a likely decision mode. If the actors are convinced of the moral correctness of their positions, they will want the conflicts to be resolved; nondecisions will have no appeal at all.

Time Dominance

As a fourth case we assume that all group members are interested only in keeping the opportunity costs represented by the loss of time at a minimum. Such a situation probably could never occur at the beginning of a meeting, because if time were immediately perceived as a significant constraint, it is doubtful that the participants would have even come to the meeting in the first place. Consequently, we assume that most meetings begin with a fairly low collective concern with the time factor. As a meeting lengthens, however, there may be situations in which time becomes the overriding consideration, thereby relegating other values to the background. This process is nicely described by Walker for the British Cabinet: "Manifestations of impatience tend to check the length of speeches. . . . This impatience is compounded of the desire of some Ministers to reach their own business on the agenda and of others simply to conclude the Cabinet in reasonable time."[37] Under such circumstances of time constraint, a majority decision seems to be the preferred decision mode because voting allows for a quick resolution of the conflict: a vote can be taken without much deliberation. However, one exception must be noted. If a decision has to be made among a complex set of alternatives, it may be very time-consuming to find the appropriate voting mechanism. A long discussion may develop concerning the sequence in which the various alternatives should be put to a vote. In such a case, the opportunity costs of time may be reduced if someone interprets the essence of the discussion in a quick and authoritative fashion. Of course, a nondecision would also bring the matter to a quick close. However, the issue would probably arise again in a later meeting, resulting in further opportunity costs in the form of lost time. The importance that the actors attach to such later opportunity costs would determine whether they "decide not to decide" in the present situation. Amicable agreement is the least likely decision mode when group members are concerned only with minimizing their loss of time, because an explicit agreement among holders of several conflicting views generally requires a fair amount of time to achieve.

Empirically Testable Hypotheses

Looking at the four "pure" cases in which all actors have only one and the same incentive has allowed us to make some simple theoretical arguments. In an actual political decision-making situation most actors will probably maximize more than one value, and different actors may maximize different values. In addition, the importance given to the various values may change during a decision-making session. As a next step we look at the possible preconditions that influence the values that are maximized in a decision-making situation. Based on previous research and our knowledge of the literature it seems plausible that the values of decision makers depend on attributes of the group within which the decision process takes place. We expect, for example, that different values are maximized in a large and a small group. It is also plausible that the kind of conflict being debated is important. We further expect that the broader context within which a conflict takes place will have an impact on the values of the decision makers. For example, it may matter how much time remains before the next parliamentary election. Finally, we assume that the decision process itself influences the values of the participants.

It may be important how many group members speak up or how many points are on the agenda of the meeting.

To put the same assumptions in a different way, we argue that the values of political decision makers depend on (1) *who* participates with them in a decision process; (2) *what* the decision process is about; (3) *where and when* the decision process takes place; (4) *how* the decision process is structured. We now arrive at the extended model in figure 2.3.

Figure 2.3

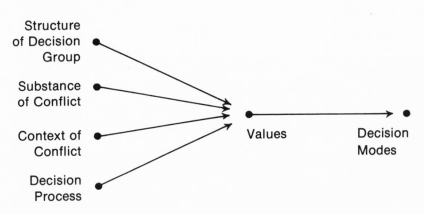

As we have stated before, we treat the values of the decision makers as an inferred variable. The empirically testable hypotheses link the preconditions of the values to the decision modes. These hypotheses are summarized in table 2.2. It contains twenty-one independent variables grouped under the four headings from figure 2.3. For each of the independent variables, the table indicates whether the probability of the occurrence of the four decision modes increases, decreases, or is unaffected. For example, for the first variable the table shows that as the size of the decision group gets smaller, the probability of majority decision decreases and the probability of amicable agreement increases, whereas the two other decision modes remain unaffected by the size of the group. We justify this hypothesis in terms of the values that are maximized in small and large groups. These justifications of the

Table 2.2   *Hypotheses to Explain Decision Modes in Face-to-Face Groups*

Independent Variables	*Probability of*			
	Majority Decision	*Amicable Agreement*	*Nondecision*	*Decision by Interpretation*
Structure of Decision Group				
1. The smaller the size of the decision group . . .	decreases	increases	unaffected	unaffected
2. The larger the proportion of high-status actors in a decision group . . .	decreases	unaffected	unaffected	increases
3. The more frequent the interactions among the members of a decision group . . .	decreases	increases	unaffected	unaffected
4. The larger the proportion of younger actors in a decision group . . .	increases	decreases	decreases	decreases
5. The more homogeneous a decision group . . .	decreases	increases	decreases	increases
Substance of Conflict				
6. The more a conflict deals not only with means but also with ends . . .	increases	decreases	increases	decreases
7. The more a conflict refers to matters of the decision group itself . . .	decreases	increases	unaffected	unaffected
8. The more a conflict involves innovative proposals . . .	increases	decreases	unaffected	unaffected
9. The more a conflict involves personnel matters . . .	decreases	increases	unaffected	unaffected

Table 2.2, continued

Independent Variables	Probability of			
	Majority Decision	Amicable Agreement	Nondecision	Decision by Interpretation
10. The more a conflict is perceived as important by the participant actors . . .	decreases	decreases	increases	increases
Context of Conflict				
11. The closer the time distance to the next parliamentary election . . .	decreases	decreases	increases	increases
12. The greater the likelihood of a referendum about the issue under discussion . . .	decreases	increases	unaffected	unaffected
13.* The more the issue under discussion has passed from the pre-parliamentary to the parliamentary phase . . .	decreases	decreases	increases	increases
14.* The more a political party is in governmental control . . .	decreases	increases	unaffected	unaffected
Decision Process				
15. The more informal the decision process . . .	decreases	increases	decreases	increases
16. The more the decision process is focused . . .	increases	decreases	increases	decreases
17. The later in a meeting an issue is discussed . . .	decreases	decreases	increases	increases

Table 2.2, continued

Independent Variables	Probability of			
	Majority Decision	Amicable Agreement	Nondecision	Decision by Interpretation
18. The higher the certainty in the information basis . . .	decreases	increases	unaffected	unaffected
19. The higher the number of proposals on the same conflict dimension . . .	decreases	increases	unaffected	increases
20. If on the same conflict dimension high-status actors author				
(a) two or more proposals . . .	decreases	decreases	increases	increases
(b) one proposal . . .	decreases	increases	decreases	decreases
(c) no proposal . . .	increases	decreases	increases	increases
21. If on the same conflict dimension: many actors speak up and distribution of opinions is				
(a) uneven . . .	decreases	increases	decreases	decreases
(b) even . . .	increases	decreases	decreases	decreases
few actors speak up and distribution of opinions is				
(a) uneven . . .	decreases	decreases	increases	increases
(b) even . . .	decreases	decreases	increases	decreases

*Specifically limited to intraparty conflicts.

hypotheses will be provided in chapter 6 in connection with the presentation of the data. For the moment we limit ourselves to a broad overview of the hypotheses in the form of this table.

It is of course probable that some interaction takes place between the twenty-one independent variables contained in this table. For example, the effect of group size on the decision modes may depend on whether a group consists more of high-status or of low-status actors. Or the effect of the political status of the actors may depend on whether their conflicts involve not only means but also goals. We will examine such interaction effects with the help of a simulation model, but constructing a simulation with as many as twenty-one variables is an extremely complicated task. Consequently, we will first try to reduce the number of variables to a more manageable size. This will be accomplished through the use of bivariate analysis in chapter 6 and discriminant analysis in chapter 7. Then, in chapter 8, we will present a reduced set of variables for which we will formulate hypotheses about the interaction effects.

CHAPTER 3

The Collection of the Data

As outlined in chapter 2, our theory aims at a broad range of applications. Manifest conflicts in face-to-face groups can take place in many different settings: for example, in cabinet meetings, in parliamentary committees, in expert commissions, and so forth. The choice of our particular data source from among these possibilities was not made arbitrarily. We followed certain strict criteria in making our selection. Listed below are the three major criteria we used.

1. *Access.* In order to get a clear picture of the decision process, it was necessary to rely not only on secondary sources such as interviews and documents but also on direct observation of the behavior of the decision makers. Consequently, we looked for political groups for which we could obtain the access necessary for participant observation.

2. *Variation.* The groups to be observed needed variation with regard to the explanatory variables of our theory. Thus, we needed, for example, small and large groups, high-status and low-status groups, and groups that had to debate both about goals and about means.

3. *Knowledge on Flow of Information.* The decision-making process a group chooses for a particular issue often depends on how the same issue was dealt with in other groups. Consequently, we needed a setting in which we could study the flow of information about issue resolution from one group to another.

We chose as our data source the Free Democratic party in the canton of Bern, Switzerland. This party fulfills in a reasonable way the three criteria mentioned above. As we will show later in this chapter, we were able to resolve the access problem. Moreover, the party displayed quite a bit of variation with regard to

41

the independent variables of our theory. Many different party groups met during the period of observation, and these groups debated a large variety of issues. There was also a fair amount of variation in the context itself, particularly because the research period covered the time before and after a parliamentary election. Finally, the choice of the party also satisfied the third criterion because we could easily monitor the movement of information in the decision-making process from one party group to another. The substance of a discussion in the bureau of the executive committee often reappeared in the executive committee, the parliamentary group, the central committee, the party convention, or some other party meeting.

It would be valid at this point to question this rather narrow empirical basis for the test of our theory. Because the theory should apply to any face-to-face political group, one may wonder what conclusions can be drawn from the study of a single political party in a single country. If a hypothesis of the theory holds for the Bernese Free Democrats, it will not necessarily hold for the British Cabinet, the American National Security Council, or the Soviet Politburo. Moreover, there are many characteristics of Switzerland that may have influenced the outcomes of the tests of the theory. One may think, for example, of the smallness of the country, its federal structure, the collegial nature of the executive, the strongly developed referendum, and Swiss neutrality in foreign policy.[1] It would of course be preferable to have good data about a large number of political groups around the world. But faced with the question of whether to do an in-depth study of a limited data set or to cover a large set of data in a more superficial way, we chose the former strategy. Of course, this does not preclude the possibility of using the latter strategy in a later project. For a discussion of further research plans see chapter 9.

As the data are far from being a representative sample of all conflicts in face-to-face political groups, it is important to specify carefully the conditions under which the theory was tested. Thus, the first part of this chapter is a rather detailed description of the Bernese Free Democratic party. Later in the chapter, the methods of data collection and the coding of that data will be discussed.

The Free Democratic Party in the Canton of Bern

The field research for this study took place from 1969 to 1970; thus, all of the information below will refer to this time period. This is important because in 1978 the three most northern districts in the Jura separated from Bern to form their own canton.[2] According to the census of 1970, the canton of Bern had a population of about 980,000. This represented 16 percent of the Swiss population, making Bern the second largest canton after Zurich. Bern was quite heterogeneous. It was one of the four linguistically mixed cantons, being predominantly German speaking with a French-speaking minority of 14 percent concentrated in the Jura districts. Religiously, it was about three-quarters Protestant, one-quarter Catholic. Bern also had a strong regional structure with a great amount of regional identification, especially in the Oberland, the Emmental, and the Jura. The development of regional identities was facilitated by the existence of high mountains and other features of the topography. During the time of this research 10 percent of the Bernese population were foreigners, and this further contributed to the heterogeneity of the canton.

Economically, agriculture was quite important with 11 percent of the population still occupied in the primary sector, 48 percent in the secondary sector, and 41 percent in the tertiary sector. For the last-named group tourism was important, as was public administration since the city of Bern is the capital of Switzerland. Bern also had a rather rural character: in 1970 the population of the city of Bern was only 162,000; other Swiss cities, in particular Zurich, are much larger.

The canton of Bern has a multiparty system. In the cantonal parliament, consisting of two hundred members, who are elected on a proportional basis, the largest group during the research period was the Swiss People's party with seventy-nine seats.[3] (The old name of this party—the Farmer, Artisan, and Bourgeois party —describes the character of the party much better than its new name.) The Social Democrats were the second largest party with sixty-three seats; the Free Democrats had thirty-seven seats; the Christian Democrats had ten seats; and all smaller parties together had eleven seats. The executive council consists of nine members, all of whom possess the same status. As is the custom in Switzerland, the seats on the Council were distributed on a proportional basis, with four seats going to the Swiss People's party, three to the Social Democrats, and two to the Free Democrats. As it is elsewhere in Switzerland, the referendum is a strongly developed tradition in Bern.

The Free Democratic party is one of the larger parties at the federal, as well as at the cantonal, level. It holds two of the seven seats on the Federal Council, the executive branch at the federal level. The Free Democrats have historical roots going back to the early nineteenth century: they were the founders of the modern Swiss Confederation in 1848. In 1969–70, the political orientation of the Free Democrats varied rather strongly from one canton to another. In Bern, the party entertained a wide spectrum of views, from a traditional "laissez-faire" liberalism to an approach more open to social responsibility. Moreover, it was about equally represented in the French-speaking Jura and in the German-speaking part of the canton. However, the two language groups were organized as two different sections of the federal party, whereas on the parliamentary level of the canton the two sections formed a single parliamentary group. (Our research was limited to the German-speaking section and the common parliamentary group.)[4] Furthermore, the Free Democrats were overrepresented among Protestants, whereas the Catholics were particularly strong among the Christian Democrats. Finally, because the canton of Bern is characterized by strong cross-cutting tendencies between political parties and interest groups, the interests of several varied economic groups were articulated in the Free Democratic party— namely, the business community, the artisans, the farmers, and the clerical employees. The main exception to this cross cutting was the trade-union movement, in which parties and interest groups overlapped to a large extent. The Free Democrats also had their own, albeit small, trade union, the Free Swiss Workers.

Decision making in the Free Democratic party takes place in a large variety of institutional settings. During our research period, we observed 111 party meetings: the parliamentary group met 16 times; the executive committee 13 times; the bureau of the executive committee 11 times; the executive committee of the party youth organization 9 times; the party convention, the central committee, and the bureau of the parliamentary group 6 times each. The remaining 44 meetings were distributed among twenty-nine committees, none of which met more than 4 times. Most of these committees with infrequent meetings were concerned with specific tasks, such as education, social policy, traffic questions, public relations, and so forth. In all, we had thirty-six different institutional settings in which we could study decision-making processes. The size of the various groups was very uneven: in 36 meetings the number of participants was 7 or less, in 42 meetings between 8 and 20, in 27 meetings between 21 and 100, and in six meetings between 101 and 156. The length of the meetings also varied widely: 18 meetings took less than an hour, 50 meetings between one and two hours, 41 meetings between two and three hours, and 2 meetings took more than three hours. In 34 meetings there was only a single agenda point to be discussed, in 24 meetings two or three agenda points, in 25 meetings four or five agenda points, and in the remaining 28 meetings there were more than five points on the agenda. As a president may have a strong influence on the decision-making pattern in a meeting, it was also important to have some variation with regard to the presiding officer: taking all of the meetings together, we were able to study 18 different presiding officers.

A significant variety of issues were discussed during the research period. Moreover, the intensity of the issues varied a great deal. On the one hand, some groups had members with very similar interests, for example, the party committee for artisan affairs, which consisted almost exclusively of artisans. On the other hand, some decision-making situations featured strongly conflicting interests: the most extreme examples of this were concerned with the Jura problem, which at the time was certainly the most explosive political question not only in Bern but in Switzerland as a whole. Actually, it was during the research period that important steps were taken for the later formation of the separate canton of Jura. In March 1970 a constitutional amendment was approved that opened the way for a series of referenda on the separation question. This constitutional amendment was hotly debated in the

Free Democratic party, particularly in the parliamentary group, which, as we have seen, consisted both of French and German speakers. The Free Democratic members of parliament from the Jura included both supporters and opponents of the separation. To be sure, the conflict about the Jura never obtained the intensity of the conflicts in Northern Ireland, Lebanon, or Cyprus, but nevertheless, the inclusion of the Jura problem in this research strongly increased the variation in the decision-making situations at our disposal. We also collected data about the status structure and the level of participation in the Free Democratic party. These data, which refer to additional important parameters of the study, are presented in the appendix.

Methods of Data Collection

The methods of data collection in this study were participant observation, interviews, and the study of documents. Of these, the most important was participant observation. The senior author had already had some experience with this method in the Swiss context, having previously observed the Free Democratic party of the canton of Bern, as well as the same party at both the federal and the local levels. Furthermore, he had observed the development of two university bills, one at the federal, the other at the cantonal level.[5] In each of these studies, the observation was of a "disguised" nature—that is, the participants in the decision-making process were not aware of being observed. This was possible because in each case the observer held an active role in the decision process, for example, as secretary of an expert committee of the Federal Council. This disguised observation had two disadvantages: first, the active role sometimes interfered with a detached and detailed observation; second, the full range of decision-making situations was not available to the observer, because he could attend only those meetings to which he had been invited in his active role. For this research, we tried to overcome these disadvantages by using an "open" style of observation in which all participants were aware that they were being observed.

This open observation caused two new problems, namely, obtaining the permission for the study and avoiding influencing the decision-making process. The senior author obtained access for participant observation through a formal decision of the executive committee of the party. At first the request drew some opposition, but this opposition eventually dissipated, primarily for the following reasons. First, the argument was made to the executive committee that the research was interested only in the causal relations among abstract variables and not in the revelation of intimate details of party activities; in this sense it was easier to get access as a political scientist than as a historian. Second, the senior author was himself a member of the Free Democratic party. Although without this membership the access problem might not have been resolved, this involvement with the party might itself have precluded a detached observation of party processes. Thus, the senior author tried to alleviate this danger by resigning from all party positions, not only at the cantonal, but at all levels. More important, he decided to renounce all plans for a later party career and to refuse any future party position. Third, the project was financially supported by the Swiss National Science Foundation, which receives its money almost exclusively from the Swiss Confederation. The support of the most prestigious Swiss foundation provided the project with a considerable degree of respectability. Finally, it may have been important that the senior author is a Swiss citizen. The argument is sometimes made in the literature that the access problem can be resolved more readily by foreigners. The opposite seems to be true in our case, primarily because it would be easier to sanction a Swiss citizen than a foreigner if party secrets were violated. The violation of secrets was a real concern for the party because during the research period (in May 1970) a general election for the cantonal parliament was held; there was a risk that the observer would reveal information about the election strategies to another party or to the public. If such an action were taken by a foreigner, few sanctions would be available for the party, for this foreigner could simply leave the country. For a Swiss citizen, on the other hand, such an abuse of privilege would result in a severe sanction. Thus, the party may have felt more in control of a Swiss than a foreign observer.

The problem of preventing the observer from influencing the decision-making processes of the party was even more difficult than the access problem. It was certainly unusual for the party to be observed on a scholarly basis. To accustom the party to the observations, they began in November 1968, two months before the initiation of the actual research period. During this "warm-up" period, several party members teased the observer that his presence made them feel like actors on stage and that they would try to give a good performance. Although such remarks did not stop completely after the actual beginning of the research period, they became much rarer. To minimize further the disturbance of the decision-making process, a relatively long research period, twenty-one months, was used. Thus, it was not possible to delay many decisions until after the conclusion of the observations, particularly because in the meantime an important general election took place. Given a shorter research period, for example, only four or five months, many decisions might simply have been postponed until the observer had left. In addition to these measures to reduce the influence of the observer on the decision making, the observer took notes rather than used a tape recorder. A tape certainly would have facilitated the observations, but it would have been such an unusual element in a meeting that it could easily have influenced the behavior of many participants. Taking notes, on the other hand, was a very common occurrence in a party meeting: many participants, as well as the secretary of the meeting, often took notes.

In larger meetings of more than fifteen to twenty participants the presence of an observer probably had little influence on the decision-making behavior; in fact, most participants tended to forget that the observer was not a normal member of the group. In these meetings the observer had no major problems with taking notes. Notes were not taken completely verbatim, but with a kind of self-developed short-hand, while the observer tried to follow the discussion as closely as possible.

Major problems did arise,·however, in the observation of very small groups. The most difficult group to observe was the so-called working lunch attended by the party president, the secretary, and the two Free Democratic members of the cantonal executive. In the beginning the observer was at times asked for his opinion and had to make it clear that he was only an observer. Needless to say, it was quite discomforting to be a silent observer at a small luncheon party. To make this role a little more bearable, the observer did take part in the informal discussion at the beginning of a lunch on topics such as the weather, the food, and sports; consequently, he was not a completely silent participant, which made both himself and the others more at ease. During these small meetings, the observer was also careful that his note-taking did not create too much of a disturbance; he had a very small booklet in which he wrote only some key notes. Immediately after the meetings he then extended these notes from memory. Although this method certainly caused some loss of information, it was an acceptable price to pay for reducing the level of disturbance.

As already mentioned, the observations covered 111 meetings during the period January 1969 to September 1970. During these twenty-one months the party held a total of 119 meetings. Because of commitments to military service and scholarly conferences, the observer could not attend 8 of those meetings.

In addition to participant observation, we studied the letters and documents of the party. The senior author obtained completely free access to the party secretariat and could check all the incoming and outgoing mail; quite often he was the first person to read the incoming mail. The availability of all party documents made it possible to monitor the decision-making process on individual issues. It was particularly interesting to see to what extent the decisions made at the meetings were implemented: if, for example, the executive committee decided that the party should send a particular letter to the cantonal government, it could be checked whether this was done and to what extent the substance of the letter corresponded to the decision of the executive committee. Working with the party documents showed with clarity that these documents do not simply mirror the events of the party, but are themselves instruments of the decision-making process. This is particularly true for the minutes of the meetings, which sometimes contained decisions that were not explicitly made in the meetings or omitted decisions that were made. Thus, the minutes had to be analyzed as components of the decision process. Relying on the minutes alone, however, would not have provided an accurate picture of the decision making in the meetings.

In addition to participant observation and the study of documents, we also employed interviews. During the research period, 318 actors participated in at least one party meeting, and we conducted a written survey with these 318 persons. The main purpose of this survey was to collect data about personal information, such as occupation, career in the party, membership in interest groups. The survey was not used to get information about the decision-making behavior itself. Our pretests had shown that most actors did not accurately remember how particular decisions had been made even if they were asked immediately after the meeting. Apparently, they became so preoccupied with the substance of the decisions that they gave only passing attention to the forms in which decisions were made. Besides, few people could be expected to remember the procedural details of a full meeting.

Of the 318 actors, 65 percent filled out the questionnaire. For those actors who did not do so, we tried to get as much information as possible from other sources. This was not much of a problem, because the questions of the survey dealt with factual information, much of which we could obtain by consulting documents in the office of the party secretariat or by asking knowledgeable party members, such as the party secretary. If the information was still unavailable, we often asked the actors themselves, either before or after a meeting.

Coding the Data

Using these methods, we collected a large amount of data. For the subsequent analysis, an appropriate way to code these data was needed. The organizational principle for the coding process was that the units of analysis were manifest conflicts in face-to-face meetings of the party. We identified 466 such conflicts, the N for our study. As already defined in chapter 2, manifest conflicts refer to situations in which a disagreement about a particular issue is verbally expressed in the formal setting of a meeting. In order to code the data, however, a more precise operational meaning was required.

In everyday language one usually speaks of a conflict only if a disagreement reaches a certain intensity. In the context of this study, however, we speak of a conflict whenever two or more actors say that they are not in agreement on a particular point. Such a disagreement may concern a trivial point like the time of the next meeting, but even such a seemingly trivial point may sometimes take on great importance because whether the next meeting will be earlier or later may occasionally influence a decision-making process.

It might have been clearer to speak not of conflicts but of disagreements. However, in everyday language a disagreement that reaches a certain intensity is no longer called simply a disagreement but a conflict. Because the term conflict is more widely used in the literature, we decided to speak not of disagreements but of conflicts.

To determine how many conflicts were involved in a particular discussion we had to distinguish among the individual *conflict dimensions*. Proposals lie on a single conflict dimension if the acceptance of one proposal precludes the acceptance of all other proposals. Ordinarily, it was quite simple to determine whether various proposals were located on a single conflict dimension or whether more than one dimension was involved. Occasionally, it was more difficult to make a judgment about the number of conflict dimensions. In these cases we have not used the criterion of whether proposals were mutually exclusive from a purely logical point of view, but whether they were *perceived* as being mutually exclusive by the participants. The basis for these judgments was the context of the discussion. A complication for the coding was that the conflict dimensions could be on various levels of abstraction. Thus, in the discussion of a bill one conflict might concern whether a new bill was even necessary, whereas other conflicts might involve details of the bill.

In order to clarify further the units of analysis, we provide a few examples from our set of 466 conflicts:

Executive committee: January 28, 1969
  —Morning flight of Swissair from Bern to Zurich should be canceled.
  —Morning flight of Swissair from Bern to Zurich should be kept.

Committee for University Affairs: February 13, 1969
—Students should be excluded from the selection process of new professors.
—Students should participate in the selection process of new professors.
—Students should participate in the selection process of new professors only if the candidates are recruited from within the university itself, but not if they come from another university.
Committee for Social Policy: March 1, 1969
—Discuss tax bill at the current meeting.
—Postpone the discussion of tax bill until the next meeting.
Committee for Propaganda: March 26, 1969
—Make the church tax into an issue for the election campaign.
—Do not make the church tax into an issue for the election campaign.
Bureau of the parliamentary group: February 3, 1969
—Mr. Christen as speaker for the parliamentary group in the Jura debate.
—Mr. Haltiner as speaker for the parliamentary group in the Jura debate.

The most important task for each conflict was to code the decision mode with which it was resolved. As this is such a crucial component of the research project, it will be discussed in detail in chapter 4. In addition to the decision mode, we coded the history in the party of each conflict. If, for example, a conflict came up in the executive committee, information was included on whether this issue had already been debated elsewhere in the party. We also coded what happened to the issue after the meeting. At this point, a further clarification with regard to our units of analysis can be added. If the same disagreement came up in several party meetings, we counted each occurrence as a separate conflict. This was a necessary consequence of the logic of the research design because the decision mode for the same conflict could easily vary from one meeting to another. This could be true even for meetings of the same group: in a first meeting a conflict might be resolved by a nondecision, in a later meeting by majority rule.

For each conflict we also coded its history within the particular meeting itself, including, for example, information on who the authors of the various proposals were, on who spoke up in the discussion, and on what the distribution of opinions was. For each actor we had a great deal of information such as occupation, political career, and so forth. This information was coded only once; whenever we referred to an actor in the context of a particular conflict, we coded only his identification number. For the analysis it was then possible to call in the relevant information from the actor cards. In addition, cards for each meeting and for each agenda point within a meeting were coded. A piece of information that referred to all conflicts within a meeting (such as the number of participants) was coded only once, but could be called in for the analysis of each conflict. The same was true for the individual agenda points within a meeting.

As a consequence of this coding device we had four sets of cards: cards for conflicts, cards for actors, cards for meetings, and cards for agenda points. It is important to remember that the units of analysis are at no point actors, meetings, or agenda points, but always solely conflicts. Probably the only way to master the huge amount of data was to use different sets of cards; even so it has taken us six years to code all of it. The most time-consuming aspect was that the material had to be prepared so that for each conflict its entire history before and after the particular meeting was available. To give an idea of the amount of data with which we were working, we had: 466 conflicts with 2 cards for each conflict; 318 actors with 3 cards for each actor; 111 meetings with 2 cards for each meeting; and 668 agenda points with 1 card for each agenda point.

How reliable and valid are these data? We have to answer this question in particular for our primary method, participant observation. Although it would have been preferable to have had at least two participant observers so that we could have compared their notes, it happened that at the time of the field research the senior author was the only available observer. Thus, there is no way to check how reliable his note-taking was. Because we were aware of this problem, the observations emphasized items that could be easily identified, such as the number of speakers in a conflict or the length of time until a parliamentary election. However, for other items the observation depended more on judgment. For instance, we tried to observe whether any actors raised their voices in a discussion, but in this particular instance we felt insecure about the reliability of the notes so the item was dropped from the analysis. The same strategy was also used in other cases in which there was doubt about the reliability of the notes, but we included some information in the analysis for which the judgment of the observer was quite important. An example is the item concerning the actors' perceptions of a conflict as a position or a valence issue. We shall comment on the reliability of such observations when we present the data.

Transferring the data from the notes of the observations to the coding categories was a relatively minor problem. If the notes indicated that a meeting was attended by eight actors, it was easy to transfer this information into a coding category. At first, the coding was done independently by two or sometimes three coders. Since no judgments were necessary, intercoder reliability was very high, more often than not reaching 100 percent. After a time, we used only one coder for each item and limited the controls to random checks. The nonproblematic nature of the actual coding process should not obscure the problems with the reliability of the notes taken during the meetings, but there is unfortunately no way to judge the severity of these problems.

In many instances, validity was no issue at all. The number of days between a meeting and the next parliamentary election is obviously a valid measurement. In other instances, however, validity was a problem. To measure the frequency of interactions among the actors of a decision group, one of our indicators was how often the group had met in the past. Yet, the frequency of such formal meetings may not really measure how often the group members interact. It might also be necessary to look at interactions outside the formal group setting. When such questions of validity arise, we will discuss them in the context of the presentation of the data.

CHAPTER 4

The Typology
of Decision Modes

In this chapter, we will discuss the coding of
our dependent variable, the mode of decision making. During the
field research, we were aware of only three decision modes, namely, majority decision, amicable agreement, and nondecision. It was
only during the coding process that we "discovered" the mode of
decision by interpretation.

First, we will consider the three more conventional decision
modes. In chapter 2, we defined at the nominal level what we
mean by majority decision, amicable agreement, and nondecision.
At this point, we should say what operational meaning we have
given to these concepts so that they were applicable to the observation of the Free Democratic party. If a vote was taken and if
this vote was not unanimous (indicating continuing dissent), we
counted the decision as a *majority decision*. In the Free Democratic party all votes were taken by raising the hands, and in all
cases an absolute majority of those voting was required to win.
We classified as a *decision by amicable agreement* a discussion in
which different opinions were expressed but the dissent vanished
at the end of the decision process. This consent could be expressed
through unanimous vote, verbal statements, or approving gestures.
Moreover, the consensus had to include all actors who spoke up
during the discussion, but not necessarily those who remained
silent. For example, if a debate occurred between only two members of a group, all that was needed for amicable agreement was
consent between these two members. Thus, it was important for
the observer to notice all approving gestures of consent. In order
to have a good view, he usually sat next to the chairman. Sharing
the same view with the chairman, the observer could notice all
of the relevant gestures, for if the chairman missed a gesture, it

was also rather irrelevant for the decision process. As indicated in chapter 2, *nondecision* is defined in a much narrower sense than the concept discussed by Peter Bachrach and Morton S. Baratz. If an issue was placed on the formal agenda of a meeting and different opinions were expressed but no decision was made among these opinions, we recorded a nondecision. A decision may be made at a later meeting or it may be postponed indefinitely. This decision not to decide at the present meeting could be either explicit or implicit. The nondecision was explicit if the chairman of the meeting proposed to leave the conflict unresolved and nobody openly objected. An explicit nondecision could also have been made through a formal vote of the group, but this situation never occurred during the research. The nondecision was implicit if the discussion simply turned to another issue without any decision being made about the present one.

Decision by Interpretation

Of the 466 conflicts observed, 12 percent were resolved by majority decision, 21 percent by amicable agreement, and 30 percent by nondecision. The remaining 37 percent appeared at first as an unclassifiable residual category. As already mentioned, it was only during the coding process that we coined the concept of *decision by interpretation*, which allows us to classify these remaining cases. Since decision by interpretation is a new concept that we wish to introduce into the literature, we must describe in more detail how we have applied the concept to our data.

In a decision by interpretation one or more of the participants interpret what they consider to be the sense of the discussion, and this interpretation is then tacitly accepted by the other participants. For example, the chairman might make the interpretation in his final summary of the discussion, as illustrated by this case taken from a meeting of the parliamentary group. Out of thirty-nine members of the group, thirty-two participated at this particular meeting. Member A proposed that in the future the important parts of a discussion in German should be translated into French. At this time 25 percent of the parliamentary group was French speaking, and the other members were German speaking; hitherto, each member had spoken in his native language, the German-speaking members in a special Bernese dialect. Member B opposed the proposal as too cumbersome and put forward the alternative that the Bernese dialect be replaced by High German. Three more participants spoke up, all supporting A. At this point the discussion stopped, and the chairman summarized the discussion, interpreting it to mean that A's proposal had won. B remained silent, neither supporting A nor asking for a vote of the whole group. If B had supported A, the decision would have been by amicable agreement. Had he asked for a vote, it would have been a majority decision. Since B chose neither of these two alternatives, but tacitly accepted the interpretation of the chairman, the decision was taken by interpretation.[1]

Sometimes the interpretation was made not by the chairman but by the secretary, writing in the minutes of the meeting. In such cases, it appeared at the end of the meeting as if no decision had been made, but the secretary reported a decision in the minutes, using his notes to interpret the essence of the discussion. This decision was then tacitly accepted at the beginning of the next meeting when the minutes of the last meeting were approved.

Decision by interpretation by way of the minutes also seems to be a common occurrence in the British Cabinet. As Richard Crossman writes, "Perhaps the great secret of Cabinet government [is] the development of the decision-drafting technique. . . . Cabinet proceedings . . . do not take down in shorthand what actually was said because they prefer to record what should have been said."[2] As a consequence, "sometimes as a member of the Cabinet you don't realize that you lost the battle. . . . But once it is there, written in the minutes, it *has* been decided—against you."[3]

The most interesting decisions by interpretation in our study occurred when an actor interpreted tacitly the decision of the group and then directed the discussion in such a way that the decision was made implicitly. For example, again from a meeting of the parliamentary group, Member A proposed that the canton issue a bond for highway construction. This proposal was supported by B, C, D, and E, speaking in order. D also introduced a procedural matter and recommended that the parliamentary group submit a motion in parliament. After these first five discussants, F spoke, taking a fundamentally different position and opposing a bond for highway construction. At this point the decision-making process took a decisive turn: B again took the floor but by-passed the question of whether a bond should be issued. Instead, he limited himself to the procedural matter, arguing that the bond should be demanded not through a formal motion but through a remark in the general discussion in parliament. The remaining discussion concentrated on the procedural question, and the final decision concerned only two procedural alternatives. The fundamental question of whether a bond should be supported at all was not raised again. The decision in this matter had obviously been made when B managed to turn the discussion away from the question of substance to that of procedure. B had assumed that the group was supporting the bond, so that details of parliamentary strategy could be settled. F, the only member of the group who had expressed opposition to the principle of the bond, decided to remain silent for the remainder of the discussion. He chose neither to support the bond in the sense of amicable agreement nor did he call for a vote.[4]

Of all decisions by interpretation in our study, 24 percent were made by the chairman, 33 percent by the secretary, and 43 percent through the structuring of the discussion. In both of the preceding examples, the interpretation was made in favor of the majority of those who expressed an opinion. Thus, one might ask whether decision by interpretation actually constitutes a distinct decision-making mode.

Distinction from Majority Decision   Is it possible that decisions by interpretation are simply majority decisions for which the voting mechanism is not made explicit? Our data suggest that this is not the case and that, indeed, decision by interpretation has to be considered as a separate and distinct decision-making mode. Of all 466 conflicts, 170 were decided by interpretation. In 85 of these 170 conflicts, the proposal that had enlisted the highest number of supporters in the discussion actually won. In 19 cases the proposal with the greatest support in the discussion lost, and in the remaining 66 cases the decision by interpretation broke a tie. These figures indicate that decisions by interpretation did not simply follow the majority position as expressed in the discussion. To be sure, the majority position won nearly five times more often than it lost, but nevertheless, in a fair number of cases a proposal won that had only minority support in the discussion. Furthermore, about two-fifths of all decisions by interpretation were made in situations in which the discussion had revealed no majority position. We conclude that to interpret the essence of a discussion does not simply mean to go along with the majority. At the same time it does not imply a complete disregard for the amount of support that a proposal has received. Often, a relative uncertainty remains about the distribution of opinions in the full group of participants. Ordinarily, only a portion of the members of a group express their opinions about a particular issue: some members may take part in the discussion without expressing an opinion, and other members may remain completely silent. This relative uncertainty is an important attribute of a decision by interpretation because it gives the interpreter more leeway in formulating the decision. The relative uncertainty about the distribution of opinions is particularly important if the discussion resulted in a tie between competing positions. Here, the interpreter uses previously gained information about the participants to formulate a decision. Thus, it is important for a successful interpreter to have a great deal of information about the opinions in the group. In the example about the highway bond, actor B was the party secretary and thus was well informed about the opinions in the parliamentary group; consequently, he was quite certain that a majority of the group supported a highway bond, although only six of the thirty-two participants had expressed an opinion. This information allowed him to interpret the sense of the discussion at an early stage and to turn the attention of the group to procedural details of the upcoming parliamentary debate.

Decision by interpretation is clearly a different decision mode from majority decision. Unlike a majority decision, a decision by interpretation does not always bring about a victory of the majority; often, it is even unclear which proposal has the highest number of supporters in the group. This element of uncertainty may well be the most important distinctive characteristic of decision by interpretation as compared with majority decision.

That a decision by interpretation will not necessarily follow the majority of the group is also stressed by Crossman for the British Cabinet. The summation by the prime minister "may not represent the discussion at all. . . . The Prime Minister can define the consensus as being what he thinks fit. Even though a majority of the opinions expressed were against him, that would not necessarily prevent him from deciding as he wishes—if he can get away with it."[5]

Distinction from Amicable Agreement   A further question is whether decision by interpretation can be sufficiently differentiated from amicable agreement. One may argue that a tacit acceptance of a decision is very close to an explicit amicable agreement. In the example above of a conflict on the language question, if member A had nodded to the summary of the chairman, it would have been a decision by amicable agreement. Here again, the crucial element of the decision by interpretation was the element of uncertainty. In many decisions by interpretation it may indeed have been true that everyone felt agreement with the decision as it was finally interpreted. However, since this agreement was not made explicit, the situation was basically different from amicable agreement. There was always the possibility that the disagreement would persist and that it would come up again in a later context, in the informal "beer-drinking" after the meeting for example. Our observation data from these informal gatherings show that discussions that ended in decisions by interpretation were often continued after the formal meetings. Sometimes the disagreements persisted, sometimes not.

Based on our observations of the informal gatherings and on unstructured interviews conducted with some of the participants, we can offer several reasons why an actor might prefer not to express his agreement or disagreement with a decision during the actual meeting. He may feel that not expressing agreement with a decision has "face-saving" advantages. He may perceive the issue as so unimportant that it seems hardly worthwhile to verbalize agreement. Or an actor may anticipate that he will lose; consequently, he will not call for a formal vote. Besides the negative psychological effects of a lost vote, a decision made by a vote generally has greater legitimacy than a decision by interpretation because it is more formalized. Thus, an actor in a losing position may prefer a decision by interpretation since the lower legitimacy of this decision mode offers more possibilities for bringing the issue up again in a later context. The crucial point is that the participants in a decision by interpretation are relatively uncertain about the persistence of the disagreement and about the possible motivations of participants for choosing not to express agreement or disagreement. This element of uncertainty clearly distinguishes decisions by interpretation from decisions by amicable agreement.

Distinction from Nondecision   A final question is whether decision by interpretation can be sufficiently distinguished from nondecision. Here, the important question is whether decisions made by interpretation are implemented. If decisions by interpretation were rarely implemented, it would matter little whether the debate ended with a nondecision or a decision by interpretation. Functionally, the two modes would be so similar that it would not be worthwhile to make a conceptual distinction between them. Our data show, however, that, to a large extent, decisions by interpretation were implemented. Of the 170 decisions by interpretation we identified during our study, 90 needed no further implementation by the Free Democratic party. These were of three types. First, some issues required that final decisions be made outside the party. For example, on the question of how much the number of students at the cantonal university should be increased, the party could only express its position; the final decision was in the hands of parliament, and the responsibility for implementation was with a governmental agency. Second, some procedural decisions were implemented during the meeting itself, for example, a decision to close discussion. Third, the implementation of certain decisions was identical with the decision itself. This applies particularly to elections and appointments: no special implementation is needed for the election of a new president, for example. Excluding these three categories, 80 decisions by interpretation remained that called for party implementation after the meeting. Sixty-five of these were actually implemented (81 percent). Although this rate of implementation is lower than those for majority decisions (97 percent) and for decisions by amicable agreement (89 percent), it is still high enough to indicate that decision by interpretation is clearly a distinctive category from nondecision.

The overall conclusion is that the properties of decision by interpretation are so distinctive in comparison with the three other decision modes that it seems reasonable to introduce decision by interpretation as a fourth decision mode.

How a Decision Is Interpreted

An interpreter proceeds in certain characteristic ways in formulating a decision by interpretation. We have already seen that, to a certain extent, he tries to follow the majority of the group. Furthermore, an interpreter often supports the opinions of the high-status group members. In the appendix, we identify a group of 15 actors with high political status in the party (see appendix 3). Our data show that these high-status actors had a greater chance of winning in a decision by interpretation than did low-status actors. Of the 170 decisions by interpretation, 65 involved the acceptance or rejection of a single proposal. Of these 65 single proposals, 20 were made by high-status actors, 31 were made by low-status actors, and 14 originated outside the meeting group. The proposals of high-status actors succeeded in 60 percent of the cases, whereas the proposals of low-status actors won in only 26 percent. Another 76 decisions by interpretation involved situations in which two proposals were on the same conflict dimension. In 15 of these, one proposal came from a high-status actor and the other proposal from a low-status actor; of these cases high-status actors won 13 and lost only 2. The remaining 29 decisions by interpretation involved more than two proposals on the same conflict dimension. Of these, 18 involved proposals made by both high- and low-status actors; high-status actors won 11 times, whereas low-status actors won 7 times. Thus, decision by interpretation clearly favors the high-status actor, but deciding by interpretation does not simply mean following the preferences of the powerful: in a substantial number of cases a high-status actor lost and a low-status actor won.

In addition to the distribution of opinions and power within a group, interpreters also took into account the order in which the proposals had been presented. The first proposal presented of two proposals on the same conflict dimension won in only 37 percent of the cases, the second in 63 percent. The results for three proposals on the same dimension were even more striking: the last proposal won in 71 percent of the cases.[6] It appears that the last proposal had an advantage because it was often presented as a compromise, and was also perceived as such. A third proposal was often formulated with the specific argument that it was designed as a moderate middle position between the first two proposals. From an objective viewpoint, it was certainly not always clear that a third proposal actually occupied such a middle position, but if no other proposal were added, the perception could easily arise that the last proposal was in fact a generally acceptable middle position. There might also have been a tendency to perceive as more important those proposals most recently articulated (temporal proximity), which would give another advantage to the last proposal. Whatever the precise explanation, our data show that the interpreters tended to favor the proposal that was presented last. Terry Sullivan also found that for congressional committees "late-proposed alternatives [had] a better chance of passage."[7]

A fourth criterion that seemed to have entered the calculations of the interpreters was the intensity with which a proposal was defended. Our data base is much weaker for this criterion than it is for the others. We tried to measure intensity with indicators such as loudness of speech and length of presentation of a proposal, but it was clear that some speakers expressed great intensity while speaking briefly and in a low voice. Objective indicators such as the loudness of voice seem much less relevant than the perceptions of the participants: whether the group members perceive a proposal as being presented with high intensity is the important question, and this perception is influenced not only by the meeting itself but also by previously gained information. Usually, group members know how a particular actor feels about a proposal even before he makes his presentation. They are also fairly well informed about whether he tends to express a great deal of intensity through certain personal mannerisms, such as the pitch or volume of his voice. It was beyond the capabilities of this project to measure how the intensity of a proposal's presentation was perceived by all group members, but using the data in an impressionistic way, it nevertheless seems quite clear that the intensely presented proposals had a better chance of winning in decisions by interpretation. This judgment is based in particular on cases of extreme intensity: when the observer had the impression that an actor fought very intensely for a proposal, the actor almost always won in a decision by interpretation.

We hope that it is clear how an actor typically proceeds in trying to interpret a decision from the essence of a discussion. He considers the distribution of preferences in the group, the power distribution, the order in which the proposals were presented, and the intensity of the presentations. As far as possible, the interpreter tries to follow the majority preference, the more powerful actors, the most recent proposal, and the proposal that was presented with the highest intensity. In making his interpretation, the interpreter uses a great deal of information that he has gained prior to the meeting. The leeway for the interpretation, however, is generally much narrower than one might think at first. The possibility that someone might contest the interpretation by calling for a formal vote is always present. If such a vote went against the interpretation, the interpreter would lose political status. Consequently, he tries to formulate the interpretation in such a way that nobody loses too much. However, this does not mean that interpretation is a purely mechanical function unreflective of power wielded by the interpreter. On the contrary, the power of the interpreter is important and stems mainly from the uncertainty of the situation: the greater this uncertainty, the larger the leeway for the interpreter.

Democratic Quality of Decision by Interpretation

One fascination of decision by interpretation is that it blurs the distinction between democratic and autocratic decision making. If we understand by democratic decision making the application of the "one man, one vote" rule, majority decision and amicable agreement are fairly democratic: in a majority decision each vote has the same weight and in a decision by amicable agreement each group member has the possibility of casting a veto and thereby preventing a decision. The "one man, one vote" rule is not applied as strictly in a decision by interpretation. To be sure, each group member has the legal right to contest a decision by interpretation and to ask for a vote, but in reality this right may at times be nonexistent. This is particularly true if a decision by interpretation is made through a clever structuring of the discussion. Inexperienced actors may get lost and not realize what is really happening. When they finally realize that a decision has been made, it may seem awkward if they try to reopen the discussion. Contesting a decision by interpretation at a belated stage often runs against a prevailing social norm. Consequently, many actors feel strong social pressure to accept a decision by interpretation and not to ask for a vote. This pressure is particularly strong if the interpreter is a powerful group member. In extreme cases of decision by interpretation, the interpreter may be so powerful that nobody dares to contest his decision. In such a case, a discussion still takes place and different opinions are expressed, but the decision is made by the interpreter alone. At times, however, decisions by interpretation appear to be quite democratic. If we understand by democratic decision making not exclusively the application of the "one man, one vote" rule but also the intensity with which an opinion is expressed, actors with an intensely held opinion should have extra clout in the decision-making process.[8] This goal can be best reached through a decision by interpretation, which allows the interpreter to include the intensity dimension in the process of decision making.

It remains to be seen whether the typology fares as well for other face-to-face groups, such as national cabinets or parliamentary committees. However, our four decision modes were exhaustive in the classification of the 466 conflicts that occurred in the Free Democratic party during our research period.

PART II

The Data

CHAPTER 5

Statistical Methods of Analysis

In chapter 2 we developed our theoretical framework for the study of the modes of decision making. In this chapter we will discuss the methodology that we will employ in the investigation of our data. The selection of a statistical model is crucially dependent on the nature of the substantive problem with which one is dealing. Therefore, the purpose of the present chapter is to provide both an introduction to the statistical procedures that we will use and a justification of their selection in terms of our substantive research problems. In so doing, we will also attempt some clarification of the major statistical problems confronting us in our research.

Before we proceed, some comments are in order concerning our general approach to theoretical modeling and empirical investigation. To a great extent any formal modeling of social or behavioral phenomena must rely on one of the most elusive human characteristics, intuition.[1] In our own research we have drawn as much as possible on the existing literature, but since we are also engaged in concept formation and hypothesis generation, much of our theory is new and stems from our own intuitive assessments of the processes at work in a decision-making situation. Moreover, as we pointed out in chapter 1, previous studies of decision making have focused too narrowly on the simple dichotomy between competitive and cooperative patterns of decision making. Our typology of decision-making modes is designed to remedy this shortcoming. Consequently, we cannot rely solely on existing literature; we must also derive new hypotheses for our new concepts.

Our primary goal is to establish a close connection between our formal theory, on the one hand, and the real-world phenomena in which we are interested, on the other. Although we are necessarily engaged in a process of abstraction, we have also maintained a high degree of complexity in our model in order that the essence of real political decisions might not be lost altogether. This has the major disadvantage that the relationships among variables in our model are extremely complex and difficult to analyze. One potential danger of this complexity is that we might get lost in a "fishing expedition"—that is, we might allow our statistical methods to determine the substantive content of our theory. It is always tempting first to run numerous analyses on a set of data and only then to begin the search for plausible interpretations of the results. Unfortunately, this procedure has an ad hoc character: given the complexity of the phenomena in which we are interested, relationships are certain to emerge from the analyses, and we can invariably find intriguing and plausible theoretical justifications for the apparent existence of such relationships.

To avoid this danger, we have developed a general research strategy for approaching the study of our data. First, we have devoted a great deal of time and effort to the elucidation of a clear theoretical framework. Second, drawing on this theoretical framework, we will formulate a number of individual hypotheses concerning the relationships among our independent variables and the modes of decision making; we construct these hypotheses *prior to any excursion whatsoever into the data*. Third, to test the plausibility of these hypothesized relationships, we will begin with the simplest possible statistical technique (bivariate contingency table analysis) and then work our way carefully to the most sophisticated techniques. At each step along the way we will be primarily concerned with the existence or absence of a posited relationship; we hope to avoid most of the temptations to depart from our theoretical framework in order to find "plausible" interpretations of otherwise unanticipated relationships.[2]

As a caveat, we should note that the analyses that follow cannot and should not be viewed as a grand test of a single model.[3] As with any attempt at modeling, many alternative models can undoubtedly be derived for the explanation of variation in the dependent variable; our model is only one of those alternatives. Consequently, we do not propose to offer the final word on this particular theory of decision making. Rather, our purpose is to investigate the general plausibility of our theoretical framework, as well as to arrive at a set of new hypotheses concerning the modes of decision making. We hope that these hypotheses might then be tested further in different contexts and refined accordingly. Therefore, what follows is not an attempt to "prove" a theory; more to the point, it is an attempt to pave the way for new insights into the decision-making behavior of politicians. Any assessment of the success or failure of this attempt must consider this underlying purpose.

We will begin with a discussion of some of the problems that confront us when we begin an empirical analysis of our data. In particular, we will address our comments to three general points: (1) the categorical nature of our dependent variable; (2) the essentially "non-linear" quality of the hypothesized relationships among variables in our model; and (3) classification as the substantive research problem in which we are primarily interested. The discussion of these points should then provide the necessary justification (in terms of our substantive theory) for the selection of the three statistical procedures that we will subsequently employ. The second part of this chapter is devoted to a brief outline of the way in which we use bivariate contingency table analysis, multivariate discriminant analysis, and simulation.

The most obvious problem is the purely categorical nature of our dependent variable. As we argued in chapter 4, there are compelling reasons for conceptualizing the modes of decision making as a nominal or categorical variable. Consequently, certain restrictions are immediately placed on the selection of appropriate statistical techniques. Foremost among these restrictions is the exclusion of Ordinary Least Squares Regression. As other authors have described in considerable detail,[4] the assumptions that one must make in order to derive OLS estimates of a model's parameters are systematically violated by observations on a nominally measured dependent variable. Specifically, the assumption that the disturbance term is normally distributed cannot hold when a dependent variable is measured at a nominal level.[5] Most important, however, the disturbance term (u) will be correlated with the independent variable (x), so that $\mathcal{E}(u_z x_z) \neq 0$; this implies that the OLS estimates will be biased and inconsistent.[6] Therefore, we cannot perform a simple linear regression on our data.

One common variation on the OLS regression theme that has received a great deal of attention in the literature in recent years is PROBIT analysis. The similarities between PROBIT and linear regression are manifold and do not need recapitulation in the present context.[7] The main difference, however, is that PROBIT is designed to deal with dependent variables that fall short of a purely interval level measurement; it is necessary to assume only that the dependent variable has been measured on an underlying ordinal scale (a "collapsing of the 'true' interval scale").[8] Unfortunately for our purposes, the relaxation of assumptions involved in the transition from interval level measurement (OLS Regression) to ordinal level measurement (PROBIT) does not go far enough: we are still unable to find a theoretical justification for the attribution of ordinality to our modes of decision making. If we were still working with a simple dichotomy between competitive and cooperative patterns of decision making, we could conceptualize a continuum running from one extreme to the other. In such a case, a technique such as PROBIT might appear more appropriate.[9] However, we have moved beyond such a unidimensional classification scheme with the introduction of both nondecisions and decisions by interpretation. Consequently, PROBIT analysis does not meet the requirements of our data, and its use would be wholly inappropriate in the context of this research.

Since we are working with a nominal level dependent variable, we must find statistical techniques that are both appropriate for this level of measurement and reasonably informative. The latter requirement is particularly crucial, for at the nominal level there are a number of appropriate statistics, and the problem then becomes one of determining whether any one of these statistics can help us unravel the complex interrelationships among our data. An obvious set of candidates for this analysis consists of the various nominal measures of association.[10] However, as we will discuss in a moment, our theoretical framework implies some serious limitations for these techniques.

Two multivariate techniques that are frequently used with a

nominally measured dependent variable are LOGIT and discriminant analysis. For our research we have decided to employ discriminant analysis, largely for reasons to be discussed shortly. A priori, we have no objections to the use of a LOGIT model, other than our preference for having a clearer understanding of our model and our data before we proceed to a more rigorous statistical test of that model. The purpose of our research at this point is basically one of hypothesis generation. Consequently, we are employing discriminant analysis in a heuristic fashion, that is, to see whether our basic hypotheses have some acceptable degree of plausibility. If our first tentative steps prove supportive of our hypotheses, then we have planned to advance the sophistication of our statistical analyses by pressing for further formalization. If and when such formalization is possible, we hope to be able to express our hypotheses (including interactions) in a LOGIT or interactive discriminant model. For the moment, however, we are interested in a lower-level confirmation of the overall plausibility of our general approach.

A second problem that we must consider in the choice of our statistical methods of analysis concerns the nature of the hypothesized underlying relationships in our model. As we have noted in chapter 2, we expect our model to be characterized by a complex set of interrelationships among independent variables. But we also assume that these relationships may not always be clearly linear or "additive" ones. In fact, as we will specify in our simulation, we must account for interaction, threshold, and dominance effects. By *interaction effects* we mean situations in which independent variables in specific combinations may have very pronounced effects on the modes of decision making even though the individual variables considered in isolation might have negligible impacts or altogether different individual effects. Although such interactions can be specified in terms of most multivariate techniques, we will not work within such an interaction framework in our first analysis of the data; instead, we will rely on our simulation for the assessment of these effects. By *threshold effects* we mean situations in which the incremental addition or deletion of one variable has no noticeable impact until a specific level of that variable (a threshold) is reached; once such a threshold is attained, the impact of that variable may or may not become "linear" in the classical sense of the term. *Dominance effects* refer to situations in which the coincidence of two or more variables leads to the "washing out" of the impact of some subset of those variables. An example of this effect is found in our data: although the status composition of a decision-making group is a crucial explanatory variable in our model, we have also discovered that its impact is most pronounced in small groups; in large groups the impact of status is virtually nonexistent.[11] This is, of course, a specific type of interaction effect.

In theory, it is always possible to incorporate these effects within the framework of a multivariate statistical model. However, explicit modifications of the methods would be necessary before we could actually test for such effects. Once again, we fall back on our basic argument that these modifications should be reserved for a later date when we have a better idea of the plausibility of our approach. If we find that conceptualizing our model in terms of interaction, dominance, and threshold effects appears warranted, more explicit tests for these effects can be developed and applied. For the moment we are satisfied to proceed at a much slower pace with a somewhat restricted purpose in mind.

Finally, we need to mention the nature of the specific research task confronting us—the problem of classification. We want to be able to classify each of our cases according to the mode of decision making that was employed in reconciling the conflict. In order to accomplish this classification, we employ the information contained in our explanatory variables. Although there are certainly conceptual similarities between such a classification problem and the prediction problem commonly associated with regression analysis,[12] we prefer to view classification as a slightly different task requiring procedures of its own. For this reason, too, we find discriminant analysis and simulation particularly compatible with our research design.

How do we actually select the statistical methods that we will then employ? First, we can exclude some of the available techniques on the basis of the preceding considerations. As we already mentioned, OLS and, to a lesser extent, PROBIT techniques are untenable from the perspective of our dependent variable: nominal level measurement ensures inapplicability of these two multivariate techniques. Given this problem with the level of measurement, two multivariate techniques remain, LOGIT and discriminant analysis. LOGIT appears on the surface to be appropriate but it requires a somewhat more sophisticated knowledge of the theoretical model than we are willing to claim at this point. This leaves us with discriminant analysis, which seems to serve our immediate purposes nicely. Further refinement of the model and the statistical methods of analysis should proceed in the direction of discriminant analysis with interaction effects and LOGIT analysis.

At this point we can also exclude the use of nominal measures of association. Here, the problem is one involving not the level of measurement but the hypothesized nature of the relationships in our model. If the pattern of interrelationships among explanatory variables is not wholly linear or additive, then we cannot expect individual bivariate relationships to be particularly pronounced: in fact, we expect them a priori to be relatively weak given the framework that we developed in chapter 2. Moreover, it is also quite unlikely that such measures of association could be fruitfully employed beyond the level of bivariate relationships. This is because the introduction of controls (that is, the shift to multivariate relationships) requires a large number of cases when nominal measures of association are employed. Without a very large N, one that is significantly larger than our 466 cases, the resulting contingency tables would be characterized by many empty cells, seriously compounding the difficulty of meaningful data analysis. In addition to these general considerations, there are also problems of spurious and hidden relationships: since we cannot introduce adequate controls, measures of association and tests of statistical significance can be potentially misleading. The obvious example here, of course, would be cases in which strong (that is, statistically significant) relationships emerge, but for reasons other than the simple bivariate hypothesis being tested. Obviously, the converse would be equally possible. Consequently, we will avoid such methods altogether rather than run the risk of confusing the issue still further.

We are left, then, with a number of possibilities. First, we can still employ simple bivariate contingency table analyses, although the extent to which we can adequately investigate the strength of the relationships is severely limited. Second, we can apply a rudimentary multivariate discriminant analysis (that is, without specified interaction effects) to our data, thus gaining some insight into the overall structure of our data. Third, we can try to specify our hypotheses in as precise a form as possible and then operationalize these hypotheses in the form of a computer simulation. Ultimately, such a simulation would seek to classify each of our 466 decisions according to the mode of decision making; this procedure would have the twofold advantage of being able to deal more effectively with the precise nature of our expected relationships as well as with the classification task that we have set out as our primary goal. Before we move on to an actual analysis of our data, we will examine each of these techniques, briefly highlighting their specific strengths and weaknesses.

Bivariate Contingency Tables

We have already noted the problems of spurious and hidden relationships as well as the inapplicability of various measures of association and statistical tests of significance. The question then arises why we use bivariate contingency tables at all. To answer this we return to our earlier discussion of our general strategy. There, we stressed the hypothesis-generating nature of the present study, and we pointed out the complexity of the task confronting us in the analysis of the data. We recommended that a strategy be adopted that begins with the simplest possible tests and works toward the most complex methods. The first step in such a strategy would logically be the formulation of bivariate hypotheses relating each of our independent or explanatory variables to our dependent variable. Following this basic design, we do find some limited purpose in the application of contingency table analysis to our data: we will simply ask the question whether a hypothesized relationship appears to hold or not. Obviously, we will be unable to provide any convincing proof of the existence or absence of the relationship. However, as a first step, this information should prove worthwhile: if our expectations systematically fail to be borne out in the cross-tabulations, we will be hard pressed to justify the applicability of our theoretical framework. If, on the other hand, our expectations fare rather well, we will be justified in taking the next step, namely, a multivariate discriminant analysis.

Multivariate Discriminant Analysis

The reader will find a detailed explanation of this technique in Robert Dorff's dissertation, "Employing Simulation Analysis in Decision-Making Theory."[13] For the present we would simply like to mention some important considerations that the reader should bear in mind. Obviously, the ability of discriminant analysis to deal with a categorical dependent variable is of prime importance to us in the selection of this technique. Moreover, the classification problem also indicates this technique as the logical selection. In addition, as we have argued, our model must be viewed as multivariate. At some point in our analyses we should attempt to examine the effects of each independent variable while simultaneously controlling for the effects of the other independent variables. Since such an examination is not possible with simple contingency table analysis, a multivariate technique is especially desirable. Two very important caveats must be kept in mind, however. First, since discriminant analysis is a linear technique, we can expect it to encounter some difficulty with the nonlinear relationships that we believe will actually characterize our data; in other words, we can hardly anticipate an ideal fit when applied to our data. Second, and even more important, we must look at the congruence, or lack of it, between discriminant analysis as a statistical model and the theoretical model that derives from our substantive theory. In our view decision making must be conceptualized as a "flow process"—that is, a process in which different variables enter the flow at various points in time. Consequently, certain variables become salient only at specific points in time. However, as with any multivariate method not designed for time series or lagged variable analysis, discriminant analysis cannot replicate the ebb and flow of an actual decision-making situation. Thus, we cannot expect discriminant analysis to tap this component of our theory. Therefore, our final step in the analysis of our data will consist of an attempt to operationalize our hypotheses in such a way that this flow process will itself become an important determinant of the mode of decision making.

Simulation

The final step in this stage of our study, then, is the creation of a computer simulation that will model this flow process. Elsewhere, we have described the theoretical nature of our simulation and its relationship to other simulation analyses.[14] Here, we would like to mention only that the precise purpose of this analysis is to arrive at a set of predictions concerning the decision mode with which a conflict was resolved. Drawing on our original data, we will try to establish a set of predictions based on the likelihood of a single decision mode being employed. In this way we will be able to compare our predictions with the actual decision mode that was used in a given situation, thereby facilitating an assessment of the general plausibility of our theoretical framework and the hypotheses that we derived from it. The particular strength of the technique is that it allows us to deal more effectively with the precise nature of the substantive theory with which we are working. In effect, the open-ended nature of simulation allows the researcher to specify his own set of parameters rather than compel him to submit his model to the restrictions of a specific mathematical model. The greatest shortcoming of this method lies in the loss of rigor when one moves from the relatively closed or rigid confines of strict statistical analysis to the loose, malleable model building of simulation. In the end we hope that we can arrive at some overall assessment not only of our model's plausibility but of the general utility of these three statistical techniques in helping us distinguish the most important relationships among our explanatory variables and the modes of decision making.

CHAPTER 6

Bivariate Analysis

In this chapter we will present the individual hypotheses relating each of the independent variables to variation in the modes of decision making. Our purpose will be both to provide the theoretical justification for each hypothesis and to report the results of some very rudimentary bivariate tests of the relationships. As noted in chapter 5, contingency table analysis can contribute only marginally to a test of the theoretical model. However, since our immediate goal in this phase of the project is to arrive at a reduced set of independent variables that we can subsequently model in a computer simulation, simple bivariate tests can help us by providing some indication of the general plausibility of a hypothesized relationship. Since the application of bivariate analysis is exclusively heuristic, we will not report the results for each and every hypothesis. Instead we will report only the most interesting results in the text; for the remainder of the bivariate analyses we refer the reader to Robert Dorff's unpublished Ph.D. dissertation.[1]

Structure of the Decision Group

Hypothesis 1.   *The smaller the size of the decision group, the higher the probability of amicable agreement and the lower the probability of majority decision; nondecision and decision by interpretation are unaffected.*

In order to demonstrate the rationale behind this hypothesis, we will first concentrate on the way in which the four values discussed in chapter 2 (power, group solidarity, rectitude, and time) may be influenced by the size of the decision group. Perhaps the most obvious impact can be seen in the opportunity costs of lost time. In a large group the number of potential speakers is higher, raising the prospect of lengthy discussions. At the same time the typical group member has relatively few opportunities to intervene in the discussion; much of his time is spent simply listening to other members. This mostly passive role, particularly when extended over a lengthy meeting, may contribute increasingly to the feeling that the time could be better invested for other purposes. Thus, the incentive grows to reduce the opportunity cost represented by this loss of valuable time. In a small group, on the other hand, discussions tend to be shorter, and everyone can participate more fully. Consequently, the decision makers generally do not perceive the time spent in the decision process as a significant opportunity cost.

Size of the group probably also influences the importance of group solidarity as an incentive. Solidarity is expected to be more important in small groups because the low number of participants leads to a high number of interpersonal interactions, and according to George Homans's well-known hypothesis, frequent interactions should be a favorable condition for solidarity.[2] Another argument, based on Mancur Olson's work, states that in a small group each actor can contribute in a more perceptible way to the maintenance of the group, whereas the maintenance of a large group depends much less clearly on the actions and inactions of individual group members.[3] Thus, in a small group a rational actor should be more motivated to work for group solidarity than the same rational actor in a large group.

Considerations of power probably have a greater impact in large groups than in small groups. The larger the number of people attending a meeting, the more that meeting takes on the character of a spectacle; the more the participants feel as though they are "performing" in this spectacle, the more power considerations will be involved. Winning or losing has a much more dramatic effect in a large group than in a small group, and scoring a point in the closeness and informality of a small group is much less spectacular than scoring the same point in a large meeting.

We can find no logical reasons why the size of the group would have an influence on considerations of rectitude. The causal linkage between the size of the group, the values, and the modes of decision making can now be made. The pressure for solidarity in a small group can best be met with a decision by amicable agreement. Two potential obstacles to a decision of this type are not particularly salient in small groups, namely, time pressure and considerations of power. If an amicable agreement cannot be achieved in a small group, the second most likely mode is probably nondecision or decision by interpretation, both of which would not disrupt solidarity significantly. A majority decision appears to be the least desirable mode since it may be detrimental to solidarity. In large groups an important consideration is the time factor; thus, majority decision is the logical alternative. A majority decision also satisfies a need for power, since it allows each participant to stand by his position. Of course, standing by one's position can result in a loss of power if that position winds up in the minority. However, since group solidarity is relatively unimportant in large groups, the majority will be largely unconcerned with what happens to the minority; thus, concessions will be unlikely. Amicable agreement should be quite infrequent in large groups, for it is both time consuming and based on a desire for group solidarity.

In a general way, our hypotheses are compatible with the experimental research of John Fox and Melvin Guyer who simply distinguish between cooperative and competitive decision-making strategies; they found that cooperative strategies are more widely used in small groups, the reason being that "individuals in small groups behave as group members, being responsive to standards of performance and the behavior of the others in the group. In large groups—those in which there is an appreciable degree of anonymity and an absence of group structure—individuals do not enter into a group process, but instead respond as independent decision makers who attempt to maximize individual gains in much the same manner as would a decision maker who was playing a game against an impassive 'nature.' In effect, what occurs when group size increases is that the individual decision maker relies more and more upon self-gain considerations in weighing a choice between cooperation and competition."[4]

Moving now to the data, table 6.1 shows the results of the cross-tabulation between the size of the decision group and the modes of decision making. It appears that our method of partitioning the size variable is effective. The partitioning depended on an intuitive sense of what we understood to be "large" and "small," as well as on our desire to have categories with roughly equivalent numbers of cases.[5] Of particular importance is the composition of the middle group. If the two extreme categories are to be meaningful partitions, we must have a middle range that does not depart significantly from the population distributions. In other words, not only must our two categories be distinct but the residual category must represent a "middle ground" as well (in this case the population averages). Here we have a substantial middle range (8–20 persons), representing 41.2 percent of the decisions. In each of our four decision categories, individual distributions for this middle category correspond very closely to population distributions. Nondecision and amicable agreement are 1.3 percent more and less frequent respectively, whereas majority decision differs by only .1 percent and decision by interpretation is precisely as expected. We can now turn to a closer examination of the two categories in which we are particularly interested, namely, the small and large groups.

Our two major expectations about group size are borne out very well by the data. Only 4.1 percent of the decisions taken in small groups are majority decisions, compared to 21.9 percent for large groups. Both of these figures represent substantial departures from the population average of 12.4 percent. The table also reveals that amicable agreement is much more frequent in small groups (28.8 percent) than it is in large groups (13.3 percent), and once again the departures from the population average (20.6 percent) are pronounced.

Although we expected no significant differences to emerge for decision by interpretation and nondecision, the table does reveal that small groups tend to postpone decisions more often (32.9 percent) than do large groups (25.8 percent), and that the former tend to reach decisions by interpretation less often (34.2 percent)

Table 6.1:   Observed Frequency of the Modes of Decision
Making by the Size of the Group (percentages
in parentheses)

Size of Group	Majority Decision	Amicable Agreement	Nondecision	Decision by Interpre- tation	Total
7 persons or less	6 (4.1)	42 (28.8)	48 (32.9)	50 (34.2)	146 (31.3)
8–20 persons	24 (12.5)	37 (19.3)	61 (31.8)	70 (36.5)	192 (41.2)
21 persons or more	28 (21.9)	17 (13.3)	33 (25.8)	50 (39.1)	128 (27.5)
Total	58 (12.4)	96 (20.6)	142 (30.5)	170 (36.5)	466 (100.0)

than do the latter (39.1 percent). A potential explanation of these differences can be found in the hypotheses that were postulated above: concerns for group solidarity in small groups could override the desirability of reaching a decision. However, each of these differences represents only a very small departure from the population averages, something less than four cases in each category. Consequently, we should not attribute undue importance to them.

When we examined the effects of size on our dependent variable while controlling individually for the remaining variables of group structure, we found that those effects remained. Small groups continued to display higher incidences of amicable agreement and lower incidences of majority decision. This relationship was reversed for large groups and in most cases appeared monotonic.

Hypothesis 2.   The larger the proportion of high-status
actors in a decision group, the higher the
probability of decision by interpretation and
the lower the probability of majority decision;
amicable agreement and nondecision are
unaffected.

In this study, political status refers to the rank that an actor has achieved in the Free Democratic party hierarchy. In order to determine variations in the level of political status we used the three traditional indicators: reputation, position, and participation. Because of its complex nature the exact operationalization of political status is discussed in an appendix. For the following analysis we simply dichotomize between 15 actors with high political status and all other actors with low political status. On this basis the following three categories of decision-making groups can be distinguished: (a) groups with only high-status actors, (b) groups with only low-status actors, (c) groups with a mixture of high- and low-status actors.

Power is hypothesized to be more important for actors with high political status. If power were not of great importance to them, they probably would not have attained their present high-status position. To be sure, some low-status actors may also be very interested in power as they attempt to scale the political ladder. But many other low-status actors simply may not have the ambition to become powerful in the political arena: in fact, they may be amateur politicians whose real interests lie outside of politics altogether. Moreover, high-status actors are probably more interested in protecting what they have and in trying to minimize losses of power, whereas low-status actors would rather try to maximize gains in power.

Solidarity is expected to be a more important value among high-status actors because they interact in the political arena more than do low-status actors. These frequent interactions should lead to feelings of identification with their fellow politicians and even to a certain sense of camaraderie. Solidarity may also be increased among high-status actors because they have to defend a common good, namely, their power.

We expect rectitude to be less important among high-status than among low-status actors. If an actor always insists on doing the "right" thing, it is difficult to compromise with him. The capacity to bargain and compromise, however, seems to be an important precondition for upward political mobility. It may also be true that in moving up the political ladder an actor learns to bargain and compromise. In either case, it seems that actors with high political status are often willing to compromise rectitude to achieve solutions.

Reducing the opportunity costs represented by time spent in the meeting is expected to be important for high-status actors because they tend to accumulate numerous political roles. Consequently, they perceive time as very scarce and try not to spend too much of it in one particular meeting. For low-status actors, on the other hand, participation in a political meeting tends to be a relatively rare occurrence; thus, they feel less of an urge to hurry on to other meetings.

The values that are maximized by the high-status actors are expected to lead to an increase in decisions by interpretation and to a decrease in majority decisions. The great importance of solidarity among high-status actors should in fact lead to many decisions by amicable agreement. But power considerations may make it difficult for high-status actors to reach explicit agreements, because they may fear conceding too early, thereby losing power. In addition, the time pressure on high-status actors may make it difficult to reach an agreement among all conflicting positions. The optimal decision mode for high-status actors should be decision by interpretation, which can be made quickly. Although not as good as amicable agreement for group solidarity, decision by interpretation is not harmful either, because it often remains unclear who the losers are. This latter aspect minimizes losses of power. With the ambiguous nature of a decision by interpretation, it is always possible to raise the issue in a later context; in this way losses may not be perceived as final. Among high-status actors, the low importance attached to rectitude should also facilitate decisions by interpretation. The diminished importance of this value implies a smaller need on the part of the high-status actor to state his position in an unambiguous manner. Consequently, the ambiguity of a decision made by interpretation may appear more desirable. Among low-status actors, we expect many majority decisions: these serve the need for rectitude by allowing each participant to articulate his position clearly. A majority decision also provides the more ambitious low-status actors with the opportunity to maximize their power by siding with winning coalitions. At the same time, the risk of losing power is not particularly great: low-status actors possess little of it anyway. Majority decisions should also be relatively more frequent among low-status actors because considerations of group solidarity are of little importance to this group. The incidence of decision by interpretation is expected to be below average among low-status actors, for they feel less of a need to safeguard power through subtle decision mechanisms. If they do not choose majority decision they will probably employ the simpler modes of amicable agreement or nondecision.

Up to this point we have dealt only with groups that consist either entirely of high-status actors or entirely of low-status actors. We turn now to the groups with a mixture of high- and low-status actors. This is not simply a middle category, as was the case with groups of intermediate size vis-à-vis large and small groups. The situation is further complicated because the precise mixture of high- and low-status actors will be of great importance. The conditions for decision making would be completely different if, for example, there were only one high-status actor among the participants or if, on the other hand, there were only one low-status actor. For the moment, we limit ourselves to the simple criterion whether high- or low-status actors are numerically predominant.

If low-status actors are in a minority, we expect the same decision-making patterns as if no low-status actors were present. The assumption is that high-status actors behave in essentially the same way whether they are among themselves only or whether they have with them a few low-status actors. The presence of some low-status actors no doubt changes the atmosphere of a meeting, by making it less intimate, for example. But we do not expect that such an influence will significantly change the modes of decision making; given both their numerical predominance and their high position, the high-status actors should remain very much in control.

An analogous argument cannot be made if high-status actors are in a minority. In such cases we cannot expect that the minority will have no influence on the choice of decision mode; high-status actors will have an impact on decision making even if they are in a minority. What decision modes should we then expect? First, we assume that, with one exception, both high- and low-status actors maximize the same values as described previously. The exception concerns the value of group solidarity for the high-status actors. Although they attach high importance to solidarity when they are among themselves, we assume that this value loses its importance if high-status actors are in a minority among low-status actors. Therefore, decision by interpretation seems a very likely decision mode. In groups of their peers, high-status actors are expected to use decision by interpretation often; they should also try to use this decision mode if they are in a minority among low-status actors. As a result of their power, they should be quite successful in achieving their desires. The frequency of majority decisions should also be above average. We have already noted that this decision mode is preferred among low-status actors, and we might expect that the high-status minority will often support this preference since group solidarity is less important in mixed-status groups. Finally, the occurrence of amicable agreement is expected to be relatively rare when a majority of low-status actors is joined by a minority of high-status actors. The impetus toward solidarity is lacking, and the common ground between high- and low-status actors that is necessary to reach a genuine agreement may also be wanting.

Only 436 of the total 466 decision-making situations are available for a test of these hypotheses. The remaining 30 cases—meetings of the party convention, the central committee, and the conference of the presidents—were too large to allow the simultaneous observation of the discussion and accurate notation of the names of all participants.[6]

In table 6.2 we distinguish four categories. At the top and at the bottom we place the two "pure" categories, all high-status and all low-status actors. For the mixed cases we distinguish between groups in which the number of high-status actors was greater than 50 percent and in which the number was less than or equal to 50 percent.[7]

Our hypotheses are most clearly supported for majority decisions. Groups consisting exclusively or predominantly of high-status actors use majority decision much less often than low-status groups. Indeed, it seems that among high status actors the importance of solidarity and the desire to minimize losses of power work against the use of majority decision. Our hypotheses are also

Table 6.2:   *Observed Frequency of the Modes of Decision Making by the Political Status of the Group Members (percentages in parentheses)*

Political Status	Majority Decision	Amicable Agreement	Nondecision	Decision by Interpre- tation	Total
All high- status actors	0 (0.0)	9 (34.6)	7 (26.9)	10 (38.5)	26 (6.0)
High-status actors > 50% but < 100%	2 (2.5)	24 (30.4)	23 (29.1)	30 (38.0)	79 (18.1)
Low-status actors ≥ 50% but <100%	31 (11.2)	49 (17.8)	87 (31.5)	109 (39.5)	276 (63.3)
All low- status actors	10 (18.2)	11 (20.0)	17 (30.9)	17 (30.9)	55 (12.6)
Total	43 (9.9)	93 (21.3)	134 (30.7)	166 (38.1)	436 (100.0)

supported for decisions by interpretation. As we expected, this decision mode is used less often when low-status actors are among themselves. For the three other categories, decision by interpretation is employed at about the same level. Thus, whether high-status actors are among themselves, numerically predominant, or in a numerical minority does not seem to make a difference; this, of course, corresponds to our hypotheses.

Our hypotheses are also supported for nondecision, for, as we expected, no marked differences appear. Finally, we find an unexpected result for amicable agreement: contrary to our hypotheses, high-status actors use amicable agreement much more than the average for the whole population. We anticipated that for high-status actors considerations of power and time pressure would counterbalance the importance of solidarity so much so that amicable agreement would be employed at only an average level. The data indicate that we underestimated the importance of solidarity among high-status actors.

With other variables of group structure controlled, the observed differences for majority decision and amicable agreement remain largely intact, whereas the results are more ambiguous for decision by interpretation. The most significant interaction occurs between status and size, with the effects of the former being most pronounced in small groups. This indicates that the interaction or combination of size and status may be more significant than the individual effects considered in isolation. The main conclusion here is that amicable agreement occurs with above-average frequency among high-status actors, majority decision with above-average frequency among low-status actors. There are no clear differences for nondecision and decision by interpretation.

Hypothesis 3.   *The more frequent the interactions among the members of a decision group, the higher the probability of amicable agreement and the lower the probability of majority decision; nondecision and decision by interpretation are unaffected.*

The members of a decision group may be meeting for the first time or they may have had many prior interactions. These interactions may have taken place within the present decision group or in various other organizational settings. Once again following the argument of Homans, we expect that a high frequency of prior interactions will increase group solidarity. We further hypothesize that considerations of power will decrease if the members of the group interact frequently because it then becomes much more possible to compensate costs in earlier games with benefits in later games. Consequently, winning or losing on a particular issue is much less dramatic in such situations than if the participants are meeting for the first time. Given the high importance of solidarity and the low importance of power, groups with a high frequency of prior interactions should choose amicable agreement relatively frequently and majority decision relatively seldom. A similar argument is made by Barbara Hinckley who uses the concept of "repetitive games," which is very nearly the equivalent of saying that the actors have had many prior interactions. She expects for repetitive games "a greater incidence of the use of accommodative strategies."[8]

We employed three indicators to measure the frequency of interactions among group members:

1. As a simple and straightforward indicator, we used the number of times a group met during the two years prior to the current meeting.
2. As an indirect measure we used the number of extra-party organizations (economic interest groups, voluntary associations, and so forth) in which individual group members hold a function. We assume that a high number of such functions increases the probability that group members will also meet outside the party.
3. As a further indirect measure we used the number of governmental functions in which the group members are involved. Here again, we assume that a high number of such functions increases the probability that the group members will also meet outside the party.

In addition, the second and third indicators were calculated in two different ways so that five distinct cross-tabulations emerged. The results of these analyses presented a complex and confusing picture.[9] Although some support for our initial hypothesis did appear, the lack of consistency across indicators and the obvious degree to which the results depended on the way in which the indicators were computed led us to doubt the validity of our measures. Consequently, we must conclude for the moment that further refinement of our measurement techniques is necessary before we can test the plausibility of this hypothesis.

Hypothesis 4.   *The larger the proportion of younger actors in a decision group, the higher the probability of majority decision and the lower the probability of the other three decision modes.*

We expect that both the biological and the political age are significant variables. By the latter we mean simply the amount of time spent in politics. We expect that younger actors will often insist on doing the "right" thing, whereas older actors may have learned through experience that ideals are hard to translate into reality. We also hypothesize that the time factor is less important for younger actors, for political meetings are still something new and entertaining for them. Older actors, on the other hand, may get bored more easily by discussions that they may have heard many times before; consequently, they may feel a stronger need to reduce the opportunity costs of time. Finally, the number of personal political acquaintances is likely to grow with age, reinforcing feelings of group solidarity.

Thus, majority decision will be a more favored mode among younger than among older actors. Majority decision allows each actor to be counted on his position, thereby serving well the value of rectitude, which is so important to younger actors. Moreover, the low level of solidarity in groups of younger actors makes it likely that they will find nothing wrong with majority decisions. Although the lack of time pressure may allow younger actors to negotiate at great length, amicable agreement should still be relatively rare among younger actors because of the high value placed on rectitude and the low level of group solidarity.

Once again, we employed multiple indicators for the independent variable.[10] On the whole, the basic hypothesis was supported for majority decision, whereas the anticipated variation in the other three modes was less distinct. However, the explanatory potential of the variable was limited by the highly skewed distribution of the data.

Hypothesis 5.   *The more homogeneous a decision group, the higher the probability of amicable agreement and decision by interpretation and the lower the probability of majority decision and non-decision.*

A decision group is fully homogeneous if all of its members share the same social attributes, such as education, occupation, regional background, language, religion, age, and sex. Homogeneous and heterogeneous decision groups are expected to be distinguished primarily by the level of internal solidarity. If the members of a group share the same social attributes, feelings of solidarity are likely to develop, and the group will perceive itself as a special entity within its environment. The intensity of internal conflicts is probably relatively low compared to the intensity of conflicts with the environment. Consequently, considerations of power will apply mainly to relations with the environment and not to relations within the group itself. Given these values, homogeneous groups should strive to utilize amicable agreement. If this decision mode is not feasible, decision by interpretation will not be too detrimental to solidarity. On the other hand, majority decision seems incompatible with the high level of solidarity in homogeneous groups, and a failure to decide (nondecision) may be perceived as a weakness vis-à-vis a potentially unfriendly environment.

In heterogeneous groups, serious conflicts take place not only with the environment but also within the group itself. Considerations of power would thus be expected to outweigh concerns for solidarity, and it would seem appealing to try to beat the opposition in a vote. If this decision mode seemed too dangerous because the group itself might collapse, a decision could be delayed for the time being.

Combining the different attributes of education, occupation, regional background, language, religion, and sex, we tried to construct a summary index for homogeneity. We had hoped to derive a category with fairly homogeneous meetings, one or two middle categories, and a category with fairly heterogeneous meetings. But the data revealed a strong cross-cutting tendency among the various social attributes. Consequently, if a meeting was homogeneous in one attribute, it was most likely quite heterogeneous in some other attributes. Thus, we found almost no cases of multidimensional homogeneous and heterogeneous groups. This raises once again the problem of insufficient variation in the data: if we cannot compare relatively pure cases of homogeneous and heterogeneous groups, the effect of this explanatory variable may not become visible. In the absence of relatively pure cases, we could still construct a summary index measuring different levels of homogeneity. But such a procedure would presuppose that we could assign weights to the different social attributes, and we were unable to find a satisfactory solution to the problem of how these weights should be assigned. Thus, we have simply analyzed the data for each individual attribute.[11]

Although we must be extremely cautious in interpreting these results, it does appear that homogeneity tends to make majority decision a less likely mode. In fact, this tendency was observed for six of the eight indicators and remained intact when we introduced controls for the other variables of group structure.[12] The effects of homogeneity were more ambiguous for the other three decision modes; however, the frequency of amicable agreement for homogeneous groups appeared to be slightly above the average.

Substance of the Conflict

Theodore Lowi has proposed his well-known distinction between "regulatory," "distributive," "redistributive," and "constituency" policies.[13] However, George D. Greenberg et al. disagreed with this typology. According to them, a single policy often has attributes of more than one of Lowi's policy types, and the perceptions may vary from one actor to another. For our part, we found the Lowi typology very appealing on the nominal level. However, we agree with Greenberg et al. that "Lowi's theory is not testable because the basic concepts are not operationalizable."[14] Consequently, the first hypothesis in this group addresses the question of whether the conflict deals only with means or also with goals.

Hypothesis 6. *The more a conflict deals not only with means but also with ends, the higher the probability of majority decision and nondecision and the lower the probability of amicable agreement and decision by interpretation.*

This hypothesis is based on the distinction between position and valence conflicts originally discussed by David Butler and Donald Stokes.[15] In a valence conflict, the actors agree on the goals and disagree only on the means to attain these goals. Butler and Stokes cite as examples for Great Britain peace, economic prosperity, and national prestige. In a position conflict, the disagreement concerns the goals themselves. According to Butler and Stokes, nationalization is such a position issue in Great Britain. We expect that the distinction between position and valence conflicts is relevant not only for election studies but also for an explanation of decision modes.

The lack of common goals is detrimental to solidarity. If the actors disagree not only on means but also on goals, winning becomes much more important; thus, power has a high priority. If goals are involved, it is not simply a question of winning for the sake of power but of winning in the "right" sense, thereby lending a high value to rectitude, too. Given the heightened importance of winning, whichever side has the necessary votes may try to outvote the other side. If the outcome of a vote is difficult to predict, a conservative strategy is to delay the decision. In a valence conflict, on the other hand, the commonly accepted goals give an overriding importance to group solidarity. Consequently, the actors will try to utilize amicable agreement. If this decision mode is not feasible, decision by interpretation may still preserve solidarity.

When the Free Democratic decision makers had to resolve a conflict, the discussion often turned on whether the disagreements concerned goals or merely means. We used such statements in the discussion as the basis for coding the conflicts as either position or valence issues. If there was some ambiguity about how the actors perceived the conflict or if the actors differed in their expressed perceptions, we coded the conflict "ambiguous whether position or valence conflict." As seen in table 6.3, this middle category comprised about half of all cases.

Our expectations concerning the effects of position and valence conflicts on the decision modes are borne out very well by the data in table 6.3. Majority decision and nondecision are used to settle position conflicts much more often than the population averages, whereas amicable agreement and decision by interpretation are used far less. Precisely the inverse relationships obtain for valence issues. The distinct effects of position and valence conflicts on the modes of decision making remain intact when we control for the other variables of the substance of the conflict.

Table 6.3:   Observed Frequency of the Modes of Decision
              Making by Position Versus Valence Conflict
              (percentages in parentheses)

Position Versus Valence Conflict	Majority Decision	Amicable Agreement	Nondecision	Decision by Inter- pretation	Total
Position conflict	28 (22.0)	10 (7.9)	54 (42.5)	35 (27.6)	127 (27.3)
Ambiguous whether position or valence conflict	27 (11.9)	45 (19.9)	64 (28.3)	90 (39.8)	226 (48.5)
Valence conflict	3 (2.7)	41 (36.3)	24 (21.2)	45 (39.8)	113 (24.2)
Total	58 (12.4)	96 (20.6)	142 (30.5)	170 (36.5)	466 (100.0)

Hypothesis 7.   The more a conflict refers to matters of the
                 decision group itself, the higher the probabili-
                 ty of amicable agreement and the lower the
                 probability of majority decision; nondecision
                 and decision by interpretation are unaffected.

The substance of a conflict may be related to the decision group
itself: for example, the disagreement may concern when to hold
the next meeting of the group. On the other hand, a conflict may
refer to a group that is quite distinct from the decision group:
for example, a group made up of natives may disagree on an issue
concerning foreign workers. Between these two extremes there are
many potential cases of partial overlap between the decision group
and the reference group of the conflict.

We hypothesize that solidarity is the main value that will be
influenced by the reference group of the conflict. The more the
decision group and the reference group of the conflict are identi-

cal, the more the importance of solidarity is expected to increase. If a group is dealing with a conflict that refers to itself, the interactions in the group may be disrupted, and even the survival of the group may be at stake. To minimize this danger, the group members will generally tend to emphasize the value of solidarity, trying to prevent the use of majority decision and to work for amicable agreement. If, on the other hand, there is no overlap between the decision group and the reference group of the conflict, the value of solidarity is not strongly involved, and it will be relatively easy to settle such a conflict by majority rule.

As seen in table 6.4, the decision group and the reference group of the conflict were identical in 88 cases; in these instances the decision groups were dealing with an internal problem of their own. The second category in table 6.4 consists of 189 cases in which the conflict referred to another group of the party. The executive committee had to decide, for example, what the agenda should be for the party convention. The least overlap between decision group and reference group of the conflict can be found in the last category, which consists of 151 decisions dealing with groups outside the party. For example, a party committee had to decide how much influence the students should have at the Bernese university. Even in such cases a certain overlap between the decision group and the reference group of the conflict may still remain: some university members may also belong to the Free Democratic decision group. Finally, 38 cases are omitted from table 6.4 because it was not possible to classify them neatly in any of the three categories.

Table 6.4 presents a rather complex picture. We find support for our hypotheses in the low frequency of amicable agreement for deciding conflicts referring to groups outside the party. But the frequency of amicable agreement does not vary from the first to the second category; it seems that solidarity is equally involved whether the conflict refers to the decision group itself or to another group of the party. Majority decisions occur with well above average frequency in conflicts referring to groups outside the party, which corresponds to our hypotheses; but contrary to our expectations, the occurrence of majority decision is also above average if the conflict refers to the decision group itself.

Table 6.4:   Observed Frequency of the Modes of Decision
                    Making by the Reference Group of the Con-
                    flict (percentages in parentheses)

Reference Group of the Conflict	Majority Decision	Amicable Agreement	Nondecision	Decision by Interpretation	Total
Decision group itself	16 (18.2)	22 (25.0)	14 (15.9)	36 (40.9)	88 (20.6)
Other party groups	6 (3.2)	48 (25.4)	56 (29.6)	79 (41.8)	189 (44.2)
Groups outside the party	34 (22.5)	19 (12.6)	59 (39.1)	39 (25.8)	151 (35.3)
Totals	56 (13.1)	89 (20.8)	129 (30.1)	154 (36.0)	428 (100.0)

We predicted no variation for nondecision among the three categories, but the data show a strong monotonic relationship: nondecision is the most frequently used mode if the conflict refers
to a group outside the party. The low number of nondecisions
for conflicts referring to the decision group itself might be explained by the importance of solidarity in such situations. If an
issue concerning the group itself is involved, failing to make a
decision could impede the capacity of the group to function; given
the high priority of group solidarity, such a development would
appear unlikely. Contrary to our expectations, decision by interpretation also shows strong variation. Here, however, the relationship is not linear: a threshold lies between conflicts dealing with
party matters and those referring to groups outside the party;
decision by interpretation is used more frequently in the former
than it is in the latter category. Here again, the value of solidarity
provides a plausible explanation: solidarity is very important for
party matters, and decision by interpretation preserves feelings of
solidarity.

Our original hypotheses were very simple: as the amount of

overlap between the decision group and the reference group of the conflict increases, amicable agreement becomes the more likely mode and majority decision the less likely mode. Since the hypotheses were not confirmed in this simple form, we will try to reformulate them post hoc. The important distinction seems to be whether a conflict refers to groups inside or outside the party. In the latter case majority decision and nondecision are used with a frequency well above the average; this could be explained by the low importance of solidarity in such situations. If the conflict involves a party matter, however, considerations of solidarity are much more important, and the actors will strive for an amicable agreement or a decision by interpretation. If a decision cannot be reached by either of these two modes, one must determine whether the conflict refers to the decision group directly or to another group of the party. In the former case majority decision seems the next best choice, in the latter case nondecision. As already argued above, the failure to make a decision about an internal matter of the decision group runs the risk of impeding the functional capacity of the group; thus, a majority decision appears to be the lesser evil. If, on the other hand, the conflict refers not to the group itself but to another group in the party, the actors may be tempted to defer their decision until they first obtain more information from other party sources. When we control for the other variables of the substance of the conflict, the relationships in table 6.4 remain largely intact, which lends a certain degree of support to our reformulated hypotheses.

Hypothesis 8.   The more a conflict involves innovative proposals, the higher the probability of majority decision and the lower the probability of amicable agreement; nondecision and decision by interpretation are unaffected.

Every conflict necessarily involves an aspect of innovation. If everyone supported the status quo, no disagreements would arise. Thus, it is necessary that someone challenge the status quo for a conflict to occur. However, differences do appear in the degree of innovation in a conflict. On the one hand, some conflicts show a clear contrast between an innovative and a status quo position: for example, in a decision-making group some actors might advocate that Switzerland give up its traditional neutrality, whereas other actors might argue for the existing policy of neutrality. On the other hand, some conflicts display little difference in innovation among the various alternatives. For example, a conflict over the federal deficit that involves merely the question of the size of that deficit would hardly be perceived as involving an innovative and a status quo position because factors like inflation and unemployment must be considered for an evaluation of budget figures. We expect that the visibility of the aspect of innovation in a conflict will have an influence on the mode of decision making.

If an innovative position can be clearly distinguished from a status quo position in a conflict, we expect the value of rectitude to be quite important. In such conflicts the decision to defend or to challenge the status quo often involves basic principles. If it is important to do the "right" thing, an actor is likely to stand by his original position and to seek a resolution of the conflict through a majority vote. On the other hand, in a conflict that does not involve a choice between an innovative and a status quo position, the value of rectitude is less important, providing more leeway for reaching a decision by amicable agreement.

The results for the aspect of innovation in a conflict are reported in Dorff.[16] Although there was a noticeable lack of variation in the data (only 17.6 percent of all conflicts involved a clear distinction between an innovative and a status quo proposal), our hypothesis concerning majority decision and amicable agreement was largely supported. Moreover, these relationships remained intact when controls were introduced for the other variables of the substance of the conflict.

Hypothesis 9.   *The more a conflict involves personnel (and not policy) matters, the higher the probability of amicable agreement and the lower the probability of majority decision; nondecision and decision by interpretation are unaffected.*

Politicians are mainly concerned with two questions: Who should do something and what should be done? The first question refers to personnel matters—appointments and elections—the second question to matters of policy. Distinguishing among conflicts according to these two broad categories, we hypothesize that considerations of solidarity are more important in personnel matters than in policy matters. Politicians often develop a certain feeling of togetherness, and this feeling is probably strongest when they are engaged in filling political positions through appointments and elections. Despite all the competition, politicians have a need to help each other in securing positions. As a consequence, we expect that amicable agreement will be used more frequently for personnel than for policy matters, majority decision less frequently.

Once again, we refer the reader to Dorff for the results of the bivariate analysis.[17] Although support for our hypothesis emerged, we must be cautious in our interpretations because the distribution of the independent variable was highly skewed. In addition to the hypothesized relationships, personnel conflicts tended to be interpreted frequently and postponed rarely. These relationships seemed to support the basic thrust of our theoretical framework, and they remained largely intact when controls were introduced.

Hypothesis 10.   *The more a conflict is perceived as important by the participants in the decision-making process, the higher the probability of decision by interpretation and nondecision and the lower the probability of majority decision and amicable agreement.*

If, for whatever reasons, a conflict is perceived as important by the participants, individual concerns with power will be strongly involved. Considerations of rectitude will also be significant, for the high importance attached to the conflict indicates that basic issues are at stake. Time pressure, on the other hand, will be weak since it seems worthwhile to take the necessary time to work out an important issue. By contrast, if a conflict is perceived as unimportant, the main consideration is not to spend too much time on it.

In an important conflict, the powerful members of the group will try to use their power in an optimal way. Majority decision and amicable agreement do not reach this optimum: in a majority decision the vote of a powerful actor is worth no more than the vote of any other actor, and in a decision by amicable agreement all the participants, and not just the powerful, have a veto power. Decision by interpretation, however, allows the powerful to maximize the use of their power resources because they can manipulate the direction of the discussion to achieve a decision conforming to their wishes. If a decision by interpretation is contested by some group members, the powerful will probably prefer a nondecision. Since time is not a factor in an important matter, powerful group members should not object to waiting for a later meeting at which support may be greater for their position.

If the actors perceive a conflict as unimportant, they will try to achieve a resolution of the conflict as soon as possible, thus saving valuable time. This may be done through majority vote or through amicable agreement (one side simply concedes). In either case the costs for the losing side are not great since the conflict has little significance. Even powerful actors may not mind losing on an unimportant issue; in fact, this may provide them with more justification for winning the important issues.

We employed four indicators for the importance of a conflict: (1) participation rate at the meeting, (2) space devoted to the issue in the minutes of the meeting, (3) space devoted to the issue in press releases, and (4) the length of the discussion. First, we assume that the turnout for a meeting provides some indication of the importance attached by the participants to the issues discussed at that particular meeting. The difficulty with this indicator is, of course, that within the same meeting some issues may be perceived as important and others as unimportant, and we do not know which issues actually affected the participation rate. Second, we assume that the more important issues receive more coverage in the minutes of a meeting and in the press release about the meeting. Arguing against the validity of this measure, however, one could point out that politicians sometimes prefer to emphasize only secondary issues and to disguise the truly important ones. Such an argument is made in the literature concerning the "symbolic use of politics."[18] Last, we assume that a lengthy discussion indicates an important issue. Here, one might argue that the length of the discussion will not necessarily depend on the importance of an issue. Moreover, the length of the discussion is conceivably influenced by the decision mode: for example, majority decisions are perhaps less time consuming than, say, amicable agreement; such a causal relationship would make it difficult to use the length of a discussion as an independent variable for explaining the choice of decision-making mode.

Given the perplexing nature of these problems, it is not surprising that the results of our analyses were quite unsatisfactory.[19] Although the hypothesis concerning decision by interpretation gained some support in the analyses, on the whole we found very little evidence to confirm or reinforce our expectations. Yet we hesitate at this point to conclude that the perceived importance of a conflict has no systematic impact on the modes of decision making. It may well be that our failure to detect such an impact is due to shortcomings in our indicators. Perhaps we could have achieved better results through direct interviews in which participants would have been asked to rank the importance of the various issues. Unfortunately, many participants had to leave the meetings quickly as a result of other commitments; thus, such interviews would have been extremely difficult to carry out. In further research, perhaps employing laboratory experiments with monetarily induced preferences, we hope to test more directly and efficiently for the effects of perceived importance.[20] For the moment we are left with a somewhat ambiguous conclusion.

Context of the Conflict

Hypothesis 11.   *The closer the next parliamentary election, the higher the probability of decision by interpretation and nondecision and the lower the probability of majority decision and amicable agreement.* (This hypothesis is specifically limited to intraparty conflicts.)

Parliamentary elections are crucial events in the lives of politicians, often determining the success or failure of a political career.

Election considerations seem to be more or less constantly on the minds of most politicians. Yet, concern with the election most likely increases as election day approaches. Consequently, we expect that the length of time before the next election will also have an influence on the choice of decision-making mode. However, the nature of this influence will probably depend on whether a decision group consists of members from different parties, like a parliamentary group, or whether all actors are members of the same party. This project deals only with the latter situation, which must be kept in mind when considering this hypothesis. The caveat that our data are limited to intraparty conflicts must be made, of course, for all our analyses. But we feel that most of the hypotheses are so general that they should apply to both interparty and intraparty conflicts. When speaking of time before the next parliamentary election, however, we expect that we must distinguish between interparty and intraparty conflicts.

The approach of parliamentary elections subjects politicians belonging to the same political party to cross-pressures. On the one hand, they would like their party to win, increasing the importance of solidarity. On the other hand, each individual politician would like to be elected; thus, considerations of individual power become important since the competition takes place primarily within the party itself. As both solidarity and power are important, neither amicable agreement nor majority decision seems a likely decision mode. A decision by amicable agreement is difficult to reach because considerations of power are so important, and a majority decision threatens group solidarity. Shortly before parliamentary elections, decision by interpretation and nondecision seem the preferred decision modes. Decisions by interpretation can be made with some actors sticking tacitly to their original positions; thus, they do not have to concede power in a very visible way. In addition, decision by interpretation is not too harmful to group solidarity, for the winners are not clearly delineated from the losers. However, if it is not possible to reach a decision by interpretation the actors will probably prefer to delay the decision until the parliamentary election is over.

Comparing the two periods before the election in table 6.5, we find that the data indicate almost exactly the reverse of our hypotheses. The period closer to the election contains not fewer but more decisions by majority vote and amicable agreement; decision by interpretation is more prevalent in the first than in the second category; and no significant difference appears for nondecision. Considering the third category in table 6.5 as well, we have tried to reformulate our hypotheses. Of course, these hypotheses have the weakness that they were formulated post hoc; but as we will see in the next section of this chapter, the reformulated hypotheses also help to explain unexpected results with regard to the likelihood of a referendum.

To describe more precisely the three categories in table 6.5, it is necessary to point out that in October of both 1967 and 1971 elections were held for the federal parliament. The federal and the cantonal elections have approximately the same importance for the Bernese Free Democratic party; this judgment is based on an assessment of the organizational efforts for and the amount of money spent on each type of election. Considering both the cantonal and the federal elections, the period from January to August 1969 appears to be an interelection period. Following this period, the serious preparations for the cantonal election began; thus, from September 1969 to election day on 3 May 1970 can be characterized as a preelection period. The remainder of the research time from May 4 to September 1970 can be viewed as a postelection period, although the federal election of October 1971 was fast approaching. How can we explain in a theoretically meaningful way the observed variation in the decision modes between interelection, preelection, and postelection periods? A good starting point is the assumption that in the interelection period politicians are more removed from the public eye than in both the preelection and postelection periods. Consequently, in an interelection period politics loses much of its salience not only for the general public but also for the politicians, who give less consideration to such political values as power, solidarity, and rectitude. Politicians are tempted to take time off from politics and to let the process of decision making drag along during this period. Thus, the vagueness of nondecision and decision by interpretation will prevail, whereas the more formalized decision modes of majority decision and amicable agreement will appear relatively seldom. In a pre-

Table 6.5: *Observed Frequency of the Modes of Decision Making by Time Reference to Bernese Parliamentary Elections of 3 May 1970 (percentages in parentheses)*

Time Reference to Parliamentary Elections	Majority Decision	Amicable Agreement	Nondecision	Decision by Interpretation	Total
Interelection: January 1969 to August 1969	14 (7.4)	28 (14.7)	65 (34.2)	83 (43.7)	190 (40.8)
Preelection: September 1969 to election day of 3 May 1970	27 (14.8)	33 (18.0)	61 (33.3)	62 (33.9)	183 (39.3)
Postelection: 4 May 1970 to September 1970	17 (18.3)	35 (37.6)	16 (17.2)	25 (26.9)	93 (20.0)
Total	58 (12.4)	96 (20.6)	142 (30.5)	170 (36.5)	466 (100.0)

election period politicians will be in the public eye to a greater extent, increasing the importance of politics. Considerations of power, solidarity, and rectitude will significantly outweigh the need for free time. The process of decision making will become more tightly organized, resulting in a shift to the more formal decision modes of majority decision and amicable agreement. However, the vagueness of nondecision and decision by interpretation still has a certain appeal because these more informal decision modes may help to mask the appearance of factions within the party during the campaign. In a postelection period the general public is still attentive to the behavior of politicians and to the way they respond to their new responsibilities.[21] Since campaign considerations dwindle in importance, the desirability of the formality of majority decision and amicable agreement further increases. Looking at table 6.5, we see that the percentage of these two modes combined rises from 22.1 in the interelection period to 32.8 in the preelection and to 55.9 in the postelection periods. At the same time, the combined percentage of the other two modes decreases over the three categories from 77.9 to 67.2 and to 44.1.[22] This is a very strong and systematic variation, which remains intact when we introduce controls for the other contextual variables. Although this result was not predicted in the original hypotheses, we have tried post hoc to make theoretical sense of it. The main point of this reinterpretation is that the likelihood of clear-cut and formalized decisions increases as one moves from an interelection period to preelection and postelection periods.

Hypothesis 12.   *The greater the likelihood of a referendum about the issue under discussion, the higher the probability of amicable agreement and the lower the probability of majority decision; nondecision and decision by interpretation are unaffected.*

In Switzerland, politicians have to submit many of their decisions to a popular referendum. Whether a referendum is necessary depends on the exact legal form of the decision, for example, whether it is a law or a decree. It is not possible to hold a referendum for certain legal forms, whereas for others it is mandatory, and for still others optional; in the latter case a minimum number of signatures must be collected before a referendum can be held.

Decision-making situations can be distinguished according to the likelihood of a later referendum on the issue. We expect that the level of this likelihood will have an influence on the mode of decision making. The hypothesis is often made concerning the

Swiss referendum that a high likelihood of a referendum increases the sense of solidarity among politicians.[23] This would hold true even across party lines, for many politicians tend to perceive themselves as belonging to an "in-group" that must defend its decisions in front of the general public. In this project, we can test the hypothesis only for intraparty conflicts, although we expect that it also has validity for interparty conflicts. Our hypothesis is that a high likelihood of a referendum increases group solidarity, thus creating a favorable condition for decision by amicable agreement and an unfavorable condition for majority decision (see table 6.6).[24]

At first, the table presents a puzzling picture. The hypotheses receive some weak support for amicable agreement, but majority decision shows exactly the opposite relationship from that which we expected. Contrary to the predictions, a strong variation appears for both nondecision and decision by interpretation. The argument that we used to reinterpret the election variable seems to make sense here, also. If we draw a distinction in table 6.6 between majority decision and amicable agreement on the one hand and nondecision and decision by interpretation on the other, a clear pattern emerges: the combined percentage of the first two modes decreases over the three categories from 48.6 to 25.1 and to 17.3, whereas the combined percentage of the last two rises from 51.5 to 74.8 and to 82.6. These relationships also hold when we introduce controls for the other contextual variables. This is analogous to our argument on the reinterpretation of the election variable: the certainty of a referendum places the politicians directly in the public eye. Thus, they feel a pressure to take clear stands on the issues—by either a majority vote or a decision by amicable agreement. As the likelihood of a referendum diminishes, this pressure also decreases, and the politicians will be tempted to use the more informal modes. Even if we omit the third category in table 6.6 because of the small number of cases, it is striking that the combined percentage of majority decision and amicable agreement is almost two times higher for mandatory than it is for optional referenda. These results indicate that the traditional hypothesis concerning the effect of the Swiss referendum must be modified. Although it is still true that the expectation of a referendum makes decisions by amicable agreement more likely, the main effect is

Table 6.6:   *Observed Frequency of the Modes of Decision*
                  Making by the Likelihood of a Referendum
                  (percentages in parentheses)

Likelihood of a Referendum	Majority Decision	Amicable Agreement	Nondecision	Decision by Interpretation	Total
Referendum mandatory	29 (28.2)	21 (20.4)	24 (23.3)	29 (28.2)	103 (38.9)
Referendum optional	12 (8.6)	23 (16.5)	58 (41.7)	46 (33.1)	139 (52.5)
Referendum excluded	1 (4.3)	3 (13.0)	5 (21.7)	14 (60.9)	23 (8.7)
Total	42 (15.8)	47 (17.7)	87 (32.8)	89 (33.6)	265 (100.0)

that the whole decision process becomes more clear-cut, increasing also the likelihood of majority decisions. On the other hand, the vagueness of the remaining two modes leads to a decline in the use of these decision modes when politicians are dealing with issues that will be put to a public referendum.

Hypothesis 13:   *The more the issue under discussion has passed from the preparliamentary to the parliamentary phase, the higher the probability of decision by interpretation and nondecision and the lower the probability of majority decision and amicable agreement.* (This hypothesis is specifically limited to intraparty conflicts.)

Many of the issues that come up in a political party are also discussed in the political system at large. We expect that the stage at which an issue is being considered in the wider political system will have an influence on the decision modes in the individual parties. It seems particularly important whether an issue is still in a preparliamentary phase or whether it has already reached the parliamentary stage. When an issue enters the parliamentary stage, most politicians will assume that the preliminary deliberations are over and that the real decisions must be made. The effect of such a movement from the preparliamentary to the parliamentary phase is probably an increase in the importance of solidarity and power. The actors in a party meeting would like their party to win in the crucial parliamentary fight, thus increasing feelings of solidarity. However, party members would also like to influence the party position, increasing the importance of considerations of individual power. If both solidarity and power are important, decision by interpretation and nondecision should be the preferred decision modes. This hypothesis corresponds closely to the one that we made for the variable of time remaining before the next parliamentary election. We expect that when an issue enters the parliamentary stage politicians will be subjected to cross-pressures similar to those associated with approaching elections. We assume that in both cases incompatibilities are likely to develop between considerations of solidarity and power, and that these incompatibilities will most likely be resolved by interpreting a decision or by delaying it. In the latter case, the party may prefer to have no common position in parliament rather than have a split position. The preceding hypotheses explictly refer only to intraparty conflicts; it may well be that a change from the preparliamentary to the parliamentary stage will have a different kind of influence on interparty conflicts.

The results of the analysis for this variable are contained in Dorff.[25] For the most part, a meaningful interpretation was difficult because the variable was applicable to less than half of the 466 cases and only 55 issues were in the parliamentary stage when they were debated, leaving us with a highly skewed distribution of the independent variable. We must conclude that no definitive evaluation can be made at this time, but the general utility of this explanatory variable seems to be rather low.

Hypothesis 14.   *The more a political party is in control of the government, the higher the probability within this party of amicable agreement and the lower the probability of majority decision;*

*nondecision and decision by interpretation
are unaffected.*[26]

If politicians of the same party have to resolve a conflict, the
mode of decision making will probably also depend on whether
their party is in or out of government. We hypothesize that a party
in control of the government puts more emphasis on solidarity and
consequently chooses amicable agreement more often and majority
decision less often than a party in opposition. We are aware that
there are plausible arguments for the opposite hypothesis: one
could reason that the desire to gain government power increases
considerations of solidarity in an opposition party. But a party in
the government has to defend one particular policy, whereas an
opposition party may even profit if it launches its attacks on the
government from different directions. Thus, we expect that the
value of internal solidarity will be more important if a party is in
the government than if it is in the opposition.

Once again the results of this analysis are reported in Dorff.[27]
Our basic hypothesis was supported by the data, although the total
number of relevant cases was rather small (193). Here, too, the
distribution of these 193 cases was highly skewed, significantly
reducing the explanatory power of this independent variable.
Nevertheless, we could make a tentative conclusion that the general hypothesis appeared justified.

Decision Process

Hypothesis 15.   *The more informal the character of the decision process, the higher the probability of
amicable agreement and decision by interpretation and the lower the probability of majority decision and nondecision.*

We expect the importance of the value of power to decrease as
a meeting becomes more informal. Actors probably do not have a
strong sense that they are being observed and evaluated by their
peers in an informal discussion; thus, it seems relatively easy to
reach an amicable agreement. In this type of situation, amicable
agreement seems very similar to decision by interpretation; the

agreement may often be given by a simple nodding of the head, and it may be rather accidental whether the chairman has seen all of the nods when he summarizes the discussion. Given this similarity between the two modes, we also expect relatively many decisions by interpretation in informal settings. In a more formal setting, however, power is more important: it is often difficult to give up one's opposition; thus, majority vote or nondecision are the preferred modes.

We judged the formality of a discussion by whether minutes of the meeting were recorded or not. According to our observations, a discussion tends to be less formal if no minutes are taken; the speakers interrupt each other more frequently and often wander from the formal agenda. Discussion tends to proceed in a more orderly fashion if minutes are taken, perhaps consciously or unconsciously helping the secretary, who must take notes.

The results of this analysis can be found in Dorff.[28] Although decisions by amicable agreement were more frequent in informal settings, decisions by interpretation were much more frequent in formal settings. Apparently the two decision modes are not as similar in informal settings, as our hypothesis states. It appears that the looseness of a decision by interpretation and the low salience of power in informal settings combine to increase the likelihood that an interpretation will be challenged, resulting in a noticeable decline in the frequency of decisions by interpretation in such settings. These relationships remained intact when controls were added for other variables of the decision process.

Hypothesis 16.   *The more the decision process is focused, the higher the probability of majority decision and nondecision and the lower the probability of amicable agreement and decision by interpretation.*

The number of agenda points in a meeting may vary a great deal. Furthermore, within each agenda point, the discussion may focus on a single issue or it may be more dispersed. Two separate indicators, the number of agenda points and the number of issues within each agenda point, provide us with measures of the focus of the discussion. If the discussion of a meeting is dispersed over several agenda items and within each agenda item over several issues, the possibility exists to compensate losses and gains within the same meeting. The actors may not always take advantage of this possibility, but if they do, the value of solidarity may take on added importance, providing a good basis for amicable agreement. Time pressure will be more acute in a highly unfocused discussion. Thus, the actors will sometimes prefer the less time-consuming decision by interpretation to amicable agreement. At the other extreme, if a meeting focuses on a single issue, the losers have no chance for compensation at a later point in the same meeting: thus, the decision will probably be made by a majority vote or it may be delayed.

As noted above, two separate indicators for the focus of the discussion were employed, and the results of the analyses are reported in Dorff.[29] Generally speaking, some of the evidence supported our hypothesis, but it was not sufficient for a conclusive evaluation. It appears that the modes of decision making are influenced more by the number of issues within the individual items on the agenda than by the overall number of items. The rationale for this difference is that participants perceive the items of the agenda of a meeting as quite distinct; thus, compensations for gains and losses across agenda items are less likely. Such compensations are more likely to occur within individual items on the agenda when a large number of issues must be resolved.

Hypothesis 17.   *The later in a meeting an issue is discussed, the higher the probability of decision by interpretation and nondecision and the lower the probability of majority decision and amicable agreement.*

Whether an issue is discussed early or late in a meeting may have an influence on the decision mode. At the beginning of a meeting, the value of power would seem to be especially important because the actors may feel as though they are performing on a stage; thus, winning or losing has a very dramatic effect. This feeling of being observed probably diminishes as the meeting progresses. Toward the end of a meeting fatigue tends to place increasing time pressure on the participants. Therefore, we expect that at the beginning of a meeting the perceived abundance of time will frequently facilitate decisions by amicable agreement. If the power factor proves an obstacle to reaching an amicable agreement, the group may often take a vote. As a result of time pressure and decreased considerations of power at the end of a meeting, the actors may often prefer that someone quickly interpret a decision or that no decision be made.

Results of this analysis, again reported in Dorff, show no support for this hypothesis.[30] In fact, the decision modes employed in the early stages of a meeting show little variation from those employed in the late stages. We conclude that a more systematic attempt to investigate the effects of timing is necessary before a conclusive evaluation can be made. For the moment it seems doubtful that this variable has a pronounced independent effect on the modes of decision making.

Hypothesis 18.   *The higher the certainty in the information basis of the discussion, the higher the probability of amicable agreement and the lower the probability of majority decision; nondecision and decision by interpretation are unaffected.*

Every group needs information to make a decision. Some information is already stored in the memories of the actors; other information is provided during the meeting itself. We are particularly interested in the extent to which there is certainty with regard to the information basis. In some meetings the actors frequently contest each other's information, whereas in other meetings there is wide agreement on the information basis. If a group is quite certain about the information basis, common group feelings are more likely to develop. There is little tension resulting from cognitive dissonance because the group members share more or less the same cognitive map. In such a situation of high solidarity, amicable agreement seems the preferred decision mode, whereas majority decision is less preferred.

The criterion that we employed for this independent variable was the explicit challenge of a participant's information by another member of the group. The results of this analysis are reported in Dorff.[31] Our basic hypothesis was supported by the data, and the relationships remained intact when we introduced controls for other variables of the decision process. In addition, decisions by interpretation occurred more frequently and nondecisions less frequently in situations of high information certainty. Although not initially anticipated by our hypothesis, these relationships support the basic thrust of the argument.

Hypothesis 19.   *The higher the number of proposals on the same conflict dimension, the higher the probability of amicable agreement and decision by interpretation and the lower the probability of majority decision; nondecision is unaffected.*

Proposals are on the same conflict dimension if the acceptance of one proposal necessarily means the rejection of all other proposals. Logically, a conflict can only take place if there are at least two proposals on the same dimension. It may be, however, that only one proposal is made explicit. The rejection of this proposal means a continuation of the status quo, the implicit second proposal. We expect that the number of proposals on a conflict dimension affects the choice of decision mode. With only two proposals the conflict is defined in either/or terms: if one proposal wins, the other simply loses. With three or more proposals actors may lose to varying degrees: a losing proposal may be relatively close to the winning proposal; thus, the loss is less severe than it is for a proposal that is further away from the winning proposal. Under these circumstances a conflict tends to be defined in "more or less" terms, which should be a favorable condition for the development of solidarity, for at least some of the losers also receive benefits. In fact, the chosen proposal may represent so much of a compromise that all participants have the feeling that they have not completely lost. An increased level of solidarity may be not only a consequence but also a cause of conflict dimensions with large numbers of proposals. In groups with high solidarity, new propos-

als are often introduced to build bridges among conflicting proposals. But whether consequence or cause we hypothesize that the
interaction of these two factors, solidarity and number of proposals,
is a favorable condition for decisions by amicable agreement.

The importance of the time factor also seems to be affected by
the number of proposals. We expect that a large number of proposals may complicate the discussion so much that the members
of the group may begin to feel time pressure. Consequently, they
will sometimes prefer a less time-consuming decision by interpretation to an amicable agreement. The corollary of this is that in
conflicts with only two proposals it may be difficult to reach an
amicable agreement, for one side would have to give in completely. The situation may also be so clear-cut that it will be difficult
to interpret a decision. We expect that with only two proposals,
conflicts will often be decided by majority vote.

It is striking that with more than two proposals about half of
the conflicts are decided by interpretation. This result corresponds
to the hypotheses, and indeed, it seems that it is easier to interpret
a decision if a large number of proposals makes a decision situation fairly complex. In such cases an interpreter has a great deal of
leeway in weighing the power, the intensity, and the numerical
strength with which the individual proposals are supported. Interpreting a decision in such complex situations may often be perceived as a time-saving mechanism.

The variation for majority decision and amicable agreement is
exactly the reverse of what we had expected. We have evidently
overestimated the importance of solidarity in situations with more
than two proposals. It seems harder than we hypothesized to reach
an agreement on a compromise proposal, and majority vote was
used fairly often to sort out the numerical support for the various
proposals. We expected no variation for nondecision, but it turns
out that with more than two proposals decisions are postponed less
often. A post hoc interpretation is that a large number of proposals
indicates high involvement of the group; thus, it may appear to be
a waste of time if the meeting ends with no decision at all. Of
course, we note that for all the interpretations of table 6.7 caution
is in order because of the skewed distribution of the data. However, we must add that all of the differences observed in the table

Table 6.7:   *Observed Frequency of the Modes of Decision Making by the Number of Proposals (percentages in parentheses)*

Number of Proposals	Majority Decision	Amicable Agreement	Nondecision	Decision by Interpretation	Total
Two	48	89	128	141	406
	(11.8)	(21.9)	(31.5)	(34.7)	(87.1)
Three or more	10	7	14	29	60
	(16.7)	(11.7)	(23.3)	(48.3)	(12.9)
Total	58	96	142	170	466
	(12.4)	(20.6)	(30.5)	(36.5)	(100.0)

remain intact when we introduce controls for the other variables of the decision process.

Hypothesis 20:   *If high-status actors author two or more proposals on the same conflict dimension, the probability of decision by interpretation and nondecision increases and the probability of majority decision and amicable agreement decreases. If high-status actors author only one proposal on the same conflict dimension, the probability of amicable agreement increases and the probability of the other three decision modes decreases. If no high-status actor authors a proposal, the probability of amicable agreement decreases and the probability of the other three decision modes increases.*

In addition to the number of proposals the political status of the authors of the proposals may be important. In the first case two or more high-status actors have made proposals on the same conflict dimension. The power of these high-status actors is heavily involved. Since they already possess high political status, they will primarily try to minimize the loss of power. A decision by interpretation provides a good way to achieve this goal because it will remain somewhat unclear just who has won and who has lost. Another option may be to take no decision at all, leaving no winners but also no losers.

In the second case only one high-status actor has made a proposal. In such a situation amicable agreement is the most likely decision mode. The need for power on the part of the high-status actor making the proposal does not conflict with similar needs of other high-status actors. Consequently, he has a good chance of imposing his proposal on the group. This will be all the easier because other high-status actors may display solidarity with him.

In the last case high-status actors author none of the proposals. Since the power of high-status actors is relatively uninvolved, it does not matter as much how a decision is made as long as it does not take too much time. Amicable agreement will probably be too time consuming, but either of the other three decision modes will suffice.

Beginning at the top of table 6.8, we move through the six categories. If a high-status actor makes a proposal and the issue is simply whether to accept or to reject this proposal, amicable agreement is used with well above average frequency, and no decision is made by majority rule; this corresponds with the predictions. The second and third categories in the table also consider cases in which the issue is the acceptance or rejection of a single proposal. But here, the proposal is made not by a high-status actor but by a participant with low political status, or it originates from a source outside the decision group (that is, from another party committee or from the government). In both categories majority decision is more frequent and amicable agreement less frequent than in the first category; this also corresponds to the predictions. Our hypotheses did not distinguish between a proposal from a low-status actor and one from a source outside the group, but the data indicate a strong difference between the two cases: of conflicts involving proposals from outside the group, 33 percent are resolved by majority decision and only 12.5 percent by amicable agreement. Perhaps a proposal from a low-status group member still elicits more solidarity than a proposal that originates outside the group. The frequency of nondecision is well above average if

Table 6.8:   *Observed Frequency of the Modes of Decision*
                        Making by the Origin of the Proposal
                        (percentages in parentheses)

Origin of Proposals	Majority Decision	Amicable Agreement	Nondecision	Decision by Interpretation	Total
Only one explicit proposal (the alternative being the status quo) Originates from a *high-* status actor	0 (0.0)	18 (32.7)	17 (30.9)	20 (36.4)	55 (11.8)
Originates from a *low-* status actor	9 (8.7)	19 (18.3)	43 (41.3)	33 (31.7)	104 (22.3)
Originates from *outside* the decision group	16 (33.3)	6 (12.5)	14 (29.2)	12 (25.0)	48 (10.3)
Two or more explicit proposals, *two or more* high-status actors make proposals	6 (6.1)	27 (27.6)	16 (16.3)	49 (50.0)	98 (21.0)
One high-status actor makes a proposal	10 (11.9)	14 (16.7)	28 (33.3)	32 (38.1)	84 (18.0)
No high-status actor makes a proposal	17 (22.1)	12 (15.6)	24 (31.2)	24 (31.2)	77 (16.5)
Total	58 (12.4)	96 (20.6)	142 (30.5)	170 (36.5)	466 (100.0)

the person making the proposal has low political status, document-
ing the low importance attached to such proposals. The decision is
less frequently postponed if a proposal comes from outside the
group, probably because there is often a set time limit within
which the group must take a position.

The fourth category in table 6.8 includes decision situations in
which at least two proposals from high-status actors oppose one
another. About three-quarters of these cases are resolved by either
amicable agreement or decision by interpretation. We had expected that decision by interpretation would be high, but we had
thought that considerations of power would make it difficult to
reach an amicable agreement, so that decisions would often be
postponed. We obviously underestimated the ability of high-status
actors to compromise; it seems that the rules of the game are more
clearly understood and followed by those who have been around
the longest and who, as a corollary, have been the most successful
in playing that game.

The fifth category deals with situations in which a proposal from
a high-status actor is competing with proposals from low-status
actors or from outside the group. Contrary to our predictions, the
frequency of amicable agreement is not above average; this con-
trasts with our finding in the first category, in which the alternative
to a single high-status proposal was the status-quo. The sixth category is similar to the third in that no high-status actor has made a
proposal, and the results are also similar: the frequency of majority
decision is above average and that of amicable agreement is below
average.

The overall picture that emerges from table 6.8 is fairly clear,
although it doesn't agree completely with our expectations. The
more high-status actors are involved in the formulation of proposals, the higher the number of decisions by interpretation and
amicable agreement. Alternatively, the less high-status actors take
part in formulating proposals, the more the decisions are made by
majority vote or postponed. This pattern holds when we introduce
controls for the other variables of the discussion.

Hypothesis 21.   *If many actors express opinions on a conflict
                     and the distribution of their opinions is very*

> *uneven, the probability of amicable agree-*
> *ment increases and the probability of the*
> *other three decision modes decreases. If many*
> *actors express opinions on a conflict and the*
> *distribution of their opinions is roughly even,*
> *the probability of majority decision increases*
> *and the probability of the other three decision*
> *modes decreases. If few actors express opin-*
> *ions on a conflict and the distribution of their*
> *opinions is very uneven, the probability of de-*
> *cision by interpretation and nondecision in-*
> *creases and the probability of majority deci-*
> *sion and amicable agreement decreases. If few*
> *actors express opinions on a conflict and the*
> *distribution of their opinions is roughly even,*
> *the probability of nondecision increases and*
> *the probability of the other three decision*
> *modes decreases.*

Relatively many or relatively few actors may address a particular conflict, and their opinions may be evenly or unevenly divided. Combining the two criteria, we can distinguish four cases: (1) many speakers with a very uneven distribution of opinions, (2) many speakers with a roughly even distribution, (3) few speakers with a very uneven distribution, and (4) few speakers with a roughly even distribution.

With many actors articulating opinions and with an uneven distribution of opinions, the minority tries to minimize its loss of power. Its best strategy would be to bring about a nondecision, but such a course of action would probably be prevented by the majority, who would like to translate their dominant position into a victory. A majority vote would not seem to be in the best interests of the minority, because such a decision mode would only affirm its defeat without procuring any gains. We expect that the minority will often concede to an amicable agreement; in this way they will at least contribute to the solidarity of the group and may be compensated through later gains.

In a broad discussion with many participants and with opinions shared about evenly among the proposals, it would be difficult to interpret a decision. The decision could be postponed, but since many actors have spoken up, the distribution of opinions may be the same in a later meeting; thus, it might seem pointless to postpone a decision. We hypothesize that this is the classic situation for deciding a conflict by majority vote. With a roughly even distribution of opinions, all actors may feel that they have a fair chance of coming out on the winning side.

In the cases in which only a few actors speak, the situation is probably perceived as not yet ripe for a decision; thus, nondecision is the most likely outcome. A possible exception is a discussion among only a few actors that begins to display a very uneven distribution of opinions. The pressure of the majority may not yet be strong enough for the minority to give in, but an attempt may be made to interpret a decision in favor of the majority. If such an interpretation is challenged, then the decision is likely to be postponed.

The results for this variable, reported in Dorff, failed to support our hypotheses.[32] In part, this probably reflects the difficulty that we encountered in managing the complexity of the variable itself: it was simply difficult to operationalize and measure effectively the actual distribution of opinions. A more useful approach may be possible in a laboratory setting in which preferences can be induced and manipulated accordingly. From our research in a real-world setting, however, it appears that the number of speakers and the distribution of opinions have no clear-cut and systematic effect on the modes of decision making.

Having theoretically justified the individual hypotheses and after obtaining the first tentative results from the bivariate analysis, we can now proceed to the more sophisticated discriminant analysis.

CHAPTER 7

Discriminant Analysis

In chapter 6, using a series of simple bivariate contingency table analyses with the modes of decision making serving as the dependent variable, we presented our hypotheses and some of the observed data for the independent variables in our model. Although some rudimentary tests were made with within-group controls,[1] the task of analyzing the complex inter-relationships among the dependent and independent variables still remains. In this chapter we will pursue these interrelationships through the use of discriminant analysis. Then, employing a simulation, we will refine and fill out this analysis in chapter 8.

As we have stressed throughout the formulation of our model and the subsequent derivation of methods with which to test our hypotheses, the total model effects may not be simply the sum of the individual effects. As with any problem involving multivariate statistical analysis, our model implies that the individual effects of our independent variables cannot be understood without looking at all of those independent variables simultaneously; in other words, we must be able to examine the effect of each independent variable on our dependent variable while controlling for the effects of the other independent variables. In a very general form this is the classic statement of any multivariate research problem.

However, as noted in chapter 5, the range of multivariate statistical techniques available to us is restricted by two closely related considerations: the "level of measurement" of our dependent variable, and the nature of the theoretical problem as defined by the substantive theory. On the one hand, the purely categorical nature of our dependent variable (as well as its polytomous form) makes OLS and PROBIT estimation techniques untenable from a statistical perspective. This is primarily because the underlying assumptions of these techniques concerning the distribution of error terms cannot be assumed to hold when the dependent variable is measured on a nominal scale; in fact, nominal level measurement ensures that these assumptions will not be met.[2] On the other hand, and perhaps even more important, the methodological problem that stems from the substantive theory is one of classification: we are interested not in predicting a single value on a continuous dependent variable for each of our observations but in arriving at best estimates of the probability that an observation belongs to one of our four decision modes. For the moment, then, our research task consists of finding a combination of our independent variables that will allow us to classify each of our original observations in one of the four categories; although an OLS technique can at times be modified to perform this kind of classification, discriminant analysis is the obvious technique for approaching this task. Moreover, it is by nature a technique that is designed to operate under assumptions more compatible with the empirical structure of a categorical dependent variable.

In this chapter, then, we present the results of a multivariate discriminant analysis of our data. But first, as a background for the subsequent discussion of the results, we offer some general comments concerning discriminant analysis as a statistical technique. Presuming that the reader is sufficiently familiar with general multivariate statistical models to understand the essential features of discriminant analysis, we provide no formal derivation of the technique itself.[3] Instead, we present only a basic overview with an emphasis on establishing an intuitive sense of how the results can be interpreted.

For the sake of simplicity, let us assume that we have a two-dimensional multivariate space defined by the independent variables X_1 and X_2.[4] We assume further that within this two-dimensional space there are three groups of observations that differ from one another only with respect to the location of the group means on the two independent variables.[5] One such situation is depicted graphically in figure 7.1.

In the figure the observations tend to cluster around the three points 1, 2, and 3. Observations corresponding to group 1 are characterized by moderately large negative scores on X_1 and mod-

Figure 7.1

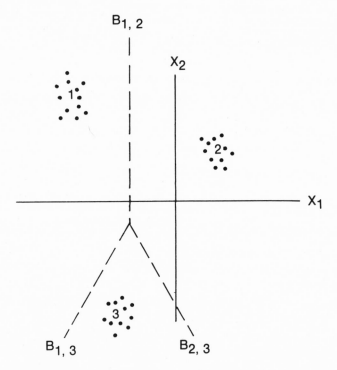

erately large positive scores on X_2. Observations comprising group 2 display small positive scores on X_1 and intermediate positive values on X_2. Group 3 observations display intermediate negative values on X_1 and large negative values on X_2. From these general characteristics we can see that if we could draw the lines representing the boundaries ($B_{1,2}$, $B_{1,3}$, and $B_{3,2}$) in the plane defined by X_1 and X_2 in such a way that they accurately partitioned that plane into three subregions corresponding to the three groups, we would have a basis for classifying a single observation into one of those groups (according to the region into which it falls). In other words, we would be able to predict the value of the dependent variable (group 1, 2 or 3) on the basis of the observed values of the independent variables. What is needed, then, is a technique that will determine first the location of these boundaries and second, on the basis of an observation's location in the two-dimensional space, the group to which that observation is most likely to belong. These two steps correspond precisely to the two main components of a discriminant analysis: the calculation of the discriminant functions (the boundaries), and the statistical classification of observations into groups according to their observed scores on a set of independent variables (prediction of the dependent variable).

Readers more conversant in statistics will recognize that a discriminant function is very similar to a set of regression coefficients: both represent lines drawn through the original multivariate space defined by the independent variables. Each one, in fact, is a linear combination of the original independent variables, and one can obtain a fairly accurate intuitive sense of a discriminant analysis through its similarities with the basic OLS model.[6] The primary similarity is that the relative contributions of the independent variables to the discrimination among groups are reflected in the size of the individual coefficients of the discriminant function: if the absolute value of the coefficient corresponding to variable X_1 is larger than that for variable X_2, we can conclude that X_1 makes a more significant contribution to the discrimination process than does X_2 (just as a higher ß for X_1 than for X_2 would represent a stronger influence of X_1 on the variation of the dependent variable). In a discriminant analysis, however, there is no direct equivalent of the R^2 statistic in a regression analysis;[7] but by focusing our attention on the number of correct or incorrect classifications we can arrive at some indication of the model's goodness-of-fit.

We now turn our attention to an assessment of this classification procedure. The problem confronting any attempt to evaluate the success of a predictive model lies with the establishment of a meaningful baseline against which to compare the model's correct (or incorrect) predictions. As the wide-ranging disagreement in the literature demonstrates, this is by no means a simple task.[8] In principle, we need only decide how many correct predictions or errors we would expect if we knew nothing about the relevant independent variables. We could then evaluate the predictive strength of a model incorporating those independent variables by gauging its improvement on the predictions generated by the baseline model. Such a procedure can be derived from the general model for defining a proportionate reduction in error measure (PRE).[9] Unfortunately, simply having this measure at our disposal does not resolve the problem of choosing an appropriate baseline; it merely tells us what to do once we have selected that baseline. Therefore, our real problem lies in selecting among a number of possible baseline models. Herbert F. Weisberg has suggested that in this search for an appropriate baseline one must decide "how predictable the dependent behavior is on the basis of chance, of its marginal distribution, of one of its correlates, or of its previous value (for time series applications)."[10] Of these, the first two seem most relevant for our problem; hence, we shall examine them more closely here.

It should be apparent that simply adopting random chance as a baseline does not resolve the problem, for we must still decide how well an appropriate random chance model would fare. Perhaps a model in which each category was predicted the same number of times as every other category would be the easiest to understand. Applied to the four decision modes this would mean that we guess each category one-fourth of the time. The expected proportion of correct predictions based on this chance model would be .25 or 25 percent.[11] Although such a model might in reality make incorrect predictions for each and every conflict, it is the expected proportion of correct predictions over the long run that determines this baseline figure.

A second potential baseline model combines the preceding random chance model with some knowledge of the marginal distribution of the dependent variable: we would guess each category only as often as its observed frequency, in essence, a type of probability matching model. Given this condition, the expected proportion of correct predictions would be .2841 or 28.4 percent.

Finally, based on our knowledge of the marginal distribution, we could simply guess the modal category each and every time. In our data, decisions by interpretation were the most frequently employed decision mode (36.5 percent). Consequently, we could predict a decision by interpretation each time with an expected success rate of 36.5 percent. But the use of knowledge pertaining to the marginal distribution of the dependent variable raises an important theoretical consideration—namely, whether the use of such information is appropriate for an evaluation of predictions made a priori. David K. Hildebrand et al. suggest that "while this approach is appropriate for measures based on prediction rules derived, *ex post facto*, from inspection of the distribution actually observed in the data, such procedures are inappropriate for evaluating propositions given *a priori*."[12] In our discriminant analysis predictions, prior probabilities were set equal (that is, .25) so that the predictions were not based on prior knowledge of the actual distribution of the decision modes. Similarly, the predictions in our simulation are a priori and are not based on the marginal distribution of the four decision modes. Therefore, it would seem inappropriate to apply either of these last two baseline models.

In the following discussion of our results, we will modify the PRE measure slightly to arrive at a measure of the proportional increase in accuracy. This measure will consist of the difference between the actual number of correct predictions obtained from the analysis and the number of correct predictions that one would expect from chance alone, divided by the number of correct predictions expected from chance.[13] This modification seems appropriate because we are primarily interested in the number of correct classifications or predictions, a feature that is highlighted by this particular statistic. We will also employ 25 percent as the number of correct classifications expected from the application of a random chance model. However, the substitution of the modal category baseline (36.5 percent) in the preceding formula still yields a measure for our predictions that is a significant improvement over the baseline expectation. So even if one adopts what we feel is an inappropriately high baseline model, our model still makes an important improvement in predictive capability.

Before we present the results of the discriminant analysis, we would like to make some additional comments concerning the relationship between this statistical technique and the theory of decision making that we have developed. In chapter 5 we pointed out that the selection of a statistical model is crucially dependent on the nature of the substantive theory one desires to test. Therefore, it seems appropriate to consider the degree of congruence between our model of decision making and the statistical model underlying a discriminant analysis.

First, it should be apparent that in terms of the entire framework laid out in chapter 2, discriminant analysis is appropriate in only a limited sense. Since we have posited a dynamic model of decision making that depends on the interaction of a number of variables, many entering the model only at specific points in the process, such a method can provide only partial insights into the data. Discriminant analysis cannot adequately take into account the complex flow of interactions that we expect will most accurately describe a decision-making situation. Although we can partially modify the model to reflect some of these considerations (for example, interaction effects), it remains quite difficult to incorporate process in a discriminant model. Moreover, discriminant analysis seeks to find the particular linear combination or combinations of independent variables that will maximize the correct number of classifications. Thus, the use of the classification results as a measure of the degree to which the data conform to a specified structure is inadequate. This is also true to a certain extent for the use of the R^2 statistic in regression analysis: the crucial question concerns the correct specification of the underlying structure and not simply the size of the R^2 (the accuracy of the predictions). It is important to realize that one can obtain extremely good predictions for the wrong reasons, so that good results are not necessarily an indication that the model is correctly specified. This is especially true in our case because, as we have argued previously, discriminant analysis is not designed to conform precisely to the specifications of our theory.[14]

Discriminant analysis cannot, therefore, *test* our theory. At a slightly different level, however, it can point to the presence or absence of a reasonably coherent structure in our data. Relating this technique both to our data and to the other techniques that we employ, we feel that discriminant analysis is best characterized as having many free parameters and being atheoretical. By this we do not mean to imply that there is no underlying mathematical theory in discriminant analysis, nor that the parameters are not estimated according to any specific criteria; we imply only that its natural congruence with our theory is not very great and that we are estimating a large number of parameters. However, our simulation operates within a rather strict theoretical framework. We derive the theory verbally, operationalize it in a computer language, and then fix the parameters in a way that we believe will most accurately reflect the underlying structure of our substantive theory and, we hope, the empirical data. In contrast to the discriminant analysis, then, our simulation is a theory-rich technique with no truly free parameters, and its congruence with our theory is perhaps the strongest argument in favor of its application.[15]

Nevertheless, we can develop strategies for dealing with this problem of congruence for discriminant analysis, and we trust that they can minimize the most deleterious effects that might occur. For example, by examining the structure that does emerge from the analysis (that is, the independent variables that contribute the most to the discriminant functions), we can check their correspondence to the structure that we have described in our original hypotheses. Good predictions will serve as an indication that a structure exists, while a comparison of the contributions of the individual variables with the original hypotheses and the results of bivariate analyses will aid us in assessing the degree to which the structure conforms to the specifications of our model. In the end, simulation can serve as a more refined check on the overall accuracy of our specifications. As a final caveat we note that what follows is certainly not the final word either for our data or for a discriminant analysis of them. But we believe that it brings us at least a small step closer to an overall understanding of the meaning of our data.

The Results

While performing the discriminant analysis, we also ran a test for the compatibility of the equal variance-covariance assumption.[16] According to that test, strong evidence exists to support our earlier supposition that the within-group variance-covariance matrices are actually different.[17] Consequently, the following discussion will focus on two sets of results. We will examine both the pooled and unpooled versions of discriminant analysis, speculating to some extent on the relationship between the two. First, we will consider the results obtained when the matrices are pooled.

In table 7.1 we still deal with the original twenty-one variables

Table 7.1:   Discriminant Analysis Results

Variable	Standardized Discriminant Function Coefficients		
	Function 1	Function 2	Function 3
Structure of Decision Group			
1. Size of decision group	.08	.09	−.48*
2. Predominance of low-status participants in the decision group	−.55*	.40*	.48*
3. Frequency of interactions among the members of the decision group			
Frequency of meetings	.02	−.39*	−.13
Number of governmental functions of the group members	−.66*	.54*	.49*
4. Age of the group members			
Biological age	.26	.10	−.06
Political age	−.06	.26	.00
5. Homogeneity of the decision group			
Homogeneity by language	−.22	.24	−.06
Homogeneity by sex	−.03	.03	−.15
Homogeneity by religion	−.07	−.32	.12
Homogeneity by education	.28	.12	−.04
Homogeneity by occupation	−.02	.19	−.15
Homogeneity by rural background	−.09	−.11	.42*
Heterogeneity by place of residence	−.40*	.07	.11

Table 7.1, continued

Variable	Standardized Discriminant Function Coefficients		
	Function 1	*Function 2*	*Function 3*
Substance of Conflict			
6. Valence nature of conflict	.58*	.03	.19
7. Reference group of conflict	−.29	.13	.19
8. Innovation aspect of conflict	.07	.04	−.05
9. Personnel versus policy conflict	.22	−.28	.02
10. Perceived importance of conflict			
Participation rate at the meeting	.20	.17	−.32
Length of the discussion	.17	−.18	−.02
Context of Conflict			
11. Time distance to parliamentary elections	−.10	−.32	.53*
12. Unlikelihood of referendum	−.05	.34*	−.46*
13. Preparliamentary versus parliamentary stage	.10	.00	−.05
14. Party control of government	−.04	−.19	−.28
Decision Process			
15. Formality of discussion	.26	−.49*	−.18
16. Focus of discussion			
Number of agenda points in meeting	.20	−.24	.43*
Number of issues within the agenda point under discussion	−.05	−.09	.07

Table 7.1, continued

	Standardized Discriminant Function Coefficients		
Variable	Function 1	Function 2	Function 3
Number of decisions in meeting	−.03	.26	.22
17. Timing of the discussion	.13	−.00	−.15
18. Certainty in information basis	.17	−.19	.20
19. Number of proposals	.09	−.19	−.36*
20. Origin of proposals	−.14	−.31	−.09
21. Structure of debate Distribution of opinions	−.01	−.26	−.12
Number of speakers with clearly expressed opinion	−.25	−.26	.00

	Centroids of Groups in Reduced Space		
	Function 1	Function 2	Function 3
Majority Decision	−.33	−1.31	−.12
Amicable Agreement	.54	−.04	.60
Nondecision	−.63	.28	.14
Decision by Interpretation	.29	.18	−.41

*Important variables are at least half as large as the absolute value of the largest coefficient.

with which we started out in chapter 2 (see table 2.2). However, as we have seen in the bivariate analysis in chapter 6, for some variables we used more than one indicator, and some of these indicators were dropped after the bivariate analysis. Thus, we have a total of thirty-three variables for the discriminant analysis.

In the table we have also reproduced the three linear discriminant functions and the centroids of each group in the reduced space. Combining this information allows us to examine not only the relative strengths of the individual variables but also the general direction of the relationships. In discussing these results, we will not go through each variable individually; instead, we will concentrate only on the most important ones. These variables are marked with asterisks in the table.

Considering first the location of the group centroids on function 1, we find that amicable agreement (.54) and nondecision (−.63) are discriminated most clearly. In other words, the distance between the group means is largest for these two decision modes. Majority decision (−.33) and decision by interpretation (.29) seem to occupy intermediate positions with the former being closer to nondecision and the latter closer to amicable agreement. The proximity of these group centroids to one another indicates a degree of similarity between them along this first discriminant function. The next task is to determine which variables contribute to that similarity and distinctiveness.

Four variables stand out for the first function: number of governmental functions (−.66), valence nature of the conflict (.58), status (−.55), and heterogeneity by place of residence (−.40). Applying these coefficients to the location of the centroids, we can observe how the variables affect our dependent variable. We need to be cautious, however, particularly when dealing with majority decision and decision by interpretation, which occupy intermediate positions. Although the two extreme positions are strongly affected by this function, the impact of the variables on the intermediate groups is less easily interpreted. The results for the number of governmental functions are very puzzling within our theoretical framework, so we will comment on these results last.

The variable of status presents a much more coherent picture. An increase in the predominance of low-status participants indicates a move away from groups dominated by high-status actors toward groups dominated by low-status actors. From the location of the group centroids we find that this movement enhances the likelihood of majority decision, which supports our earlier hypothesis that low-status actors should vote proportionately more often than their high-status counterparts. Low status also leads to a reduction in the likelihood of amicable agreement, once again confirming our expectations. Further support is found in the increased likelihood of nondecision associated with groups dominated by low-status actors, as well as in the decreased likelihood of decision by interpretation. The latter decision mode, in particular, was presumed to be a mechanism more often employed by high-status actors.

The variable of heterogeneity by place of residence refers to the percent of the group who had been long-time residents of Bern.[18] As this variable increases, heterogeneity by place of residence increases. We find considerable support for our original expectations here: increasing heterogeneity enhances the likelihood of majority decision, reduces that of amicable agreement, increases the chances of nondecision, and reduces the chances of decision by interpretation. This is a reasonably clear relationship and one that was almost wholly anticipated by our hypotheses.

Another variable contributing strongly to this discriminant function concerns the distinction between conflicts dealing primarily with ends (position issues) and conflicts dealing primarily with means (valence issues). As this variable increases, we move from position issues, through a middle range of relatively mixed cases, to a set of valence issues. Support for our original expectations is evident here, also: valence issues seem to produce a reduction in the likelihood of majority decision and nondecision and an increase in the likelihood of amicable agreement and decision by interpretation, whereas position issues present exactly the opposite probabilities.

Commenting now on the puzzling results with regard to the number of governmental functions, we must remember that we used this variable as an indicator for the frequency of interactions among the group members outside the Free Democratic party. We expected that a high frequency of such interactions would increase the number of decisions by amicable agreement and decrease the number of majority decisions. The first function shows exactly the opposite result.[19] Furthermore, a high number of governmental functions increases the number of nondecisions and decreases the number of decisions by interpretation; these results do not fit well with our hypotheses, either. We will not attempt to reinterpret these data at this time, but we will point out that in the bivariate analyses a great deal of ambiguity surrounded all of the indicators for the frequency of interactions.[20]

Looking at the discriminant function as a whole and trying to characterize it according to the major variables, we have a function that tends to take on its highest positive value in the presence of the following conditions: a group structure that is characterized by a predominance of high-status actors who have lived most of their lives in Bern and who have not accumulated a large number of governmental functions and a conflict that can be characterized as a valence issue. When these conditions obtain, we find that non-decision and, to a lesser extent, majority decision are unlikely to occur, whereas decision by interpretation and particularly amicable agreement are the most likely decision mechanisms. With the exception of the number of governmental functions variable, the results conform quite well to our hypotheses.

Before considering the second discriminant function and the important variables associated with it, we must make note of one additional caution concerning the interpretation of the contributions of individual variables. Because these functions are calculated in decreasing order of importance, it is quite likely that in the individual contributions some apparent contradictions will arise: for example, one variable might imply an increase in a decision mode on function 1 and a decrease on function 2. This can occur because, as with a factor analysis, the second discriminant function is, in essence, picking up information not picked up by the first function. Consequently, we must again proceed with caution in attributing significance to any single relationship.

Five important variables can be discerned in the second discriminant function: frequency of meetings $(-.39)$, status $(.40)$, number of governmental functions $(.54)$, unlikelihood of a referendum $(.34)$, and formality of the discussion $(-.49)$. The centroids of the four groups on this function show an almost exclusive discrimination of majority decision from the other three decision modes, although these three also vary somewhat. As we found in the bivariate analyses, the likelihood of majority decision actually seems to increase as the frequency of the group meetings increases. The variables of status and number of governmental functions are now exactly reversed in their effects on majority decision: low status and a high number of governmental functions now decrease the likelihood of a vote. We will not endeavor to subject this result to further scrutiny, but will treat it as a possible consequence of the *partialling out* that occurred with the first discriminant function.[21] The coefficient for unlikelihood of a referendum, however, strongly supports our reinterpretation of the effect of this variable—namely, that when a referendum is either certain or quite likely to occur, the resultant visibility of the issue and the politician induces the latter to take a clear stand. This clarity of position is most easily facilitated with a majority decision. As a referendum becomes increasingly unlikely (that is, as the independent variable increases), the chances of a majority decision decline (and quite sharply judging from the distinctiveness of this decision mode). Nondecision also appears to be more likely as the possibility of a referendum becomes more remote. Finally, decisions taken in formal discussions are more likely to be majority decisions.

Although perhaps not as clearly as the first, this second function can also be characterized by the major variables: it would tend to take on its highest negative value (that is, favoring majority decision) when the group structure is characterized by frequent meetings, a predominance of high-status actors, and a low group average for number of governmental functions; a referendum is certain; and the decision process is formal. Under these conditions, after having controlled for the information contained in the first discriminant function, the results indicate that a majority decision would be the most likely outcome.

The third and final discriminant function is still more diffuse than the second, indicating the decreasing importance of the functions. Eight variables appear to make significant contributions to the discriminant function: size of group $(-.48)$, status $(.48)$, rural homogeneity $(.42)$, number of governmental functions $(.49)$, time distance to parliamentary elections $(.53)$, unlikelihood of a referendum $(-.46)$, number of agenda points $(.43)$, and the number of proposals $(-.36)$. The location of the group centroids indicates that this function discriminates primarily between amicable agreement and decision by interpretation.

The contribution of the variable of size of group is quite straightforward and very much in line with our original expectations: as the group gets larger, the chances for amicable agreement decrease, whereas those for decision by interpretation improve. This is the classic trade-off alluded to earlier—namely, that decision by interpretation should become more desirable when a group is too large to permit lengthy, unstructured discussion. This tendency is reinforced by the contribution made by the variable of number of proposals: as more proposals are put forth, the chances for amicable agreement are reduced, whereas those for decision by interpretation rise. This conforms very well to our theoretical reinterpretation discussed in chapter 6 and indicates the possibility of a relatively close relationship between these two decision modes. In addition, although less clearly discernible, increases in meeting size and the number of proposals are associated with increases in the likelihood of majority decision and decreases in the likelihood of nondecision, both highly plausible relationships that we have mentioned in our earlier discussions.

The reappearance of status and number of governmental functions continues to complicate the interpretation of the results: low status is now associated with an enhanced likelihood of amicable agreement (although the chances for decision by interpretation are still reduced), whereas an increase in the variable of number of governmental functions finally conforms to our expectation of a greater likelihood for amicable agreement. Once again, we cannot offer any satisfactory interpretation of these phenomena other than to restate the complexity problem. However, we feel more comfortable leaving this problem unresolved than trying to stretch our data and the interpretations beyond a reasonable degree of certainty.

As the bivariate analyses indicated, homogeneity with regard to rural residence (an increase in the rural homogeneity variable) seems to enhance considerably the chances of amicable agreement, whereas urban homogeneity seems to favor decision by interpretation.[22] The two trends observed previously for the effects of approaching parliamentary elections also emerge in this third discriminant function: amicable agreement becomes more likely, whereas decision by interpretation becomes less likely. In addition, as we saw in the second function, although not as strong as the other relationships, this variable was also associated with an enhanced likelihood of majority decision, a relationship first observed in the bivariate analyses.

Our original expectation concerning the number of agenda points appears to be borne out by these data: an increase in this variable enhances the likelihood of amicable agreement. Moreover, the reinterpretation regarding decision by interpretation appears warranted since there is a reduced likelihood of this mode as the discussion becomes less focused. The effects of the unlikelihood of a referendum on the modes of decision making, already noted in the second discriminant function, emerge even more clearly here. The increasing unlikelihood of a referendum, indicated by an increase in this variable, is associated with a decreased likelihood of amicable agreement and an increased likelihood of decision by interpretation. The latter relationship was observed previously, and a reinterpretation was offered (see p. 107); the emergence of the relationship here seems to lend further credence to the reinterpretation and indicates that the relationship is apparently durable. The relationship of this variable with amicable agreement was suppressed slightly in the bivariate analyses, but now appears to provide further support for our original hypothesis—namely, that if a referendum is certain, the party will attempt to maximize solidarity through amicable agreement.

Interpreting this function on the basis of the variables contributing to it is difficult because of the relatively large number of variables. However, this function tends to take on its highest positive value when the following conditions exist: a group structure characterized as a small group, as dominated by low-status actors, as primarily homogeneous with regard to rural residence, and as having members with a high average number of governmental functions; a context consisting of impending or recently held elections and a high possibility of a referendum on the issue; and a highly unfocused discussion (many agenda points) with only a few proposals on the issue. In such situations it is likely that a decision by amicable agreement would be employed and unlikely that a decision by interpretation would result. This particular situation conforms very well to our original hypotheses in which we expected many decisions by amicable agreement (small, homogeneous group with high interaction potential) and relatively few majority decisions and nondecisions; the exception of course is the low-status condition. The additional decline in decision by interpretation, perhaps not what we would expect given only this particular

Table 7.2 :   Classification Results: Pooled
                     (percentages in parentheses)

| | | Predicted Group Membership | | | |
Actual Group	No. of Cases	Majority Decision	Amicable Agreement	Nondecision	Decision by Interpre- tation
Majority Decision	43	30 (**69.8**)	4 (9.3)	4 (9.3)	5 (11.6)
Amicable Agreement	93	12 (12.9)	47 (**50.5**)	16 (17.2)	18 (19.4)
Nondecision	134	16 (11.9)	17 (12.7)	76 (**56.7**)	25 (18.7)
Decision by Interpre- tation	166	22 (13.3)	28 (16.9)	27 (16.3)	89 (**53.6**)

Percent Correctly Classified = 55.5

group structure, seems to result from the absence of high-status
actors, the context (proximity of elections and certainty of referendum), and the decision process (lack of focus and few proposals).

Before summarizing these findings, we will examine the results
obtained when we apply these discriminant functions to the classification of our original observations. The results are reported in
table 7.2. The main diagonal in the table shows how many observations from each of the four groups were correctly classified. Obviously, we do the best with majority decision, classifying 30 of the
43 cases correctly (nearly 70 percent).[23] Nondecision is next with 57
percent, followed by interpretation with 54 percent and amicable
agreement with 51 percent. These individual percentages may be
somewhat deceptive, however, since they do not take into account
the number of times a category was guessed. As noted earlier, we
prefer to examine the proportional increase in accuracy over the
chance model that accrues from the addition of this information.
Of all the observations taken together we were able to classify 55.5

percent correctly. Since we have adopted 25 percent as the baseline, the calculation for the improvement deriving from this analysis is

$$\frac{55.5 - 25}{25} = \frac{30.5}{25} = 1.22$$

According to this measure, we were able to improve our classification by 122 percent. This increase represents a substantial improvement in our ability to classify the data.[24]

Before moving to an evaluation of the substantive interpretations arising from these results, we will consider the results obtained when we relax the assumption concerning the equality of within-group variance-covariance matrices. Since this essentially implies that our decision rule will no longer be a linear function but a higher-order quadratic function, we cannot report the individual contributions made by the independent variables to the discriminant functions.[25] Consequently, we are compelled to rely only on the improvement in the accuracy of our classifications (see table 7.3).

Again, we focus on the overall classification results and the entries on the main diagonal. It should come as no surprise that we have improved our overall accuracy: we have demonstrated elsewhere that working with the unpooled matrices takes into account a more accurate representation of the group distributions and the resulting probabilities.[26] In essence, we have simply reduced some of the gray area that resulted from the forced pooling of the variance-covariance matrices. Consequently, we are now able to classify all of the majority decisions correctly, and our overall accuracy of classification climbs to 77.1 percent. Using the same baseline as above, this gives us a 208.4 percent increase in accuracy. This is obviously quite an improvement over the chance model, indicating that a significant amount of information is contained in these variables. Unfortunately, we cannot say with any assurance that the variables that emerged as important in the pooled version are the same variables that led to this 77 percent accuracy. We have attempted, however, to check the various cases individually to see if the previously misclassified cases were gen-

Table 7.3:   Classification Results: Unpooled
                    (percentages in parentheses)

Actual Group	No. of Cases	Predicted Group Membership			
		Majority Decision	Amicable Agreement	Nondecision	Decision by Interpre- tation
Majority Decision	43	43 (100.0)	0 (0.0)	0 (0.0)	0 (0.0)
Amicable Agreement	93	5 (5.4)	69 (74.2)	7 (7.5)	12 (12.9)
Nondecision	134	4 (3.0)	14 (10.5)	102 (76.1)	14 (10.5)
Decision by Interpretation	166	4 (2.4)	22 (13.3)	18 (10.8)	122 (73.5)

Percent Correctly Classified = 77.1

erally borderline cases, thus indicating that the better guesses obtained here might be attributable to the more accurate calculation
of the probabilities rather than to a substantially modified set of
linear combinations of the variables. Although this is certainly
quite speculative, we do find that in the vast majority of the cases,
previously misclassified cases are now classified in what were for-
merly the second most likely categories. We conclude that we are
probably justified in attributing this improvement more to the ad-
justment in the classification rule than to an entirely new combination of our independent variables. However, since we cannot
systematically test the plausibility of this conclusion, we will not
rely too heavily on the results. The primary justification for including this analysis is heuristic: it does give us some idea of the
structure of the data. In comparing the results of our simulation
to those obtained from the discriminant analysis, we will use the
pooled results because we have more certainty about the precise
nature of the linear combinations and subsequent classification
rules.[27]

Summary

On the whole, we find these results both informative and encouraging. When we force a pooling of the variance-covariance matrices, the important relationships among dependent and independent variables bear a close resemblance to our original expectations. The improvement in our ability to classify the observations according to the mode of decision making represents a valuable gain on what one might expect from chance alone. We conclude from this that, at least according to the procedures employed by discriminant analysis, a discernible and significant underlying structure does exist to relate our independent variables to the modes of decision making.

Considering all three discriminant functions and concentrating only on the most important variables, we find that group structure is a key determinant of the differences among decision modes; in all three functions, variables reflecting characteristics of group structure are the most numerous. Of these, status and number of governmental functions seem to be the most consistently important variables for discriminating among our four decision modes.[28] However, the context and substance of the conflict, as well as the decision process, also contribute to the variation in likelihoods of the various decision modes. This conforms very well to the model of decision making that we developed in chapter 2: group structure is the first variable that enters our flow process and hence may be considered the most important simply because it sets the stage for the actual decision making that follows; this structure is then mediated by the context within which the conflict takes place, the type of issue being considered, and the ensuing decision process. Although discriminant analysis cannot deal adequately with the flow of this process, it does appear to highlight the relative temporal importance of each set of variables.

The application of this technique has provided us with some additional insights into the data. More than anything else, it has served to reinforce many of our initial hypotheses as well as to strengthen the plausibility of some of our reinterpretations. The reasonably good correspondence between the relationships uncovered here, the results of the bivariate analyses, and our original hypotheses means that, to some extent, we can use the discriminant results in helping us select the most important variables for inclusion in the simulation.[29] The classification results also provide us with some basis for evaluating our simulation. We know that we can classify over 50 percent of the decisions correctly with discriminant analysis, and we hope that our simulation will fare at least as well if not better.

Discriminant analysis has proved useful. Its primary utility lies in its ability to handle a large number of variables and to control for the potentially confounding factors in the data. Monitoring the correspondence between the interrelationships among dependent and independent variables in discriminant analysis and the earlier results helps us to verify that the technique is not ranging too far afield from the actual structure of the data; it also represents a first step in the verification of our hypothesized structure since we are not confronted by wholesale divergencies or contradictions. In this way, we are better equipped to gain a meaningful overview of the complex system elucidated in our framework of analysis (see chapter 2).

CHAPTER 8

Simulation Analysis

In this chapter we will present our simulation of the decision-making process. As discussed previously (see p. 78), the purpose of this simulation is to arrive at a set of predictions of the actual decision modes employed in the 466 conflicts. In effect, we will attempt to design a classification process based on our theoretical framework. To do this, we want to construct a simulation that accurately reflects our hypotheses concerning the threshold, dominance, and interaction effects among our variables. However, we want to arrive at the most parsimonious model that will still allow for accurate classification of the decision modes. At a general theoretical level, parsimony is desirable because it implies that extraneous or redundant information has been excluded; this allows us to gain a clearer insight into the structure of the data, unencumbered by potential "noise" arising from redundancy. But parsimony is also necessary before we can hope to operationalize our theory in a computer simulation. If we were to proceed with all thirty-three independent variables, as we did in the last chapter, the model would be so complex that we would be virtually unable to deal with the myriad combinations. The program itself would be so unwieldy that our insights would more than likely be confounded rather than facilitated.

Therefore, before proceeding with the construction of our simulation, a logical first step is a reevaluation of our independent variables. We will summarize the findings of chapters 6 and 7 and attempt to arrive at a reduced set of independent variables. Our criteria for evaluation will be (1) the degree to which a variable conforms to our theoretical expectations, and (2) the importance of the variable as indicated in the bivariate and discriminant analyses. In this way we hope to arrive at a set of hypotheses that are theoretically meaningful and not simply post hoc reinterpretations. Consequently, we do not take the results of the bivariate and discriminant analyses as the final determinant of our decision to include or exclude a variable; we give primary consideration to the substantive theory and the hypotheses that we derived from it. Although our previous analyses will at times aid us in arriving at a decision to include or exclude, we will feel free to reintroduce variables that might not have appeared important or to exclude variables that did appear important. First, we will review and evaluate the independent variables and restate our central hypotheses, and second, we will discuss the simulation and the results that we obtained.

Group Structure

We began with five characteristics of group structure: size of the group, political status of the group members, frequency of interactions among group members, biological and political age of the group members, and homogeneity of the group. In our bivariate analyses we discovered that size and status were important and, for the most part, tended to support our initial hypotheses. In the discriminant analysis both variables again played significant roles in distinguishing among the various decision modes. Consequently, we included these variables in our simulation.

The multiple indicators that we used to analyze frequency of interactions among the group members presented an extremely confusing overall picture. Whereas we expected our indicators to provide some measure of the likelihood of interactions, the often unexpected and mutually contradictory results suggested many problems with these indicators. Plausible reinterpretations, short of complete post hoc revision, did not seem obvious; thus, we concluded that little could be gained from employing any of these indicators in the simulation. This was particularly true for the number of governmental functions. This variable, which appeared to be quite important in the discriminant analysis, confronted us with the problem of meaningful interpretation: although the variable seemed to contribute a great deal to the discrimination among the four decision modes, we could not find an acceptable substantive interpretation for its apparent effect on the mode of decision making. Although the temptation existed to come up with some ad hoc reinterpretation of the variable's theoretical meaning, we saw little value in such far-reaching revisions. Had a meaningful reinterpretation been possible—that is, one that we could have justified readily in terms of our substantive theory—we would have been inclined to incorporate this variable in the simulation. Without this theoretical justification we ran the danger of allowing our methods to determine the substance of our theory. Consequently, we chose to exclude this variable although we hoped that a theoretically meaningful simulation could still fare well without it.

Preliminary indications were that the biological and political age of group members affected the mode of decision making, but the strength of the relationships did not appear overwhelming. In fact, only majority decision and nondecision were affected consistently, and this effect was more pronounced with the former than with the latter.[1] However, in the discriminant analysis neither political nor biological age was among the more important variables. Given this lack of clear and strong relationships, we doubted that these variables could contribute much information to our simulation. Therefore, we excluded them too.

Homogeneity of the group posed many problems for our interpretation of the results. One of the biggest problems lay in determining whether the absence of a particular attribute might also constitute homogeneity, albeit of a different variety. We encountered this difficulty with university education, full-time political occupation, residence in Bern, and urban-rural residence. Although the bivariate analyses indicated that all of these variables were somewhat important, only the two indicators dealing with place of residence emerged clearly in the discriminant analysis. This was at least partly a result of the skewed distributions, since strong homogeneity was generally a rather rare occurrence. But this indicated that little could be gained from the addition of this information to the simulation: since most of the cases fell into one (or at most two) of three categories, we were not able to garner much information about the vast majority of the cases. We confronted the same problem with the Bern residence variable, in which we had only 38 cases in the homogeneous category.[2] Although we might have been able to observe some variation in the modes of decision making, the overall variation in the independent variable was so restricted that we would not have been left with very much information concerning our 466 conflicts (we would have learned something only about the 38 cases). The urban-rural variable was marginally better because the urban homogeneous groups handled slightly over 22 percent of the cases.[3] Still, the variation in this variable was hardly overwhelming. Moreover, there was an operational problem concerning the definition of urban and rural since in many cases it was necessary to make a somewhat arbitrary distinction between rural and urban. Consequently, we decided to proceed without any homogeneity variables. If the initial results had proved unsatisfactory, we might have returned to these variables for further information. For the moment, however, we had reduced group structure to two variables: size of the group and political status of group members.

Substance of the Conflict

We began this study with five variables relating to the substance of the conflict: importance of the conflict, position versus valence issues, reference group of the conflict, innovation aspect of the conflict, and personnel versus policy conflicts. Of these, only position versus valence issues appeared significant in both the bivariate and discriminant analyses. The support for this variable was strong not only in the empirical tests but also in the correspondence with our substantive theory. Clearly, we felt a necessity to include this variable in our simulation.

Importance did not fare as well. The biggest problems with this variable were the unpredictable fluctuation within each indicator and the lack of empirical-theoretical congruence among indicators. Our fourth indicator (space provided in minutes) also lacked explanatory power because we had only two categories and a less than pronounced variation between them. Rate of participation seemed to fare much better than the other indicators, but its use would have necessitated a reformulation of our hypotheses emphasizing the value of free time. Since this variable emerged only in the third discriminant function, we excluded it from the initial version of our simulation. Again, we did this for two reasons: the rate of participation as an indicator of importance did not correspond as closely as we would have liked to our original hypotheses, and its effects on our dependent variable had not as yet been demonstrated clearly in the empirical tests. However, this is certainly a variable to which we might want to return if further information is required.

Personnel versus policy conflicts was excluded from further analyses because of the lack of variation in our data. Although the evidence supported the hypotheses derived from our substantive theory, we could not gain very much knowledge about our decisions from the variable. Similarly, the innovation aspect of a conflict, which for the most part supported our theoretical expectations, contributed only marginally to our knowledge of the actual decision modes. Here again, the problem lay in the substantial lack of variation in our data. As a result of these skewed distributions, we excluded both of these variables from the simulation.

Finally, we come to an evaluation of reference group. This variable presented some clear support for our hypotheses in the bivariate analyses, although it did not appear very strong in the discriminant analysis. Nevertheless, the variable did provide us with some valuable insights into the data. On the one hand, the trends that we observed previously appeared durable: they did not disappear when controls were added. On the other hand, our reinterpretation concerning the unanticipated effects on decision by interpretation and nondecision did not appear implausible: decision by interpretation seemed to be facilitated by a strong overlap between the decision group and the reference group, whereas nondecision was more characteristic of conflicts pertaining to groups other than the decision group itself. We made use of this information by incorporating this variable in the simulation. In sum, we now had two variables relating to the substance of the conflict: position versus valence issues and reference group of the conflict.

Context of the Conflict

We had four variables for context of the conflict: time before and after parliamentary elections, likelihood of a referendum on the issue under consideration, preparliamentary versus parliamentary stage in the decision process, and party control of government. The first two variables posed an interesting dilemma for our evaluation of their utility. On the one hand, the results of the bivariate analyses led us to some substantial reinterpretations of our initial hypotheses. On the other hand, both variables appeared to make significant contributions to the discrimination among the four modes of decision making. Thus, we were inclined to proceed with the incorporation of these variables in the simulation. This was not only because they emerged as important in the discriminant analysis but also because the results of the bivariate analyses appeared to justify some theoretically plausible reformulation of our hypotheses. In particular, the addition of visibility to the parliamentary elections variable anticipated a similar reinterpretation concerning the variable of likelihood of a referendum. Although hardly an adequate test for validity, this correspondence between the two variables did serve to reduce the danger that we were simply reformulating our hypotheses post hoc. A good check on the value of such reinterpretations is whether the addition of one further consideration can account for unexpected variation in other variables as well.

Neither of our other contextual variables proved useful here. Although support for our initial hypotheses was evident in the bivariate analyses, the variables lacked substantial explanatory power: we had a relatively large number of cases for which the variables were inapplicable and a relatively small number of cases for which they were applicable but the distributions were skewed. Moreover, because of the somewhat peculiar nature of the Swiss political system, the distinction between party control and opposition control of government can be quite fuzzy.[4] For these reasons we chose to exclude these two variables and rely only on the time before and after parliamentary elections and the likelihood of a referendum as components of the context of a conflict.

Decision Process

We began with the following variables: formality, focus, timing, information basis of the discussion, the number and origin of the proposals, and the number of speakers and the distribution of opinions. Information basis was excluded because of the highly skewed distribution of our data. The focus of the discussion posed problems of interpretation because of the empirical contradictions between the two indicators. Even though the number of agenda items did contribute significantly to the discriminant analysis, the lack of a clear substantive interpretation of this variable led us to exclude it from further analyses. The number of speakers and the distribution of opinions also posed insurmountable problems of theoretical interpretation: although the initial hypotheses received some support, empirical results largely belied any easy interpretation of their meaning. Empirical results of the bivariate analyses also pointed out the necessity of reevaluating the effects of the timing of the discussion on our dependent variable, but the discriminant analysis did not bear out the significance of this variable.

Formality of the discussion displayed a somewhat confusing picture in the bivariate analyses. Although some evidence supported our original hypotheses, some was notably contradictory.[5] Yet this variable did seem to make a substantial contribution to the discriminant analysis, particularly in discriminating between majority decision and the other modes of decision making. However, we were once again inclined to exclude this variable from the simulation because we lacked a truly plausible reinterpretation. In addition, our concerns with parsimony were such that we preferred to proceed with a minimal amount of easily interpretable variables rather than with a host of variables that we could have simply tossed into the pool. We recognize, however, that in this variable we do have some potentially valuable information, and if further revisions of the simulation are necessary, we will consider the reintroduction of formality of the discussion.

Similarly, we decided not to incorporate the variable of number of proposals in our simulation, although not without some reservations. In our earlier treatment of this variable we devoted a good deal of time to a reconsideration of its effects. In the end we argued that an increase in the number of proposals could conceivably contribute to an enhanced complexity of the decision-making process. We believed that this reinterpretation was plausible, and the results of the discriminant analysis indicated that this variable contained some valuable information. However, for the purposes of our simulation this information appeared somewhat less useful, primarily since only two categories were meaningful, and these two showed little substantial variation between them. Once again, our desire for parsimony and theoretical clarity led us to exclude this variable, although, as before, we will want to return to this information if revisions and modifications of the simulation prove necessary.[6]

This left us with one independent variable for the decision process: origin of the proposals. Although this variable contributed only mildly to the discriminant analysis, there were compelling reasons for including it in the simulation. First, the initial bivariate analyses indicated that this variable contributed substantial support to our hypotheses. Although some reinterpretations were necessary, none of these represented a major departure from our theory; rather, they were primarily shifts of emphasis. Second, to perform the discriminant analysis we were forced to combine two tables from the bivariate analysis into one, ultimately resulting in a substantial loss of information.[7] Fortunately, our simulation allows us to incorporate this information without running any risks of complicating the interpretation of results. Since our simulation is not based on a linear estimation of the model's parameters, correlation between independent variables does not pose the same problems for our analysis. Although at times we might be using redundant information, our theory is specifically designed to incorporate such redundancy as meaningful information.[8] Therefore, we feel that this variable illustrates well the differences between the other two techniques and our simulation: certain information may be particularly valuable in one case and virtually useless (or even misleading) in another. The decision process will be represented in our simulation by the single variable, origin of the proposals.

Central Hypotheses of the Simulation

The reduced model with which we will construct our simulation consists of seven variables. The variables and the sets from which they are drawn are as follows:

Group Structure
  Size of the group
  Political status of the group members
Substance of the Conflict
  Position versus valence issues
  Reference group of the conflict
Context of the Conflict
  Time before and after parliamentary elections
  Likelihood of a referendum on the issue
Structure of the Discussion
  Origin of the proposals

For the sake of clarity we will now briefly restate our hypotheses, including reinterpretations. For the actual derivation of these hypotheses, we refer the reader to the previous discussions in chapter 6.

Hypothesis I	*Size of the group.* The larger the group, the greater the likelihood that majority decision will be employed and the smaller the likelihood that amicable agreement will be employed. No hypothesized influences on decision by interpretation and nondecision.
Hypothesis II	*Political status of group members.* When a group is composed solely or predominantly of high-status actors, the likelihood of amicable agreement is greater and the likelihood of majority decision is smaller. No hypothesized influences on decision by interpretation and nondecision. (In terms of an interaction effect between these two variables, we expect that the effects of high status will be most pronounced in small groups.)
Hypothesis III	*Position versus valence issues.* A position issue increases the likelihood of majority decision and nondecision and decreases the likelihood

of amicable agreement and decision by interpretation.

Hypothesis IV   *Reference group of the conflict.* The more a conflict is concerned with the decision group itself or the party, the greater the likelihood of amicable agreement and decision by interpretation and the smaller the likelihood of nondecision. No hypothesized influence on majority decision.

Hypothesis V   *Time before and after parliamentary elections.* The smaller the interval to the parliamentary elections (before or after), the greater the likelihood of majority decision and amicable agreement and the smaller the likelihood of nondecision and decision by interpretation.

Hypothesis VI   *Likelihood of a referendum.* The greater the likelihood of a referendum, the greater the likelihood of majority decision and the smaller the likelihood of nondecision and decision by interpretation. No hypothesized influence on amicable agreement.

Hypothesis VII   *Origin of the proposals.* (1) One Proposal: A proposal originating from a high-status actor increases the likelihood of amicable agreement and reduces the likelihood of majority decision. No hypothesized influence on nondecision and decision by interpretation. A proposal originating from a low-status actor increases the likelihood of nondecision and majority decision and reduces the likelihood of amicable agreement and decision by interpretation. A proposal originating outside the decision group enhances the likelihood of

majority decision and reduces the likelihood
of amicable agreement and decision by interpretation. Nondecision is unaffected. (2) Two
or more proposals: At least two proposals from
high-status actors increases the likelihood of
decision by interpretation and amicable agreement and reduces the likelihood of majority
decision and nondecision. One proposal from
a high-status actor encountering opposition
from at least one proposal from a low-status
actor reduces the likelihood of amicable
agreement but does not affect the other three
modes significantly. The absence of a proposal
from a high-status actor increases the likelihood of majority decision and reduces the
likelihood of amicable agreement and decision
by interpretation. Nondecision is unaffected.

From this set of basic hypotheses we will construct our simulation.

Constructing the Simulation

We have now completed the review and evaluation of our independent variables and have selected seven of them to be incorporated in our simulation. The hypotheses that we restated
briefly in the last section will comprise the core of the simulation,
but we must still translate these verbal statements into a series of
machine readable commands that can be executed by the computer. Moreover, we must finally deal with the nature of the dominance, threshold, and interaction effects that we think most accurately characterize our data; at a basic level this involves some
operationalization of the anticipated differences in importance of
the independent variables. Therefore, before we proceed to a
description of the simulation and the hypotheses incorporated in
it, it is necessary to pitch our discussion at a very general level
and to examine some of the most general relationships among
the variables.

We can construct a preliminary flow chart of the relationships

Figure 8.1

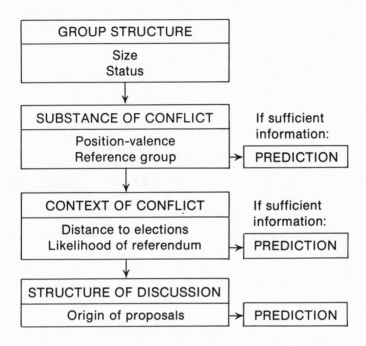

among our four sets of independent variables from the theoretical framework developed in chapter 2 (see figure 8.1). The first variable that enters the process is group structure. A decision group takes on relatively fixed structural characteristics from the moment it convenes.[9] In particular, each group is either small, medium, or large and consists solely or predominantly of high-status or low-status actors. From our theory and the individual hypotheses that we restated in the previous section (hypotheses I and II), we expect that group structure alone will not suffice for the prediction of a single decision mode. Our theory presumes that certain tendencies should be evident under specific structural conditions, but that an actual outcome will remain largely indeterminate until further information becomes available. In other words, although certain structural combinations will clearly favor one or two decision modes over the others, group structure alone should rarely (if ever) be sufficient for determining a single decision mode. Therefore, our simulation makes note of the specific characteristics of the group structure but passes directly to the next variable (substance), rather than take the path to the predictions.

Once the meeting is convened, the group confronts an agenda of issues. In each decision-making situation, then, the next salient question concerns the nature of the conflict. In other words, the actual substance of the conflict begins to interact with the characteristics of the group structure. In our model we distinguish between conflicts dealing with actual goals (position) and conflicts dealing with means (valence). Further, we consider the reference group of a conflict to be an important determinant of the way in which the decision-making process unfolds and, ultimately, of the decision mode actually employed. However, we also expect that the criterion of position-valence will be somewhat more important than the reference group, although the interaction between the two remains crucial. Our assumption follows from the argument that the position-valence nature of a conflict will be the primary characteristic of its substance: political decision-makers will consider this factor first, and only secondarily will they consider the reference group of a particular issue.

In general, we also assume that the combined information of structure and substance will not suffice for specific predictions. Our reasoning here is that the group structure and the substance of the conflict, although of primary importance in determining the resulting decision mode, will not always lead in the same direction; hence, some indeterminacy must remain. Moreover, as we will soon see, most combinations of these two sets of variables will serve only to narrow the range of possible decision modes, rather than restrict that range to a single mode which we could then predict. An exception to this indeterminacy occurs with small groups comprised solely of high-status actors or solely of low-status actors. Although we will elaborate later on some of the specific hypotheses and predictions, we note here that for this subset of conflicts we could take the path leading to prediction.

The context of the conflict is the third factor to affect the flow of the decision-making process. The two variables that we employ here are the time interval before and after parliamentary elections and the likelihood of a referendum. As noted previously, one might argue that the time interval to elections should enter the process earlier than we have stated; however, the logic of our theory indicates that concern with elections will become salient only if the particular issue being considered is somehow relevant to the upcoming elections. Concerns with electoral impact should normally become salient only after the substance of a conflict is apparent and the preliminary discussion has taken place.

The final variable concerns the decision process. Once a meeting is convened, an issue determined, and the impact of contextual variables ascertained, the actual progress of the discussion will help determine which values change and which remain fixed. As pointed out in chapter 2, we do not assume that the values for every actor will remain invariant: in fact, we make the explicit assumption that these values change "from actor to actor and, for each actor, from situation to situation [and even] for the same actor during the decision process itself" (see p. 26). We anticipate that the origin of the proposals will be a major factor in effecting change in these values and, hence, in the decision mode that is employed.

We now have all the necessary elements in order to proceed with our simulation: we have selected the variables, restated the central hypotheses, and constructed a flow chart of the essential relationships among our independent variables. The next step is to move from general relationships among variables to specific hypotheses that lead to predictions. However, an exhaustive treatment of every hypothesis and prediction would be cumbersome and tedious. Therefore, we will provide only an overview of the simulation through four selected examples. The purpose of these examples is to illustrate how we arrived at the predictions and to provide the reader with an intuitive grasp of the procedure.[10]

Before proceeding, however, we would like to comment briefly on the nature of our predictions. Whenever we reached a point at which we felt a prediction was possible, we tried to establish a set of expectations for all four modes of decision making. Rather than simply select a single decision mode as our prediction, we also tried to decide whether another mode appeared so unlikely that it could be excluded: in other words, we were interested not only in deciding which mode was *most* likely to occur but also in deciding which mode was *least* likely to occur. This implies that we will also have a middle category in which a given decision mode is expected to occur but with much less frequency than the predicted mode. In part, this reflects a fundamental premise of our theory: although some probabilistic or likelihood tendencies should be evident in these data, no completely deterministic relationships are anticipated. Since there is still a great deal of room for individual maneuver and design, indeterminacy must remain an integral component of any decision-making process. Consequently, it may not always be possible to select a single decision mode as the most likely, or even when such a selection is possible, we may not be able to decide how all of the other modes will be affected. Although we hope to avoid as much of this indeterminacy as possible, it is more meaningful to incorporate uncertainty by admitting its existence in specific situations than to assign a prediction somewhat arbitrarily to an uncertain or indeterminate case. Since we argue that, to some degree, human behavior must remain indeterminate, we will not attempt to find determinacy where in fact none exists.

We would also like to emphasize that these predictions were formulated *before* we looked at the actual or observed distributions. However, we have included both the predictions and the empirical results in our final flow chart. This should not be taken as an indication that the predictions were formulated post hoc on the basis of the observed modes of decision making.

To save space we have used symbols in the flow chart to represent our predictions. Brackets indicate that a mode is expected *not* to occur, and parentheses indicate a middle position. The decision mode at the top of the list is our single prediction, and our calculation of a success rate will depend exclusively on this single selection. As David K. Hildebrand et al. suggest, allowances must be made for variation in the scope of a model's predictions: more stringent criteria should be applied to multiple predictions than to single-outcome predictions.[11] We have made single-outcome predictions wherever possible in this simulation, thus facilitating evaluation. But our model indicates that such purely deterministic outcomes are quite unlikely given the range of maneuver available to decision makers. As a result, we should not expect these single-outcome predictions to achieve the same rate of success as, say, predictions of congressional roll-call voting.[12] Constraining our simulation to single-outcome predictions is not entirely arbitrary, but it does suggest that a truly meaningful evaluation of the model would have to go beyond the simple calculation of a success rate offered here. We will return to this point in our conclusions at the end of this chapter. We turn now to a discussion of our four examples.

Path I   *Small group, all high-status participants, valence issue.*

For the first example the reader should follow path I in the flow chart, which is to be found between pages 156 and 157.[13] The first variable, group size, has three categories: small (≤ 7), middle-sized (8–20), and large (>20). Hypothesis I suggests that if the group is small, the probability of amicable agreement should increase, whereas that of majority decision should decrease. As we have indicated, however, the information concerning group size alone is insufficient for narrowing our choices to a single decision mode. Consequently, we proceed to the next variable, status, for additional information. In our example we pursue the path that corresponds to groups comprised solely of high-status participants. Once again, amicable agreement appears to be the most likely decision mode and majority decision the least likely, as indicated by hypothesis II. Although both variables now indicate a high likelihood of amicable agreement, we still believe that the information pertaining solely to group structure is insufficient for a prediction. Obviously, the decision to stop the input of information and to make a prediction is a relatively subjective one. Nevertheless, it is a decision that is shaped by the theoretical framework with which we are working, and it therefore reflects the underlying theory of decision making that we outlined in chapter 2. Ultimately, of course, the test of our decisions regarding the extent of necessary information will be the degree to which our predictions prove correct.

We now follow the path from the box labeled "all high-status participants" to the one labeled "position issue." If a group is dealing with a conflict that involves means rather than ends, it is deciding a valence rather than a position issue. Therefore, we follow the appropriate path to the box labeled "valence issue." Hypothesis III indicates that a valence issue should enhance the likelihood of amicable agreement and decision by interpretation while decreasing the likelihood of majority decision and nondecision, primarily because of the relative lack of divisiveness of such issues. Now we are ready to make our predictions; let us examine these variables once more to see how the predictions unfold.

First, the size of the group is a favorable condition for amicable agreement and an unfavorable one for majority decision (hypothesis I). Second, the status composition of the group favors amicable agreement, whereas it makes majority decision increasingly unlikely (hypothesis II). Therefore, the characteristics of group structure strongly indicate that amicable agreement will be employed and majority decision avoided. Finally, the substance of the conflict (disagreement over means rather than ends) favors amicable agreement and decision by interpretation over majority decision and nondecision. Thus, a single prediction becomes possible because all three variables favor amicable agreement as the most likely decision mode. Moreover, all three variables point to a very low likelihood of majority decision, hence we can predict that majority decision will not be employed in these situations. Decision by interpretation might be expected to occur because it is unaffected by the first two variables and favored by the last, but the frequency of decision by interpretation should not be as high as that of amicable agreement. Similarly, we might anticipate an occasional nondecision because it, too, is relatively unaffected by the first two variables; the valence nature of the conflict, although an unfavorable condition for this decision mode, should not be sufficient for making nondecision as unlikely as majority decision.

The results in the flow chart indicate that we have correctly predicted 60 percent (6 of 10) of the decisions that were made under these conditions. Furthermore, we correctly predicted an absence of majority decisions, a further sign that our model has a fairly strong predictive capability. But it should also be apparent that this example is a very simple one for two obvious reasons.

First, the amount of information required for our predictions was quite small (three variables). Second, all of the variables seemed to point unanimously in the direction of amicable agreement, which admittedly made it possible to make our predictions with so little information. Unfortunately, this example is not representative of all cases in which we made predictions. Therefore, in our subsequent examples we want to increase both the complexity and uncertainty associated with the predictions so that the reader can get some sense of how the simulation works and of the way in which the predictions were formulated.

Path II   *Small group, all high-status participants, position issue.*

For the second example we follow the same path through the group structure variables, but this time we consider a decision involving a position issue. As it did in the previous example, group structure (small group, all high-status participants) strongly favors amicable agreement and reduces the likelihood of majority decision. However, hypothesis III indicates that for a position issue we should expect a higher frequency for majority decision and non-decision and a lower frequency for amicable agreement and decision by interpretation. Clearly, no single decision mode is unanimously indicated. Nevertheless, we can still make a prediction if we can reach some conclusions about the relative importance of these variables in this specific context. For example, it seems that group structure works so strongly against majority decision that, even when considering a potentially divisive position issue, such groups should not resort to the voting mechanism. At the same time the increased likelihood of amicable agreement indicated by the characteristics of group structure should be offset to a large extent by the substance of the conflict; hence, it is quite unlikely that a true consensus will be found in these groups when the disagreement concerns ends rather than means. Therefore, we predict that neither amicable agreement nor majority decision will be employed in this situation. Moreover, as we observed in the previous example, group structure has no hypothesized influence on the two remaining decision modes, so there is no further indication here whether one mode is more likely than another. The substance of the conflict, however, indicates that the likelihood of nondecision should be enhanced, whereas that of decision by interpretation should be reduced. Since their concern with solidarity should generally override concerns with individual gains and losses, we expect these groups to postpone potentially divisive issues rather than force a decision. Therefore, we predict that nondecision should be the most frequently employed decision mode in such a situation. Decision by interpretation is relegated to the intermediate category because it is rendered unlikely by only one of the three variables; consequently, we anticipate that it might be employed on occasion to resolve a conflict. Although this example is not as clear-cut as the previous one, it indicates that we are able to reach certain conclusions about predictions even when all the variables do not point toward a single decision mode. The key question now is: How do these "less obvious" predictions fare?

Once again, the flow chart indicates that our predictions turned out rather well. Although the number of cases is very small (4), we were able to predict 75 percent of them correctly. Moreover, we were again correct in our prediction concerning the modes that were least likely to occur, and the single case that was not a nondecision fell into our second most likely category, decision by interpretation. This example should illustrate that, even though some situations may not present obvious indications of the relative likelihoods of the decision modes, reasoning according to our theoretical framework does lead to quite accurate predictions. Moreover, our assessment of the model will more than likely understate the accuracy of the predictions: although we make no claim that we expect *only* nondecision (after all, we have an intermediate category for a reason), the assessment of percent correctly classified assumes that we have done so. In addition, we have no way of building our predictions of the least likely decision modes into an evaluation of the model. Thus, we feel that the single measure of correct classifications provides only a very crude measure of the predictive accuracy of our model, and one that is likely to understate systematically the degree of that accuracy.

Path III: *Middle-sized group, predominantly low-status*
                   participants, valence issue, reference group:
                   decision group itself or party, referendum
                   uncertain, and preelection period.

We turn now to an example in which the predictions are much more difficult to make on the basis of the independent variables. Path III leads first to a middle-sized group (8–20 participants). The intermediate value on the size variable provides no basis for choosing among our four decision modes, so we move directly to a consideration of the status composition of the group. Following path III, we find that in this example the group is composed predominantly of low-status participants.[14] Once again, the intermediate value of the independent variable does not allow us to limit the alternatives at this point. Since these groups still contain a fair number of high-status participants, the tendency of low-status actors not to employ amicable agreement should be at least partially offset. At the same time, although we expect low-status participants to use majority decision relatively often, the size of these groups is such that this decision mode should be somewhat less likely. However, we cannot make any specific predictions until further information is obtained; thus, we follow path III to the next variable, substance of the conflict.

As the reader will observe, path III leads us through a position to a valence issue, or conflicts dealing with means rather than ends. Hypothesis III suggests that such conflicts should enhance the likelihoods of amicable agreement and decision by interpretation while reducing those for majority decision and nondecision. Although this additional information provides us with the first real basis for narrowing down the alternatives, it still does not allow us to make a prediction of a single decision mode. Therefore, we look to the reference group for more information on the substance of the conflict. In our example, path III indicates that the conflict refers to the group itself or to the party. Hypothesis IV indicates that this overlap should favor amicable agreement and decision by interpretation at the expense of nondecision. Yet this additional information still provides no basis for choosing between the two favored modes since both are supported by the last two variables.

To resolve this indeterminacy, therefore, we must turn to the information concerning the context within which the conflict is resolved. The particular combination of the contextual variables associated with path III (referendum uncertain in a preelection setting) is one in which we expect the visibility of the politicians to be low (see p. 107). This low visibility enhances the likelihood of decision by interpretation and nondecision (hypotheses V and VI).

It is now possible to formulate predictions. A quick review of the variables should serve to illustrate how we arrived at this point. As noted previously, the structure of the group (size and status) provides no basis for choosing among the four decision modes. The addition of information concerning the substance of the conflict points to increased likelihoods of both amicable agreement and decision by interpretation, but does not allow us to choose between them. The context of the conflict favors decision by interpretation and nondecision, but not amicable agreement. Thus, we anticipate the use of decision by interpretation as the most frequent decision mode. Since amicable agreement was favored right up until the addition of the contextual information, it seems likely that this decision mode will also be employed. However, we expect decision by interpretation to occur more often than amicable agreement. The likelihood of majority decision was not enhanced by any of the variables, so we predict that it will not be employed in these situations. Although nondecision was favored by this particular combination of the referendum and parliamentary elections variables (context), the reference group and the valence issue (substance) work strongly against this decision mode; hence, we conclude that nondecision should not be employed either.

As the flow chart demonstrates, the results of our predictions are not very good. Only 8 of the 28 conflicts that conformed to these conditions were resolved by the predicted decision mode (decision by interpretation). Moreover, the decision mode that we predicted would occur somewhat less frequently than our favored mode actually occurred more often (amicable agreement = 11). And finally, whereas we predicted that nondecision would not be employed in these situations, it was not only employed but was employed as often as the predicted category (nondecision = 8).

Perhaps the only encouraging result was obtained with majority decision. Our prediction that votes would not occur was well supported: only 1 of the 28 conflicts was resolved with this mode. According to our single prediction measure, the results obtained in this example yield a successful classification rate of 28.6 percent.

Obviously, we have not fared very well with these predictions; this deserves additional discussion. First, two of the more important independent variables in this example had observed values in intermediate positions. This contributes both to the uncertainty of our predictions and, perhaps, to the indeterminacy of the decision-making process. Because of the particular logic of our theory, we anticipate the most difficulty with predicting outcomes in groups that display a mixture of characteristics. Second, since the values of the group structure variables did not help to narrow the choices, we had to incorporate far more information than in the preceding two examples. Although this additional information enabled us to make predictions, it is clear that more information does not necessarily translate into improved predictions. Quite the contrary, the addition of more information usually indicates increased ambiguity and a need for additional decision criteria. Nevertheless, the finding that our results are better when a relatively small number of variables line up and point to a single, most likely decision mode is not a negative finding. Rather, it suggests something important about the predictability of human behavior in these decision-making contexts: small groups may be more predictable by nature than larger groups. This is an important finding for the study of decision-making behavior in face-to-face groups.

Finally, we encourage the reader to examine the flow chart to see how other predictions in these intermediate categories fared. Although we wanted to include at least one example in which our predictions were not particularly successful, we do not mean to suggest that all of our predictions in these categories were equally unsuccessful. In fact, cases in which the independent variables suggested a certain distribution of the decision modes and in which the observed distribution was significantly different from the predictions were relatively rare. However, other situations arose in which the ambiguity was such that we were simply unable to make a single prediction based on the independent variables. In these cases we made no attempt to guess the outcomes and instead labeled our predictions *indeterminate*. Our last example will illustrate just such a situation.

Path IV:　　　　*Large group, predominantly low-status participants, position issue, reference group: outside party.*

Path IV leads the way through the variables to our prediction of indeterminate. The size of this group is large (greater than twenty), which is a favorable condition for majority decision and an unfavorable one for amicable agreement. The status variable, however, falls in an intermediate position, providing us, for the moment, with little additional information concerning the likelihoods of the four decision modes. We therefore turn to the substance of the conflict in an attempt to resolve the remaining ambiguity. As path IV indicates, this example deals with a position issue, a characteristic that should favor majority decision and nondecision. The conflict also refers to a group outside the party, which should favor nondecision. Therefore, it appears that both majority decision and nondecision should occur most often. However, we must return for a moment to the status composition of this group and recall that a number of the high-status participants are quite likely to occupy the leadership positions within these groups. Consequently, it also seems possible that these high-status actors will attempt to structure and guide the decision-making process in large, somewhat cumbersome groups.[15] A preferable decision mechanism for these actors, particularly when a large group is confronted by a number of alternatives, is decision by interpretation. This leaves us with three possible candidates for the most likely decision mode. When we tried to resolve this indeterminacy through the incorporation of additional information, we were unsuccessful. Thus, we concluded that, within the context of our theoretical framework, we had no reasonable basis for choosing among the three decision modes. We felt confident in saying only that amicable agreement should rarely, if ever, be employed.

The results contained in the flow chart reveal two interesting features. First, as we predicted, amicable agreement seems to be a highly unlikely decision mechanism in these situations: only 1 of the 23 conflicts was resolved by this decision mode. Second, given the frequencies of the other three modes, indeterminate appears to be a very accurate label for such situations: each mode occurs nearly as often as the other two. Thus, our decision not to force a single-outcome prediction appears justified. Again recalling our argument from the beginning of this chapter (see p. 158), it is theoretically more meaningful to incorporate indeterminacy in the model than to constrain quite arbitrarily the predictions. In reality, decision-making situations will certainly arise that will defy prediction on the basis of our theoretical framework. The anticipation of the unpredictable nature of these conflicts should itself be taken as an indication of the merit of our approach.[16]

Conclusions

Those who wish a more comprehensive discussion of the simulation should consult Robert Dorff's unpublished dissertation, in which he describes all of the possible combinations and the predictions associated with each.[17] For the moment we will return to the problem of evaluating the performance of our simulation.

The entire classification process covered 436 cases. From our universe of 466 decisions we had to omit 30 cases that had missing values on some of the seven independent variables included in the simulation. We predicted indeterminate for 25 of the remaining 436 decisions, leaving us with 411 cases for which we made a single-outcome prediction.[18] In 237 cases (57.7 percent) our predictions were correct. Judged by the standard of evaluation discussed previously (see pp. 125–27), this figure represents a substantial improvement in our ability to classify each decision: measured against a baseline of 25 percent, which presumes that we have no a priori knowledge of the distribution of the four modes, our 57.7 percent rate of correct classification constitutes a 131 percent proportional increase in accuracy. Even if we were to employ the higher but less theoretically appropriate baseline of 36.5 percent (modal category), our simulation would still achieve a significant 58.1 percent proportional increase in accuracy over the chance model. Regardless of the specific measure employed, the improvement in predictive capability achieved by our model seems indisputable.

Of course, these measures do not include the other components of our predictions, which also proved remarkably accurate. For example, we have no method of combining this measure of success with the successful prediction of decision modes that were *not* employed. Moreover, as we noted previously, the success rate as calculated here presumes that our theory was making single-outcome predictions; in fact, this was often only approximated in our more probabilistic framework. In highlighting this feature, however, we do not wish to claim a greater success rate than our measures indicate; such a claim would have to be supported by more tests and measures that we do not have at this moment. Instead, we wish only to stress the inherent difficulty in evaluating this kind of predictive model and to restate that no single measure will provide a wholly adequate assessment of the model. We hope to develop more meaningful evaluation criteria as we refine our investigative and analytical techniques. For the moment we suggest that our model performed rather well—just *how* well is a question that defies an easy answer at this time.

Beyond its ability to classify nearly 58 percent of the decisions correctly, the most important general substantive result of the simulation is that our predictions fared much better with small groups, particularly those comprised predominantly of high-status participants. What does this finding imply? It could mean that the decision-making behavior of high-status actors interacting in small groups is relatively strongly predetermined by the characteristics of the decision situation. The norms in these groups could indicate quite clearly the kind of behavior that is expected, and the high-status actors would then tend to follow these norms, to which they have been socialized while gaining experience and success in the political arena. In large groups consisting mainly of low-status actors, social constraints on the decision-making behavior of participants would be less severe. The choice of a decision mode to resolve a particular conflict would depend much more on idiosyncratic characteristics of the individual participants and, perhaps, even on chance.

It is not easy to evaluate the success rate of our simulation.

In none of the decision-making situations would we expect a success rate of 100 percent, and we have certainly done much better than we might expect from chance alone. But is our success rate high enough so that we can attribute the incorrect predictions to idiosyncratic elements and to the operation of chance? For the moment the answer is an inconclusive "not yet," but the possibilities for successive research efforts that seek to build on this general approach appear to be very promising, indeed.

The simulation as it stands is still very crude. We have completed only an initial analysis of the data, and the simulation reflects the somewhat tentative and preliminary nature of our approach. Nevertheless, the results appear very encouraging and seem to call for further investigation. As we indicated in chapter 5, the thrust of that investigation should be toward finding increasingly more formalized and specific expressions of the relationships among independent variables. Such formalization and specificity might exist in a discriminant analysis with interaction effects or, in keeping with our desires for verisimilitude and congruence between our substantive and mathematical models, in a simulation with increasingly constrained weights for the variables. The problem with weighting the independent variables, however, emerges quite clearly from the preceding discussion of the simulation: the weights themselves change with the changing conditions of the decision-making situations. In other words, no single variable will have a consistent effect on the modes of decision making across the entire range of cases. Although we hope to reach the point at which we will be able to specify these weights more accurately than we can at this time, we doubt that we can ever achieve complete specificity. Moreover, since our theory posits such changes in the parameters of the model, the use of any linear estimation technique will always encounter difficulties with our data: the number and variety of potential interaction effects would make a completely accurate specification of the model prohibitively complex. And of course, the costs of incorrect model specification for a linear estimation of the parameters include biased estimates, a highly undesirable outcome when the nature and extent of the bias remain unknown.

In the end, we are encouraged by but not complacent about

these results. On the one hand, our methodology has served a useful purpose and has yielded results that appear to lend a significant degree of credibility to our overall approach. On the other hand, we still have a long way to go in the refinement and validation of these results before we can reach a conclusive evaluation of our theoretical framework. Nevertheless, we conclude that there is ample evidence to support the logic and utility of our approach. We can therefore close this phase of the research on a positive note even as we begin to confront the perplexing problems ahead.

PART III

The Outlook

CHAPTER 9

**Strategies for
Further Research**

We have already acknowledged that the empirical basis for this test of our theory is relatively narrow (see chapter 3). Therefore, the next logical step is the application of the theory to some other universe of face-to-face groups. In so doing, we must choose between two fundamentally different approaches: we can study either groups that are very similar or groups that are very dissimilar to the various committees of the Free Democratic party. The two strategies would serve quite different purposes.

We would choose the first strategy if we wished to examine how the change in a particular parameter influences the theory. If, for example, we were interested in whether the ideological location of a group on a left-right continuum has an impact on any of the hypotheses of the theory, the best choice would probably be to study the Bernese Social Democratic party. Thus, many important parameters could be held constant for both studies, but we would have a clear variation in ideological orientation. If in this "quasi-experimental" setting a hypothesis supported in the Free Democratic party were refuted in the Social Democratic party, the ideological orientation of a group would have to be incorporated as a relevant theoretical parameter. If a hypothesis were supported in both parties, it would, of course, take on a more general character.

We would choose the other strategy—namely, to study groups that are as different as possible from the committees of the Free Democratic party—if we wanted to examine the universality of a hypothesis. If a hypothesis supported in this study survived the test of the British Cabinet or even of the village assembly in the Sudan mentioned in chapter 2, it would indeed have a very general character. However, this second strategy has one great disadvantage: it would be impossible to modify a refuted hypothesis since the studies would differ in so many relevant dimensions.

Whether studying generally similar decision-making groups or largely dissimilar ones, one could choose from a variety of approaches to carry out the study. Obviously, one could simply replicate the present study through participant observation, interviews, and analysis of documents, perhaps drawing on the strengths and weaknesses of our endeavors to improve the overall technique. Unfortunately, one would still be compelled to work with data for which external validity is quite high but internal validity is much more difficult to guarantee. The design and implementation of relatively precise laboratory experiments is another basic approach. This technique emphasizes internal validity, but sometimes sacrifices external validity. The primary advantage of such an approach would be the added precision and rigor with which one could examine specific theoretical relationships. But since this technique does not ensure the applicability of the results to the kinds of decision situations that occur in the real world, one should be skeptical about pursuing this method exclusively.

Since compromise is an often employed means of resolving conflict, it is appropriate that just such a resolution is suggested in the present dilemma. First, we assume that the issues of external and internal validity can never be resolved; at best, we can only pursue strategies that seek to ameliorate the worst consequences of the inability to satisfy these two criteria. Second, as noted above, we believe that our approach in this project has favored external validity over internal validity, in that our problems and data have specific relevance for the actual politics of decision-making behavior. This has meant, of course, that in the analysis of our data we have not always been able to conform to the scientific ideal of the controlled laboratory environment; hence, we always have some doubt about the results. Therefore, we feel that a fruitful approach might well lie in a combination of these two general techniques, laboratory experiments and participant observation. Using this combination, one could simultaneously replicate the observation of an actual decision-making group and design and perform certain laboratory experiments that would test more specifically and under more controlled conditions for the existence of hypothesized relationships. Although such a combined strategy would not resolve the issues of external and internal validity, it would bring a wider range of techniques with concomitant differences in strengths and weaknesses to bear on an otherwise imposing research task. Of course, the precise nature of the experiments, as well as the decision group that one chooses to observe, will depend on one's own interests and expertise and on the specific kinds of relationships that one wishes to investigate.

Comparing Political Parties

For further research using the same theoretical framework, we could change the units of analysis. Rather than look at individual conflicts, we could look at aggregates of conflicts for whole political parties. At this level of analysis the present study would constitute a single case characterized by a particular distribution of decision modes. We could then examine whether other political parties have a different distribution of decision modes—for example, whether they have a larger or smaller proportion of majority decisions than the 12 percent observed in the Free Democratic party. To explain such variation, we could refer to the variables in the theory presented here. Thus, one would expect, for example, that political parties with many conflicts about position issues would have a high frequency of majority decisions and nondecisions. But in moving from the level of individual conflicts to the level of political parties, we would have to extend the theory to include variables referring to properties of political parties themselves. As an example, we might expect the frequency of the individual decision modes to depend on whether we are dealing with a mass or a cadre party.[1] At this level of analysis we might also extend the research to other political groups, such as labor unions or business associations.

Comparing Political Systems

A bigger challenge would be to investigate the decision modes used at even higher levels of aggregation—to compare the distributions of the four modes for whole political systems. This would bring us to the level of analysis of the literature on consociational theory discussed in chapter 1. It would certainly not be unproblematic to apply our micro-level theory to this macro-level, because we would also have to consider systemic variables such as the economic structure and the international position of a country. Yet, we hope that our micro-level theory would at least be of heuristic value for the formulation of meaningful theory at the macro-level.

Before we could even begin to theorize at the macro-level, however, we would have to solve the imposing problem of how to measure the distribution of decision modes for whole political systems. Although it is relatively easy to determine how frequently a particular political party uses the various decision modes, the same task poses severe problems at the systemic level. For example, how can we measure in a reliable and valid way whether decisions by interpretation are used more widely in Italy than they are in France? We do not claim that we already have a satisfactory answer to such methodological questions, but we will discuss some of the issues and indicate possible directions in which further research in this area could go.

In his most recent book Arend Lijphart uses an impressionistic approach. He compares the decision modes in a fairly large number of countries in both the First and the Third worlds, still applying the relatively simple distinction between consociational and competitive decision modes.[2] With our own fourfold typology the problem would be greater, but even his twofold scheme clearly demonstrates that the impressionistic soft-data approach has severe limitations.

On the basis of a careful study of the literature, Lijphart uses his expert judgment to describe each country. The following examples are indicative of his approach:

> The Italian case remains a clear example of centrifugal democracy, but even here a few qualifications are in order. At the local level, one often finds cordial relations and fruitful cooperation among Christian Democratic, Socialist, and Communist party and government officials. At the national level, the "opening to the left" represented the bridging of the segmental cleavage between Christian Democrats and Socialists. The next step toward a grand coalition spanning the political spectrum from Christian Democrats to Communists—the "historic compromise" pro-

posed by Communist leader Enrico Berlinguer in 1973—would entail the introduction of the principal element of consociational democracy.[3]

Writers on Canadian politics disagree on how the country should be classified in the typology of democratic regimes. Presthus states that it "fits nicely" into the consociational category. But McRae thinks that "the existing Canadian political system, even at its best, must be viewed as a very imperfect example of consociational democracy." An "average" of these two views is probably the most nearly correct interpretation: Canada fits approximately in between the centrifugal and consociational types.[4]

The two authors who have written about Israel from the point of view of the consociational model are cautious in their judgment as to how well the country fits the model. Paltiel merely states that "the consociational approach provides a fruitful framework for analyzing political integration and the nature of democracy in Israel." And Gutmann concludes that, "although not a consociationalism in the accepted sense of the term, the Israeli ruling coalition is based on some of its elements." Like Canada, Israel may be regarded as a combination of consociational and centrifugal democracy.[5]

A Malay-dominated emergency council ruled until 1971 when parliamentary government was restored, but only after the parliament first voted to entrench the privileged position of the Malays in the constitution and to ban all further public as well as parliamentary discussion of these sensitive provisions. The Alliance leaders resumed their efforts to build grand coalitions both by co-opting communal parties into the Alliance and by entering into post-election coalitions. Because of the limitation of the freedom of expression and the increasing political and economic discrimination in favor of the Malays, it is doubtful that Malaysia after 1971 can be regarded as either fully democratic or fully consociational.[6]

Lijphart's judgments about the four countries, as well as most of the other judgments in his book, seem plausible in our view. However, what seems plausible to one reader may appear implausible to another. Brian Barry's critique of the consociational literature, which we considered in chapter 1, is a good illustration of this point. Barry's disagreements about the classification of particular countries raise the issue of the reliability of the measurements. We do not doubt that Lijphart has a profound knowledge of the countries about which he makes judgments, but it remains somewhat unclear what weight he attributes to the various elements when he makes his summary judgments. In the Italian case, for example, Lijphart mentions some consociational elements at the local level, but he doesn't make clear what precise importance he attaches to the local, as compared to the national, level. Because of the lack of explicit criteria for the formulation of summary judgments, other scholars, even when using the same literature and the same data, could come to wholly different conclusions.

To increase the reliability of their studies, other scholars rely heavily on so-called hard data. They look, for example, at roll-call votes in parliament. If done with great care, collecting such data usually poses no significant problems with reliability. Moreover, if the intention is merely to make statements about voting patterns in parliament, validity is no real problem, either. However, if such data are used as indicators for the decision modes in a political system as a whole, major problems of validity do arise. Decisions by roll-call vote in full parliament will rarely be made by interpretation, because this decision mode is generally precluded by formal rules. Yet, in other parts of the system, for example, in the cabinet or in parliamentary committees, decisions made by interpretation might be quite frequent. Consequently, relying on roll-calls in the full parliament would lead to a very distorted picture of the overall decision-making patterns in a country. It is obvious that this lack of validity cannot be offset by a high level of reliability, for if an indicator does not measure what it is supposed to measure, it is no consolation that the measurements are reliable.

Satisfying Both Reliability and Validity

Current research about decision modes at the systemic level seems to fall into one of two extreme positions: an impressionistic soft-data approach that lacks reliability or a hard-data approach that lacks validity. Is there no middle ground that combines satisfactory levels of both reliability and validity? Before we try to suggest such a middle ground, we must first exclude the option of simply applying the methodological instrument that we have used at the micro-level of the Free Democratic party to the macro-level: it is simply not feasible to observe all decision making at the systemic level.

In practical terms no one would have the time, the money, and the manpower to undertake such a project. In addition, the access problem for participant observation most certainly could not be resolved for many important decision arenas, such as cabinet meetings. Limiting the study to a random sample of all conflicts also seems impossible because it would remain unclear from what universe of cases the sample should be drawn. Beyond these practical considerations lies a more fundamental problem: at the macro-level, conflicts occur not only between individuals but also between groups. Consequently, merely observing decision making in face-to-face groups would not provide a complete picture, especially since conflicts at the macro-level are not simply the sum of all conflicts at the micro-level.

One possible way to study decision modes at the macro-level is to look at specific issues. For example, one could analyze how a country is reacting to the problem of the safety of nuclear plants. To provide a good comparative basis, the countries included in the study would have to face similar issues. In this respect, nuclear safety is a good example because this issue has come up at about the same time in very similar terms in many countries. For each country one would have to identify the groups and the individual actors participating in the decision process. Then one would have to determine the conflict structure and the arenas in which the conflicts were debated. On this basis one could look at the decision modes and see what modes prevailed in what arenas and for what conflicts. One could perhaps see that a particular conflict was solved by amicable agreement in the cabinet, by interpretation in the parliamentary committee, and by a majority vote in the full parliament.

An obvious method for studying decision making about individual issues would be the analysis of written documents, which could include minutes of parliamentary debates and other meetings, press releases, reports by journalists, and so forth. As we learned in this project, however, such documents are not simply a mirror of the decision process; quite often the author of the minutes does not simply report a decision, but interprets a decision from the sense of the meeting. If one wishes to know what actually happened in a meeting, one must try to obtain documents from as many different sources as possible. As a second method, one could interview some of the key actors. However, our experience in this project indicates that interview answers are often a very imprecise reflection of the actual decision process. The respondents may try to distort reality in their favor, or they may simply not remember the precise development of the decision process. But if we remember this weakness, interviews with key actors might still help clarify the information found in the documents. At some point one must piece together all of the available information; and to do this one must finally rely on judgment. To put these judgments on a more solid foundation, one might use a third method of inquiry by submitting the tentative judgments to knowledgeable persons, such as other scholars and journalists.

Using this methodological approach, one should be able to describe the decision process on a particular issue with some degree of reliability and validity. The results should be more reliable than Lijphart's because it is easier to make a judgment about a particular issue than about a political system as a whole. The results should be more valid than if one had used only hard data such as roll-calls because one could study a broader range of the decision process. The same methodology could be used to analyze several issues for each country. In addition to nuclear safety, one could study other issues that appear in similar ways in various countries, such as control of rising health costs, purchase of new fighter planes, and regulation of abortion.

Would it be possible to aggregate these case studies so that one could obtain a measure for investigation at the systemic level? The major problem would be that the decision modes would probably vary a great deal from one issue area to another. It is certainly conceivable to assign weights to the various issue areas and thus to construct a summary index at the systemic level, but the assignment of such weights would necessarily be quite arbitrary.

To investigate decision modes effectively at the systemic level, one would have to find indicators that apply at this level of analysis. What reliable and valid indicators would measure the distribution of decision modes for whole political systems? Although the answer is not obvious, one possibility would be to develop such indicators on the basis of our micro-theory of decision modes. For example, we have seen that small groups tend to make many decisions by amicable agreement and few by majority vote. Based on this finding, one could assume that political systems with many small decision groups might also make many decisions by amicable agreement and few by majority vote. Thus, the size of the decision groups could be used as an indicator for the prevailing decision modes at the systemic level. Other indicators based on our micro-level theory might be the degree of participation of low-status actors in the decision process, the frequency of position versus valence issues, or the strength of the popular referendum. However, we must caution that these indicators are not unproblematic, because one cannot always deduce occurrences at the macro-level from those at the micro-level.

CHAPTER 10

Implications for Normative Democratic Theory

In the previous nine chapters we tried to describe and explain various political decision modes. In this final chapter we wish to address the normative question of whether some decision modes are preferable to others. To answer this question, we must first determine the goals to which the different decision modes might contribute. One source for the generation of these goals would be an abstract philosophical system.[1] Here, however, a more modest approach will suffice. We will state and briefly justify three values that are of particular importance to us.

1. *Participation.* The members of a political system should have ample opportunities to participate in an efficacious way in the decision-making process of the system. To have such input is the most basic democratic criterion.

2. *Innovation.* On the output side, a political system should be innovative enough in its performance that it can adapt to new challenges. This does not mean that any innovation is better than the status quo, but it means that there must be realistic possibilities to change the status quo in a significant way.

3. *Peacefulness.* The relations between the groups and the individuals of a political system should be peaceful. This does not mean that we expect an absence of conflicts; this would be neither realistic nor desirable.[2] Peacefulness implies an absence of physical violence and, as far as possible, of psychological and structural violence, too.[3] Defined in this way, peacefulness corresponds to an important criterion of human dignity in that the integrity of human beings must not be damaged.

In principle, it would be possible to study empirically the causal relationship between political decision modes, on the one hand,

182

and participation, innovation, and peacefulness, on the other, but one has to be aware of many difficulties. One problem is that the consequences of variation in the decision modes are often noticeable only at the aggregate level. For example, whether a particular conflict is decided by majority rule or by interpretation may have no immediate effect on the levels of the three variables. An effect can often be detected only when a specific decision mode predominates over a longer period of time. Consequently, one would have to compare aggregates of conflicts, not individual conflicts. One could look at a political party with a predominance of majority decisions and compare it with another party in which decision by interpretation predominates. The question would then be which of these two parties has higher levels of participation, innovation, and peacefulness. It would be even more important to compare whole political systems because it can be assumed that our three values are most strongly influenced at the systemic level. In chapter 9, however, we saw how difficult it is to classify political systems according to the distribution of decision modes. It would probably be equally difficult to measure participation, innovation, and peacefulness as dependent variables. Of course, one could attempt to measure peacefulness with a very simple indicator such as the number of deaths from domestic violence,[4] but such an indicator would be not only simple but also simplistic because it would not tap the important phenomenon of structural violence, such as that experienced (before the outbreak of physical violence) by blacks in South Africa and Rhodesia. Similar problems would arise for the measurement of participation and innovation. Moreover, the demonstration of the exact causal relations among four such complex variables as decision modes, participation, innovation, and peacefulness would present many problems. We referred to some of these problems in our discussion of the literature on consociational theory in chapter 1.

All of these difficulties should not discourage empirical studies about the effects of political decision modes on our three important values. The further research suggested in chapter 9 should indeed have as its main direction a clarification of these causal relations, but we cannot postpone our normative discussion until these empirical results are available, because the questions have an immediate and urgent relevance for the political environments of many countries; moreover, constantly waiting for further research is an abdication of responsibility. In addition, the definitive research answer will probably never be found since controversy will always remain.[5] This is particularly true if broad values such as participation, innovation, and peacefulness are involved. Although we have no real "hard" data to offer, we would still like to discuss at this point how these three values might be influenced by the prevailing decision modes. This discussion will mainly be of a speculative nature. As far as possible, we will refer to the literature and, when appropriate, to information drawn from our study of the Free Democratic party.

Decision Modes and Participation

First, we will examine the possible impact of the various decision modes on the level of participation. A standard hypothesis in the literature is that majority rule encourages participation more than does amicable agreement.[6] Two main arguments support this hypothesis. First, politics played by majority rule is simply a better spectator sport than politics played by amicable agreement. With majority rule, the question of who is going to win is always exciting, and if the battle for the votes is close, the needs of the "homo ludens" are well served and citizens are motivated to attend political meetings. If a conflict is decided by amicable agreement, the winners are not clearly distinguished from the losers, and thus, politics as a game loses much of its attraction. Second, majority rule seems the clearer, more efficacious mode, especially to the less articulate actors. With majority rule, each actor in a decision group has the same weight when it comes to the counting of the votes. Thus, even the actors who are not articulate enough to speak up in a meeting may hope for some influence. Although with amicable agreement each actor has a veto power since the opposition of a single actor makes it impossible to reach a decision by amicable agreement, this veto power cannot be used through a simple gesture of the hand; nor is it possible under most circumstances to take the floor and simply say no. Ordinarily a position must be argued formally, thus placing the less articulate actors at a strong disadvantage. This is particularly true in large meetings like party conventions in which a certain courage and experience are needed to speak up and defend a position. Lacking this skill, many actors might be discouraged and withdraw from further participation.

Politics played by the rules of decision by interpretation can be the most exciting to watch but at the same time it can be the most difficult to understand. Observing the Free Democratic party, we were fascinated by all the subtle maneuvers that occurred when this mode was employed. To interpret a decision tacitly and to direct the subsequent discussion as if a formal decision had been made requires considerable skill and experience. One might expect that a predominance of decisions by interpretation would attract many interested spectators who enjoy watching the subtleties of the process. Unfortunately, the process tends to be understood only by the main participants, so that the average citizen may derive little pleasure from watching something that he does not fully understand. A decision by interpretation is often made before most participants realize what is going on. Thus, for most people, politics played by interpretation may not only be a bad spectator sport, but it may also lead to a low level of political efficacy. This is because no positions are expressed in a vote, and contrary to amicable agreement, the actors do not have a veto power. Before many actors have noticed, a decision has already been made, and the discussion has passed on to the next point on the agenda. In principle, of course, it is always possible to return to an earlier agenda point, but such a move often seems awkward and goes against strong group norms. On the whole, it seems that decision by interpretation encourages participation even less than does amicable agreement.

Nondecisions seem to be as bad for participation as are decisions by interpretation. To be sure, it may be fascinating to observe how some key actors subtly maneuver the discussion so that no decision is made. However, very few people will understand this process, particularly if the decision to postpone the issue is made implicitly, as it often is. This maneuvered and unspoken aspect of nondecisions may cause many actors to feel that they have no real influence.

On the whole, we expect that majority decision is the most favorable for participation, amicable agreement somewhat favorable, and both decision by interpretation and nondecision least favorable. In the appendix, we have recorded some data about the level of participation in the Free Democratic party of the canton of Bern. During the time of our research, the party had approximately 10,000 registered members, of whom 318 held positions at the cantonal party level. Thirty-five percent of these 318 party members did not speak at any meeting during the twenty-one months of our observations. Sixty-nine percent did not contribute a single proposal to the conflict situations that we observed. Of all proposals that entered these conflict situations, 37 percent originated from the four most active participants, and 64 percent from the 14 most active ones. Such data may give the impression that participation in the party is low, which would support our hypotheses since majority decision was the least frequent decision mode (12 percent) and decision by interpretation (37 percent) and nondecision (30 percent) the most frequent. But we must be very cautious in drawing such conclusions because we have no systematic basis for making comparisons with other political parties. Unfortunately, we could not find any other study in the literature that had comparable data. Thus, we cannot exclude the possibility that other parties have even lower levels of participation. It is also possible that the 12 percent of majority decisions in the Free Democratic party is, comparatively speaking, not particularly low. Consequently, we are not really sure whether we can say that the Free Democrats have low levels of both participation and majority decisions. Given this uncertainty, we provide the data in the appendix about participation in the Free Democratic party only to facilitate a rough comparison if other scholars are interested in replicating this study in another party.

Even if further comparative studies were to demonstrate a correlation between a low frequency of majority decisions and low levels of participation, causality would still present a problem. One could argue that low participation is not the consequence but the cause of a low frequency of majority decisions, or that the two variables are linked in a complex feedback process. It is also conceivable that no direct causal linkage exists between the two variables and that both variables depend on a third factor.

Decision Modes and Innovation

Second, we will consider the possible impact of the various decision modes on the scope of innovation. According to a widely shared view in the literature, decisions by amicable agreement tend to be less innovative than majority decisions. On the basis of laboratory experiments, Samuel A. Kirkpatrick et al. note "greater shifts among majority rule groups over consensus rule groups."[7] Summarizing the literature dealing with experiences drawn from the "real world," Arend Lijphart states that for consociational decision making "the gravest problem is that of immobilism."[8] The hypothesis that amicable agreement tends to be noninnovative is based on the argument that the more conservative group members have a kind of veto power with this decision mode. If these members feel that a proposed change departs too radically from the status quo, they can always threaten to withdraw their support, meaning that no decision would be made and that no change would take place. The more innovative group members do not have this leverage in a decision by amicable agreement: if they believe that a proposal is not innovative enough, a withdrawal of support is likely to make things even worse because making no decision only strengthens the status quo. In these situations majority rule provides the innovative group members with the possibility of outvoting their conservative colleagues. Of course, many majority decisions also reinforce the status quo. But a vote at least provides the opportunity for reaching decisions over which the most conservative group members have no veto power.

The commonly accepted hypothesis that majority decisions tend to be more innovative than do amicable agreements can be challenged if a distinction is made between decision *making* and decision *implementation*. Too much emphasis has been placed on how decisions are made and not enough on how they are implemented.[9] If a very innovative decision is made but never implemented, the overall result is a reinforcement of the status quo. In such a case, decision making is simply window dressing, a symbolic use of politics.[10] The implementation of majority decisions might face so much obstruction from the losing minority that many of these decisions would never be put into effect. Although decisions by amicable agreement may be less innovative, they are supported by all group members and, thus, have a better chance of being implemented. It is this argument that Lijphart has in mind when he writes that "consociational democracy may appear slow and ponderous in the short run but has a greater chance of producing effective decisions over time."[11]

For decision by interpretation it is also possible to make arguments for both sides. It may seem that a decision by interpretation allows great potential for innovation because it makes it possible for a minority to impose its will on the remainder of the group. If powerful innovators know how to use this decision mode to their advantage, decision by interpretation might indeed offer the best chances for innovation. But, as pointed out in chapter 4, the use of decision by interpretation tends to favor high-status actors, and these actors may be more inclined to defend the status quo than to be innovative: because they have more to lose than to gain, high-status actors will tend to prefer the certainty of the status quo to the uncertainties of change. Decisions made by interpretation might also be rather noninnovative because they might be difficult to implement. Since an interpretation is not made in as formalized a way as is a majority decision or a decision by amicable agreement, a decision by interpretation often lacks the legitimacy of decisions made by the other two modes. Because of this lack of legitimacy, it would be relatively easy to challenge a decision by interpretation in the implementation phase. Generally speaking, we hypothesize that decisions by interpretation are rather strongly oriented to the status quo.

Since a nondecision by definition leaves the status quo unchanged, further comments on this mode are unnecessary.

As we have already shown in chapter 4, majority decisions in the Free Democratic party had the highest chance of being implemented (97 percent), followed by decisions by amicable agreement (89 percent) and decisions by interpretation (81 percent). In

chapter 6, we identified 53 conflicts in which an innovative proposal was clearly opposed by a status quo proposal. It is interesting to
note that an innovative proposal had the highest chance of winning
with a majority decision (68 percent), the second highest chance
with amicable agreement (55 percent), and the lowest chance with
a decision by interpretation (40 percent). These data seem to indicate that majority decisions contribute most to innovation, decisions by interpretation least. But again, we have to be cautious
with our conclusions. Obviously, it would be much better to study
the relationship between decision modes and innovation at the aggregate level, for example, by comparing various political parties.
It remains to be seen whether such studies will in fact support
the hypothesis that a predominance of majority decisions contributes to innovation whereas a predominance of decisions by interpretation reinforces the status quo.

Decision Modes and Peacefulness

Finally, we will offer some speculation about the causal linkage
between decision modes and peacefulness. First, we look at the
level of peacefulness among the decision makers themselves.
Here, we expect a feedback loop in which a high frequency of
majority decisions and a high level of hostility reinforce each other:
if many decisions are made by majority rule, hostility among decision makers is likely to increase and such an increase in hostility
leads in turn to many decisions by majority rule. Conversely, the
use of amicable agreement, decision by interpretation, and nondecision is likely to contribute to peacefulness among decision
makers, and this peacefulness would seem to be a favorable precondition for the employment of these three decision modes.

A predominance of majority decisions should increase hostility
among decision makers, both for direct and indirect reasons. First,
we expect that majority rule would tend to heighten feelings of
hostility among losing minorities. Such a tendency would be absent only if, over a large number of votes, each actor had an equal
chance of winning and the importance of his winning votes corresponded to the importance of his losing ones. In most cases,
these preconditions will not be fulfilled for there are usually some

actors who perceive that they are outvoted more often than they win and that their losses concern more important issues than do their victories. With a nonmajoritarian decision mode, the level of hostility among the losers should be lower, and it may even be that nobody will perceive himself as losing. If a decision is made by amicable agreement, for example, the compromise may be so good that no one will feel disadvantaged. However, amicable agreement may sometimes be brought about by social pressure. In such cases, some actors may feel just as hostile as they would have if they had been outvoted by a majority. In a decision by interpretation, losers have some consolation because their loss is not as explicit as it is in a vote. In a nondecision the question of who loses seems to be postponed, but in many cases the implicit winners are the supporters of the status quo, which may cause hostility in the actors who support innovation. In conclusion, we do not agree that nonmajoritarian decision modes do not ever cause hostility, but we do expect that the level of hostility caused by decisions of these types is lower than it is with majority rule.

To give a more indirect argument why majority decisions tend to cause more hostility among decision makers than do nonmajoritarian decisions, we introduce here innovation and participation as intervening variables. According to the hypothesis developed earlier in this chapter, innovation and participation tend to be supported by the use of majority rule. In decision-making situations with a significant degree of innovation and participation, hostility among the decision makers seems more likely because more actors are involved in more disagreements.[12] Figure 10.1 shows both the direct and the indirect causal linkages between decision modes and the level of hostility among decision makers.

Hostility among decision makers seems to be not only a consequence but also a cause of majority decisions. Figure 10.2 describes the hypothesized feedback processes. In order to reduce the complexity of the model we concentrate on only a few key relationships. As we have already argued, a high frequency of nonmajoritarian decisions tends to decrease the levels of innovation, participation, and hostility. If innovation, participation, and hostility are at low levels: (a) decisions tend to be made by small

Figure 10.1

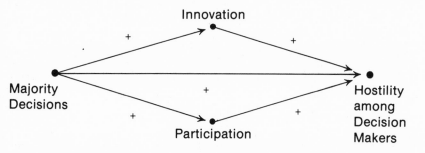

groups of high-status actors; (b) conflicts tend to deal with means rather than with goals; and (c) decision making tends to shift from the parliamentary to the preparliamentary phase. These last three tendencies are favorable conditions for nonmajoritarian decisions, thus closing the feedback loop.

Figure 10.2

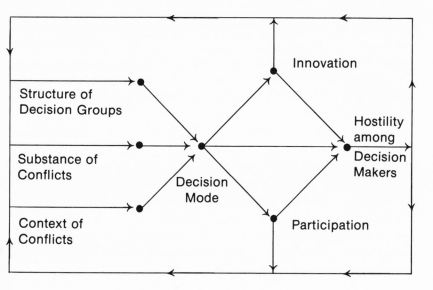

Will a continuation of this feedback process eventually eliminate majority decisions? Not necessarily, for we must also take into account the hostility factor at the mass level. Parallel to the feedback process just described, we have another feedback process with hostility at the mass level as the key variable, and we expect that the two feedback processes are interrelated. In this second feedback loop, a high frequency of nonmajoritarian decisions tends to lead to an increased malaise at the mass level. By malaise we mean an unfocused attitudinal hostility: distrust, animosity, and hatred that are directed not against specific persons but against the leaders in general or, even broader, against the political system itself.[13] We hypothesize that the causal linkage between nonmajoritarian decisions and malaise operates through the two variables of innovation and participation, as described in figure 10.3. We have argued before that nonmajoritarian decisions tend to decrease innovation and participation. With a low level of these two variables, the political system tends to be seen by its members as static, not readily lending itself to effective influence by citizens. Under these conditions, citizens may easily develop feelings of frustration that will be directed in an unfocused way against the system as a whole.

Figure 10.3

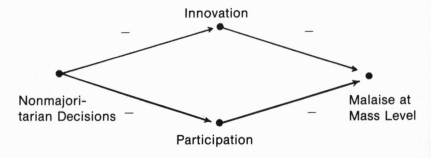

A strong malaise at the mass level may influence the decision modes through a feedback process. If citizens develop a strong sense of malaise, they may either withdraw from the political system or try to change it ("exit" or "voice," to use Albert O. Hirschman's terms).[14] Following the latter course, they may try to change the structure of the decision groups, by demanding an increase in their size and a faster circulation among leadership positions, the substance of the conflicts, by introducing more position as opposed to valence issues, or the context of the conflicts, by shifting the emphasis from the preparliamentary to the parliamentary phase. If such grass roots efforts are successful, the frequency of majority decisions is likely to increase, which should reduce the malaise. It is also possible that the decision makers themselves will try to prevent the development of malaise at the grass roots level. They may anticipate that a predominance of nonmajoritarian decisions could lead to increasing malaise among the citizens, thus threatening the survival of the political system. As a response, the decision makers might take measures that would lead to a higher frequency of majority decisions. They could, for example, place a limit on the length of tenure in party offices, or they could shift the emphasis of the decision-making process from the preparliamentary to the parliamentary phase. The response of the decision makers might also be more direct: for example, they could consciously try to use majority decision more often.

As these examples illustrate, our model includes specific voluntary elements—that is, factors that can be manipulated by human design. By incorporating this voluntarism in the model we are rejecting narrow social determinism and allowing for a certain degree of free choice.[15]

What level of hostility did we detect in the Free Democratic party? In 6 of the 466 conflicts party members criticized each other personally. By a personal critique we mean, for example, a claim that someone cannot be trusted or is incompetent. At the informal gatherings outside the meetings, personal critique was more frequent. As described in the appendix, we observed 414 informal discussions of various topics, and in 19 percent of these discussions a party member was criticized in a personal way. Do these data indicate a high or a low level of hostility among the Free Democratic decision makers? An answer cannot be given before comparable data for other parties are collected. Further research would also have to include an analysis of hostility at the mass level.

We have discussed the possible influence of political decision modes on the levels of participation, innovation, and peacefulness. Can we now say which is the best decision mode if our goal is to increase these three values? The answer is obviously difficult because we have little data to support our speculations. Moreover, it is impossible to maximize all three values at the same time, because they are influenced in different ways by the decision modes. Consequently, we must look for the decision mode that provides the most satisfactory trade-offs among the three values. But what kind of balance shall we seek among these values? For example, how much innovation are we willing to concede to get more peacefulness? In our view, such questions cannot be answered in the abstract but only for concrete cases. An increase in peacefulness is certainly much more valuable in Northern Ireland than it is in Switzerland. Before formulating a recommendation, we first need to determine where the major problems lie in the specific case. Such a case-by-case approach seems more fruitful than an abstract statement about the "best" decision mode. We will illustrate this method with a brief discussion of Switzerland.

The Case of Switzerland

In our opinion lack of innovation is the greatest problem confronting Switzerland today. Karl W. Deutsch has also argued that Switzerland has a rather small scope of innovation when compared to countries with similar levels of economic development.[16] Some well-known examples of the retarded capacity of innovation of the Swiss system include the late introduction of female suffrage and the continued nonparticipation of Switzerland in the United Nations. Another example is the slowness with which Switzerland has reacted to such problems as the expansion of higher education, protection of the environment, conscientious objectors, and abortion. From a conservative viewpoint, the reduced scope of innovation may of course be applauded; we would also not deny that a political system sometimes reacts too quickly, leading to problems of oversteering. A possible example of this is West Germany, where many reforms in higher education have been undertaken very quickly, resulting in severe problems such as the chaos in connection with the introduction of the *numerus clausus* at the universities. Thus, we do not agree that the most innovative solution is always the best, but we do not like the Swiss tendency to let other countries take the first steps in new directions and to follow only when the major risks have been eliminated.

The scope of innovation in a political system can be increased in many ways. We are particularly interested in knowing whether a change in the mode of political decision making can accomplish this. Our speculations indicate that an increase in the use of majority decision will tend to increase the scope of innovation. Switzerland also has a lot of room for such a change since majority decisions are relatively rare. Majority decisions are also desirable because they tend to contribute to a higher level of political participation. In Switzerland, this would be a welcome contribution because complaints about a lack of participation have become more and more frequent. Before recommending such a change, however, we must check whether an increase in the number of majority decisions could have negative side effects. We must acknowledge that an increase in the use of majority decision introduces the danger of disrupting peaceful relations among the various cultural groups. However, contemporary Switzerland is so peaceful that this danger is probably minimal, especially if the increase in majority decisions is relatively moderate. Thus, we can conclude that within the parameters of our value system an increase in the employment of majority decision can be recommended for Switzerland. An obvious deduction from this recommendation is that Switzerland should abandon its "magic formula" for the composition of the Federal Council; the competitive principle of majority rule should replace the grand coalition of the four major parties, which has governed Switzerland since 1959. But such a recommendation must consider the institutional setting within which this change takes place, and it is here that the difficulties begin, with the two most important aspects of the institutional setting in Switzerland, the referendum and the federal structure of the country.

The referendum is a very powerful weapon for every member of the opposition; at times, it even allows a minor party to defeat a proposal of the government. If one or two of the major parties were to leave the government, it would be relatively easy for them to defeat proposals of the government through the use of the popular vote. As a consequence, the government would be unable to implement major components of its program. Thus, the change to a competitive formation of the cabinet would decrease rather than increase the innovative capacity of the system. One remedy would be to abolish the referendum, but such a change would probably influence another component of our value system negatively— namely, the level of participation. One of the great strengths of the Swiss system is that it offers the citizens the opportunity not only to elect their representatives but also to decide substantive matters in the referendum.

The federal structure of the country is another obstacle to a change from the traditional formula. In the Swiss federal system the political parties have their organizational strength at the cantonal level, and the federal parties remain relatively loose associations of cantonal parties. As a consequence, the federal parties cannot always count on the support of all of their cantonal sections. Thus, it would be difficult to form a governmental coalition of a minimal winning size because such a coalition would constantly be confronted with the danger of losing the support of some of its cantonal sections, thereby losing its majority in the federal parliament. The remedy for this is, of course, that the Swiss parties be centralized and disciplined so that a governmental coalition could count on the unquestioned support of all of its members. However, such a change would also mean the end of the strongly developed federalist system, and this would involve high costs for our three values of participation, innovation, and peacefulness. Generally speaking, it is easier under a federal structure for a citizen to take part in a country's political life. Further, federalism often contributes to innovation because new experiments can be launched in limited areas of the system. In Switzerland, federalism also helps to maintain peaceful relations among the subcultures because sensitive issues like school and church affairs are handled primarily at the cantonal and local level. The abandonment of the federal structure would certainly facilitate the introduction of the competitive formation of the cabinet, but the costs seem to be prohibitively high.

We conclude that it would be no simple matter to implement

the recommendation for more majority decisions. The obvious solution of dissolving the grand coalition of the four major parties seems to entail more costs than benefits. Thus, we have to search for a solution within the existing pattern. Here, we see ways to increase the number of majority decisions without changing the traditional structure of the cabinet. Even at this time, conflicts among the four major parties are often resolved by majority rule, both in parliament and in the referendum, but in the general public the norm prevails that majority decisions should be avoided among governmental partners. Yet the criticism is often made that the four parties represented in the Federal Council are unable to arrive at common solutions. Steps should therefore be undertaken to change this norm: the governmental parties should be not discouraged, but encouraged to make their differences visible. Thus, citizens would be confronted with clearer alternatives in the referendum, which would help to revitalize this important institution of participation. As already occurs in practice today, the losers would not always be on the same side. The various cleavages in Switzerland are cross-cutting to such an extent that different coalitions are likely to develop from issue to issue. It is just such a system of changing coalitions that we would like to advocate. One may object that this system will not have sufficient leadership to move the country forward. However, we would argue that the high flexibility of a system of changing coalitions would allow for a great deal of innovation. The probability of innovative solutions would certainly be higher than it is with a grand coalition in which each decision requires the consent of all participants. A system of competitive cabinet formation, on the other hand, has the attendant risk that most changes will simply move back and forth because as each party comes to power it will tend to counterbalance the changes implemented by the previous cabinet. (Britain is a good illustration of this pattern.) If all major parties are represented in the cabinet, but are nevertheless allowed to form shifting coalitions, the political system may develop a finely tuned steering capacity. This is particularly true if the referendum is strongly developed so that the citizens can play an important part in the process of decision making. Such a system would have a very short feedback loop, allowing for constant correction in the direction of the development. If a particular decision caused widespread dissatisfaction, a different coalition could correct the course of further development. This seems to correspond to what Deutsch calls a high learning capacity of a system.[17]

The implementation of this proposal for Switzerland would be relatively simple. The major parties would still have a proportionate share of the seats in the Federal Council, but they would use more majority decisions than heretofore to settle conflicts. The greatest change would be that the parties would use majority rule without feelings of guilt. They would recognize that a system of shifting coalitions is a legitimate alternative to both rigid grand coalition and majority-opposition types of government.

We have formulated our proposal only for the specific conditions of Switzerland, and we do not claim that it should be applied to all other countries. But we hope that our Swiss example has a certain paradigmatic significance in indicating the possibilities and the limitations for political scientists who wish to give advice to politicians. We see an initial limitation in the impossibility of telling the politicians what values they should pursue: since such recommendations cannot be made solely from an objective, scientific basis, we consider it both possible and desirable that political scientists make their own political values explicit. An extensive dialogue between politicians and political scientists about their respective values seems important for fruitful collaboration. Political scientists can then use their theoretical knowledge to determine the ways in which specific values can be best attained. Such scientifically founded advice can be given in general terms, but obviously cannot include subtle details. In the example of Switzerland it seems possible to say that the postulated values could be best attained if more emphasis were placed on majority decisions. It also seems possible to recommend that the grand coalition of the four major parties not be dissolved. But our theory does not provide any specific advice for some more detailed questions. An example is the controversial issue whether votes in the Federal Council should be made public. The arguments concerning this issue are so varied and subtle that it would be dishonest and arrogant to claim that scientifically based advice can be given.

What we have done for Switzerland could be done for any other country. Depending on the situation that exists within a country, the recommendations could be very different from those offered for Switzerland. In Northern Ireland, for example, we see the biggest problem, not so much in the lack of innovation, but in the high level of hostility between Protestants and Catholics. Consequently, we would recommend not more but fewer majority decisions. We would probably also conclude that the necessary preconditions for amicable agreements are not available. A practical recommendation could be that in joint Protestant-Catholic meetings, decisions by interpretation should be used more often. In order to be useful, such a recommendation would have to be specified for the existing institutional setting of the country. From this perspective, it seems necessary that political scientists have a profound historical and institutional knowledge of a country before they approach the politicians with recommendations.

Appendixes
Notes
Bibliography
Index

Latent Conflicts in the Free Democratic Party

By *latent conflicts* we mean issues that are not articulated in the formal setting of a group meeting. Peter Bachrach and Morton S. Baratz use the term *nondecisions* to refer to such latent conflicts.[1] We agree with these two authors that the "predominant norms, precedents, myths, institutions, and procedures" often prevent important issues from reaching the political arena.[2] We also agree that "nondecision making" is often "perpetuating 'unfair shares' in the allocation of benefits and privileges."[3] Therefore, it is certainly important to question why some issues enter the political arena, whereas other issues are kept outside.

Unfortunately, the debate about nondecisions is rather confusing.[4] One source of confusion is the term "nondecision" itself. In everyday language one usually speaks of a nondecision if an issue is formally debated in a meeting but no decision concerning the substance of the issue is made. Employing this usage, we treat nondecision as one of our four decision modes in this project. "To decide not to decide" refers to the formal setting of a meeting. For an issue that is filtered out before it reaches the formal agenda, it is clearer to speak of a latent or unarticulated conflict. Another source of confusion is that the concept of latent conflict is used in several different ways; at least four meanings can be distinguished:[5] (1) the political decision makers talk informally about an issue, but they do not set it on the agenda of their formal meetings; (2) the political decision makers are aware of an issue, but they discuss it neither formally nor informally; (3) some groups in the population are aware of an issue, but this issue is not communicated to the political decision makers; (4) a society has an underlying conflict, but no one in the society is aware of this conflict; thus, it does not develop into an issue.

The greatest confusion in the discussion about latent conflicts results from the question whether such a conflict can be studied with empirical methods. The critics of Bachrach and Baratz argue that it is usually not feasible to study latent conflicts with valid and reliable data. Bachrach and Baratz acknowledge that "the product of the research may well be impressionistic or ill-supported by data" but insist that such research is still necessary because latent conflicts are such an important phenomenon for the understanding of the political world.[6]

In this project we have tried to study latent conflicts in the first meaning of the term mentioned above. Participant observation was also extended as much as possible to the social gatherings before and after the meetings of the Free Democratic party.[7] It was, of course, impossible to observe all discussions at these occasions since they usually took place at different tables and sometimes even in different rooms; nor do we claim that the observations covered even a random sample of all informal gatherings. It is probable that we missed a great portion of the most intimate discussions among close party friends; at any rate, the observer was quite logically excluded from all discussions involving only two persons. Despite these caveats, however, the observations give at least some impression of the discussions that took place outside the formal party meetings.

Altogether, we observed the discussion of 414 topics at these informal occasions. The judgment that the discussion had changed to a new topic was based on the perceptions of the participants themselves; such a change was usually introduced with phrases like "to change the topic," "going to another point," and so forth. To be included, a topic had to be discussed by at least two participants: if a first speaker was not followed by someone else, this was not counted as a debated topic.

Comparing the discussions at the informal gatherings and at the formal meetings, two points stand out. First, the two types of discussion covered quite similar topics. In table A-1, we compare the informally debated topics with the 466 conflicts that we identified at the formal meetings. A single difference is visible in this table: the functioning of other parts of the political system was discussed more often at informal gatherings than it was at formal

Table A-1 :   *Debated Topics by Issue Areas (percentages)*

*Issue Areas**	*Informal Gatherings* (N = 414)	*Formal Meetings* (N = 466)
Elections and appointments	24	25
Functioning of the Free Democratic party	19	18
Functioning of other parts of the political system	19	5
Cultural affairs (education, science, art, religion, media, sports)	9	11
Social policy (health, welfare, social security, housing, working conditions)	4	9
Infrastructure (traffic, energy, environment)	6	9
Economic and financial affairs	10	14
Protection of the state (justice, police, military)	4	2
Jura question	5	7
Total	100	100

*Foreign policy is missing as an issue area since we observed a cantonal party.

meetings. This difference can easily be explained by the high number of role accumulations between the party, various interest
groups, and the parliament. When actors with such role accumulations meet informally, it may certainly be expected that they will
often talk about their roles outside the party. At formal meetings,
however, they will be more restricted to their party roles. With
this one exception, the topics debated informally and formally were
quite similar.

A second point that we noted in our comparison was a clear
difference in style between informal gatherings and formal meetings. At informal gatherings, issues were discussed in more personalized terms than they were at formal meetings. For example,
in a conflict between two options for a new road, the discussion

at a formal meeting typically dealt with such nonpersonal factors as the length and costs of the road; at informal gatherings the discussion was more likely to deal with who was supporting which option. At informal meetings the talk was not only more about persons, but such personalized discussions were usually more critical than they were at formal meetings. We counted, both for formal and informal meetings, how many times party members were criticized in personal terms. This meant not simply the expression of a disagreement of opinions, but a direct critique of the person as well: for example, the remark that he could not be trusted, was incompetent, or lacked leadership qualities. Of the 414 informally discussed topics, a present or absent party member was criticized in personal terms in 78 cases (19 percent). Of 466 conflicts at formal meetings, on the other hand, such personal critiques were articulated in only 6 cases (1 percent). Thus, personal critique was much more frequent at informal than at formal meetings.

How shall we interpret the similarities and differences between informal gatherings and formal meetings? Bachrach and Baratz argue that knowing the issues that are prevented from reaching the formal agenda helps us to make inferences about the power structure of an organization. For example, if economic and financial issues were often filtered out between the informal and the formal stages of the discussion, their interpretation would be that the rich were interested in preventing issues of distribution of the wealth from appearing on the formal agenda and that, consequently, these economic and financial matters were seldom discussed. Our data, however, do not support such an argument. The Free Democratic decision makers talked both formally and informally about largely the same issues; no evident social norm demanded that certain issues be stopped at the informal stage. But a clear social norm prevented the personal critique of other party members from passing from informal gatherings to formal meetings. Following the analysis of Bachrach and Baratz, one could analyze which people or groups benefited from the operation of such a norm. One could then conclude that these persons had the real power because they were able to shape the norms of agenda setting. We tried to determine who in the Free Democratic party was most concerned that personal critiques did not reach the formal agenda. Despite several trials, this search was completely unsatisfactory. The methods proposed in the literature are so vague that they were of no help. Interviews with the participant actors would not have been of great utility because, according to Bachrach and Baratz, the actors may not even be conscious of their interests. Even if we could have determined who was interested in a particular norm of agenda setting, we could still not necessarily have concluded that these actors also created this norm. A norm develops in a very complicated way, and it is sometimes shaped by persons for whom it represents a disadvantage. But perhaps persons who reinforce a norm that does not work in their favor act out of "false" consciousness. The real power holders find subtle and efficient ways to make others work for them, a further documentation of their power. All of these arguments are so fuzzy that it seems impossible to do a serious analysis. Of course, it is also possible that the interpretation of our data is very trivial: it may simply be a characteristic of any organization that personal critique is more frequent in informal settings.

Turning to the other meanings of the concept of latent conflict, the major problem is not how to interpret the data but how to get to any data at all. If an issue is not communicated to the political decision makers and, even more if no one in the population is aware of an issue, the data situation gets very difficult indeed. One could study marginal groups such as farm workers or homosexuals in order to detect issues that have not reached the political decision makers. Comparisons with other countries and other historical times might reveal conflict dimensions of which a particular population is unaware. One could then analyze the mechanisms and the power structure that keep such issues out of the political arena or even out of the awareness of the population. We agree with Bachrach and Baratz that these are fascinating and important questions, but no methods have as yet been suggested with which to study them in a satisfactory way.

Participation in the Free Democratic Party

The attendance rates for the 111 meetings that we observed are given in table A-2.

Table A-2: *Attendance Rate at Party Meetings*

Attendance rate (percentage)	Number of meetings (absolute)	(percentage)
100	5	4
81–99	20	18
61–80	32	29
41–60	44	40
40 and less	10	9
All meetings	111	100

Twenty-two percent of all meetings were attended by more than 80 percent of the committee members. In 49 percent of the meetings, the attendance rate was 60 percent or below.

During the time of our research, the Free Democrats in the canton of Bern had approximately 10,000 registered party members. A total of 318 persons held positions at the cantonal level, which is the level that we have studied. Table A-3 indicates the number of meetings at which these 318 actors actually spoke. About two-thirds of the 318 actors with formal positions in the party spoke at only one or at none of the meetings. Fourteen actors spoke at more than twenty meetings; among these very active participants, the party secretary and the party president stand out, speaking at 85 and 79 meetings respectively.

Party members made a total of 694 proposals in the 466 con-

Table A-3:   *Number of Actors Speaking at Party Meetings*

	Number of Actors (absolute)	(percentage)
At no meeting	111	35
At one meeting	97	30
At 2–3 meetings	49	16
At 4–10 meetings	30	10
At 11–20 meetings	17	5
At more than 20 meetings	14	4
Total	318	100

flicts that we identified. Table A-4 shows to what extent the 318 actors with formal positions in the cantonal party contributed to these proposals. During the twenty-one months in which we observed the party, 69 percent of all party members with formal positions did not contribute a single proposal to the party discussions. The 14 percent who made more than 10 proposals each actually contributed 64 percent of all proposals. The concentration of participation among a few actors is even more visible in that the four most active party members together made 37 percent of all proposals; the party secretary was the most active person with 112 proposals.

Table A-4:   *Number of Actors Presenting Proposals at Party Meetings*

	Number of Actors (absolute)	(percentage)
No proposal	219	69
One proposal	37	11
2–3 proposals	24	8
4–10 proposals	24	8
11–30 proposals	10	3
More than 30 proposals	4	1
Total	318	100

Political Status in the Free Democratic Party

To measure the status of the individual actors in the Free Democratic Party we applied three traditional indicators—*reputation*, *position*, and *participation*—to the 318 actors who held a formal position in the cantonal party. For the indicator of reputation we solicited the opinions of nine judges who were the party members with the highest rank in the formal party hierarchy, namely, the members of the bureau of the executive committee and of the bureau of the parliamentary group. In a personal interview each judge was asked to rank all 318 persons according to the following categories: (a) strong influence in the cantonal party, (b) moderately strong influence, (c) weak or no influence.

This reputational test allowed us to classify the 318 persons into the following groups:

	Number of Persons
1. Unanimity among all judges—strong influence	1
2. Near unanimity among all judges—strong influence (no more than two judges dissenting)	4
3. Judges split (at least two judges for strong influence, but also at least two judges dissenting)	10
4. Near unanimity among all judges—no strong influence (no more than two judges dissenting)	14
5. Unanimity among all judges—no strong influence	289
Total	318

Thus, 90 percent of all party members having a formal position at the cantonal level were perceived as having no strong influence on the affairs of the party. For another 5 percent, the judges were nearly unanimous that they had no strong influence. This leaves only 5 percent, or 15 actors, for whom a substantial number of the judges indicated strong influence. Even among this group only 5 actors emerged for whom the judges were unanimous or near unanimous in attributing a strong influence.

For the indicator of position the question is whether the actors with the highest reputation also have the highest formal positions in the party. The executive committee and the parliamentary group form the top of the formal party hierarchy, each having about the same rank, and each group has a bureau with a more limited membership. During the time of our research, the executive committee had twenty-five members, and its bureau, four, whereas the parliamentary group had thirty-four members, and its bureau, ten.

The 5 actors who had a clear reputation for strong influence in the party were all members of both the executive committee and the parliamentary group. Two of them also belonged to both bureaus, and a third belonged to the bureau of the parliamentary group. Thus, we see that the actors with the highest reputation were also at the top of the formal party hierarchy.

The data for the 10 actors who followed the top 5 in reputation confirms the conclusion that high reputation tends to accompany high formal status. Four of these 10 actors were members of both the executive committee and the parliamentary group; 3 were members of only the parliamentary group, and 1 was a member of only the executive committee. The remaining 2 had no formal position at the top of the formal party hierarchy. However, they were both journalists, which gave them a particular power base in the party. With the exception of these two journalists, those members who had high reputations also held high formal party positions. This does not mean, however, that those with high formal status necessarily had high reputations. Twelve members in the executive committee received no rankings of high reputation. Thus, a high formal status seems a necessary but not a sufficient precondition for a strong influence in the party.

Our third indicator of political status is participation. We observed a total of 111 meetings; our data show at how many of these meetings each actor spoke. The 5 actors with the highest reputations spoke at an average of 45 meetings each, whereas the 10 actors with the next highest reputations spoke at an average of 26 meetings each. The remaining 303 actors holding a formal position in the cantonal party spoke at an average of 2.3 meetings each. High reputation clearly goes together with speaking up at party meetings. This conclusion is confirmed if we consider the number of proposals that an actor introduced into the discussion. In the 466 conflicts that we identified at the 111 meetings, group members articulated a total of 694 proposals. The 5 actors with the highest reputations made an average of 37 proposals each, whereas the 10 actors with the next highest reputations made an average of 19 proposals each, and the remaining 303 actors made an average of only 1.1 proposals each. Finally, the 5 percent with the highest reputations made 53 percent of all proposals.

Overall, we get the following picture from our three indicators: a small group of 5 to 15 persons has a truly high status in the party. The members of this group are respected for their influence, they hold high formal positions in the party hierarchy, and they participate extensively in party life.

Notes

Chapter 1

1. Gerhard Lehmbruch, "A Noncompetitive Pattern of Conflict Management in Liberal Democracies," pp. 90–97; Arend Lijphart, "Consociational Democracy," pp. 207–25.
2. Gabriel Almond et al., eds., *Crisis, Choice and Change*, pp. 648–49.
3. Lehmbruch, "Noncompetitive Pattern," p. 97.
4. Brian Barry, "Political Accommodation and Consociational Democracy," pp. 477–505.
5. Lijphart, "Consociational Democracy," p. 216.
6. Lehmbruch, "Noncompetitive Pattern," p. 93.
7. Raimund Germann, *Politische Innovation und Verfassungsreform*; Barry, "Political Accommodation," pp. 477–505.
8. Hans Daalder, "The Consociational Democracy Theme," p. 615.
9. Douglas W. Rae and Michael Taylor, *The Analysis of Political Cleavages*.
10. Dusan Sidjanski et al., *Les Suisses et la politique*.
11. The question was: "Which of these terms *best* describes the way you usually think of yourself? Genevois (for example), Swiss Romand (for example), Swiss."
12. Henry H. Kerr, *Switzerland: Social Cleavages and Partisan Conflict*.
13. For an older but still valuable source, see Hermann Weilenmann, *Pax Helvetica oder die Demokratie der kleinen Gruppen*.
14. For a detailed discussion of Austria and the Netherlands, see Jeffrey Obler et al., *Decision-Making in Smaller Democracies*.
15. See, for example, Martin O. Heisler, ed., *Politics in Europe*.
16. Lijphart, "Consociational Democracy," pp. 213–14, 224.
17. Barry, "Political Accommodation," p. 488.
18. This description of political decision making in Switzerland relies heavily on Jürg Steiner, *Amicable Agreement versus Majority Rule*.
19. See, for example, Erich Gruner, *Die Parteien in der Schweiz*;

Leonhard Neidhart, *Plebiszit und pluralitäre Demokratie*; Paolo Urio, *L'Affaire des Mirages*.

20. See Christopher Hughes, *The Parliament of Switzerland*; Beat Alexander Jenny, *Interessenpolitik und Demokratie in der Schweiz*; Gerhard Kocher, *Verbandseinfluss auf die Gesetzgebung*.

21. Peter Gilg, "Parteien und eidgenössische Finanzpolitik," pp. 41–74.

22. For a more elaborate analysis of Austria, Belgium, and the Netherlands, see Obler et al., *Decision-Making in Smaller Democracies*.

23. Rodney P. Stiefbold, "Segmented Pluralism and Consociational Democracy in Austria," p. 121.

24. Kurt Steiner, *Politics in Austria*, pp. 418–19.

25. Gerhard Lehmbruch, "Das politische System Oesterreichs in vergleichender Perspektive," pp. 35–56. "Bereichsopposition" can be translated as opposition politics restricted to certain issues, and "Bereichskoalition" as coalition politics restricted to certain issues.

26. Heinz Fischer, "Empirisches zur Arbeit des Nationalrates in der XIII. Gesetzgebungsperiode," pp. 77–94.

27. Anton Pelinka, "Repräsentative und plebiszitäre Elemente im österreichischen Regierungssystem," pp. 33–47.

28. Raoul F. Kneucker, "Austria: An Administrative State," pp. 95–127.

29. Manfried Welan, "Vom Proporz- zum Konkurrenzmodell," pp. 151–76.

30. Arend Lijphart, *The Politics of Accommodation*.

31. James A. Dunn, Jr., "Consociational Democracy and Language Conflict," pp. 9–16.

32. Eric A. Nordlinger, *Conflict Regulation in Divided Societies*.

33. Martin Heisler, "Patterns of European Politics," pp. 42–43.

34. Leo Panitch, "The Development of Corporatism in Liberal Democracies," pp. 65–66 and n. 5.

35. Philippe C. Schmitter, "Modes of Interest Intermediation and Models of Societal Change in Western Europe," pp. 7–38, and Gerhard Lehmbruch, "Liberal Corporatism and Party Government," pp. 91–126.

36. Charles Lewis Taylor and Michael C. Hudson, *World Handbook of Political and Social Indicators*.

37. G. Bingham Powell, Jr., *Social Fragmentation and Political Hostility*, p. 38. *Lager*, literally "camp," is a term often applied to the two major Austrian parties.

38. Arend Lijphart, *Democracy in Plural Societies*.

39. Harold E. Glass, "Subcultural Segmentation and Consensual Politics."

40. William T. Bluhm, *Building an Austrian Nation*, p. 62.

41. Klaus Zapotoczky, "Religion als Grundwert," pp. 162–75.

42. Erich Bodzenta and Norbert Freytag, "Soziale Ungleichheit," pp. 100–136.

43. Lijphart, *Politics of Accommodation*, pp. 103–38.

44. Germann, *Politische Innovation und Verfassungsreform*.

45. Ronald Inglehart and Dusan Sidjanski, "Dimension gauche-droite chez les dirigeants et électeurs suisses," pp. 994–1025.

46. Max Imboden, *Helvetisches Malaise*.

47. Obler et al., *Decision-Making in Smaller Democracies*.

Chapter 2

1. Peter Bachrach and Morton S. Baratz, "Two Faces of Power," pp. 947–52.

2. Richard Crossman, *Inside View*, pp. 47–48.

3. Ibid., p. 50.

4. Patrick Gordon Walker, *The Cabinet*, p. 151.

5. Gary B. Nash, *Quakers and Politics*, p. 165.

6. Sherif El-Hakim, "The Structure and Dynamics of Consensus Decision-Making," pp. 55–71.

7. Ibid., p. 63.

8. Ibid.

9. Ruth A. Gudinas, "Wisconsin Winnebago Political Organization."

10. Personal communication from James W. White, University of North Carolina at Chapel Hill.

11. In a personal letter in November 1978, Kay Lawson offered the following comment on the concept of decision by interpretation: "My observations of the local meetings of the Rally for the Republic of France suggest to me that your concept has wide application, and provides new language for talking about problems many of us have known to exist without knowing exactly how to say so."

12. Based on unsystematic observation at the political science departments of the University of North Carolina at Chapel Hill, Michigan State University at East Lansing, and the Universities of Geneva and Mannheim.

13. George B. Rabinowitz, "Popular Perceptions of Public Figures and Their Implications for Candidate Strategies," p. 3.

14. Franz Lehner and Hans Gerd Schütte, "The Economic Theory of Politics," p. 146.
15. Kenneth R. MacCrimmon and David Messick, "A Framework for Social Motives," p. 99.
16. Mancur Olson, Jr., *The Logic of Collective Action*; James Q. Wilson, *Political Organizations*.
17. See Robert A. Dahl, "Power," pp. 405–15.
18. This definition follows the tradition of Max Weber and Robert A. Dahl. See Dahl, "Power."
19. Olson, *Logic of Collective Action*, esp. p. 65.
20. Wilson, *Political Organizations*, p. 33.
21. Olson, *Logic of Collective Action*, p. 60; Wilson, *Political Organizations*, pp. 33–34.
22. Steven J. Brams, *Game Theory and Politics*, p. 215; William H. Riker, *The Theory of Political Coalitions*, p. 22. Riker is aware that there may be other incentives, but he considers them so unimportant that they can be overlooked.
23. Jürg Steiner, "Why So Few Minimal Winning Coalitions?"
24. Wilson, *Political Organizations*, p. 30.
25. Ibid.
26. Ibid., p. 34.
27. Ibid.
28. Edward J. Lawler and George A. Youngs, Jr., "Coalition Formation," p. 14. See also John M. Orbell and Geoffrey Fougere, "Intra-Party Conflict and the Decay of Ideology," pp. 452–53.
29. Harold D. Lasswell, *On Political Sociology*, p. 197.
30. Wilson, *Political Organizations*, p. 30.
31. Ibid., p. 34.
32. Ibid., p. 35.
33. We omit, for example, erotic incentives, as does Olson, *Logic of Collective Action*, p. 61.
34. Brams, *Game Theory*, pp. 9–11.
35. Formal coalition theory is, of course, interested in this specific subset of all decision situations.
36. Albert O. Hirschman, *Exit, Voice and Loyalty*.
37. Walker, *The Cabinet*, p. 107.

Chapter 3

1. These and other characteristics of Switzerland were discussed in an earlier work, Jürg Steiner, *Amicable Agreement versus Majority Rule*.

2. In a national referendum (24 September 1978) the Jura was accepted as a new canton.

3. Election of May 1970.

4. When we speak of the Free Democratic party, we refer to the section in the German-speaking area of the canton of Bern. The section in the French-speaking area is called the Radical Liberal party.

5. Steiner, *Amicable Agreement.*

Chapter 4

1. Meeting of 7 September 1970.

2. Richard Crossman, *Inside View,* pp. 48, 55.

3. Ibid., p. 48.

4. Meeting of 7 September 1970.

5. Crossman, *Inside View,* pp. 50–51.

6. We have an insufficient number of cases for analysis with more than three proposals on the same conflict dimension.

7. Terry Sullivan, "Voter's Paradox and Logrolling," p. 37.

8. This argument was suggested to us by Arend Lijphart in a personal conversation in November 1976.

Chapter 5

1. For a discussion of the role of intuition in the process of model building, as well as a broader treatment of other important factors in this process, see Ralph M. Stodgill, ed., *The Process of Model-Building in the Behavioral Sciences,* especially the article by William T. Morris, "On the Art of Modeling," pp. 76–93.

2. See, for example, Stodgill, *Process of Model-Building,* p. 81.

3. Ibid., pp. 80–82.

4. Representative examples include John Aldrich and Charles F. Cnudde, "Probing the Bounds of Conventional Wisdom"; J. Johnston, *Econometric Methods;* Lawrence S. Mayer and Philip M. Burgess, "Contrasting Regression and Correlation Analysis with Discriminant Analysis for Investigating Nominal Measures of Behavior."

5. Of course, in the case of dichotomous dummy variables some modification of the interpretations of regression estimates can lead to meaningful analysis. However, when dealing with four nominal categories, it becomes extremely difficult to specify four separate analyses with dummy variables in order to account for all of the possibilities. It is doubtful

that such a procedure can provide any useful insights into the relationships among our variables.

6. For example, see the discussion in Aldrich and Cnudde, "Probing the Bounds of Conventional Wisdom," pp. 575–79.

7. For example, ibid.

8. Ibid., p. 580.

9. Although it is possible to modify the PROBIT technique to deal with nominal level dependent variables, we prefer not to enter into such a discussion here.

10. For example, Kendall's tau$_b$ (unsigned) and lambda (λ_b).

11. See p. 89.

12. Robert H. Dorff, "Employing Simulation Analysis in Decision-Making Theory," pp. 248–52.

13. Ibid., pp. 223–48.

14. Ibid., pp. 15–25.

Chapter 6

1. Robert H. Dorff, "Employing Simulation Analysis in Decision-Making Theory," chaps. 5–8.

2. George Homans, *Social Behavior*.

3. Mancur Olson, *The Logic of Collective Action*.

4. John Fox and Melvin Guyer, "Group Size and Others' Strategy in an N-Person Game," p. 337.

5. Other partitions were performed to cross-check for any significant loss of information. These additional checks revealed no major changes in the data; hence the original partition was employed.

6. A particular difficulty was that some latecomers always sneaked in when the discussion had already begun.

7. For an additional check on the validity of this partition compared to one employing a threshold of one-third, see Dorff, "Employing Simulation Analysis," p. 142.

8. Barbara Hinckley, "Introduction to Special Issue on Coalitions and Time," p. 488. See also Ian Budge, "Consensus Hypotheses and Conflict of Interest."

9. See Dorff, "Employing Simulation Analysis," pp. 116–24.

10. Ibid., pp. 126–29.

11. Ibid., pp. 129–41.

12. An important interaction effect also emerged between size and homogeneity: the effect of homogeneity was most clearly visible when groups were small, whereas it often "washed out" for larger groups.

13. See the series of three articles by Theodore Lowi: "American Business, Public Policy, Case-Studies and Political Theory"; "Decision Making versus Policy Making"; "Four Systems of Policy, Politics, and Choice."

14. George D. Greenberg et al., "Developing Public Policy Theory," p. 1536.

15. David Butler and Donald Stokes, *Political Change in Britain*, p. 177.

16. Dorff, "Employing Simulation Analysis," pp. 156–57.

17. Ibid., pp. 158–59.

18. Murray Edelman, *Politics as Symbolic Action*.

19. See Dorff, "Employing Simulation Analysis," pp. 163–68.

20. See Robert H. Dorff and Jürg Steiner, "Political Decision-Making in Face-to-Face Groups."

21. For example, one might think of the relatively common practice in the United States of evaluating presidential performance after the first one hundred days of a new term.

22. The number of nondecisions remains about the same from the first to the second category. But from our theoretical perspective we think it more important that the combined percentage of nondecision and decision by interpretation decreases monotonically across the three categories.

23. Leonhard Neidhart, *Plebiszit und pluralitäre Demokratie*.

24. In table 6.6, we distinguish among mandatory referenda, optional referenda, and cases in which a referendum is legally precluded. The table contains only 265 cases because the criterion of likelihood of a referendum applies only to issues that must be acted on by parliament; internal party matters are excluded. For the interpretation of the data we must note that the third category contains very few cases.

25. Dorff, "Employing Simulation Analysis," pp. 185–86.

26. In the canton of Bern, as in Switzerland in general, the seats in the cabinet are distributed among all major parties on a proportionate basis. The Bernese cabinet has a fixed number of seats (nine), two of which were held by the Free Democrats during our research period (the Department of Education and the Department of Police and Military Affairs). All cabinet seats have the same formal weight, and each cabinet member is the head of a department. The cabinet meetings are presided over by a chairman, an office that rotates annually among all cabinet members according to seniority. The system often works in such a way that the individual cabinet members are rather autonomous in their departments; thus, the political parties feel particularly responsible for the

departments that are headed by their own representatives. At the same time, all other parties tend to place themselves in a kind of opposition to a department that is not under their direct influence. This peculiar feature of the Swiss political system has given us some basis to test the effects of the party control of government. We distinguished the issues according to the criterion of whether they fell inside or outside the jurisdiction of the two departments headed by Free Democratic cabinet members.

27. Dorff, "Employing Simulation Analysis," pp. 189–90.
28. Ibid., pp. 194–95.
29. Ibid., pp. 197–99.
30. Ibid., pp. 201–2.
31. Ibid., p. 204.
32. Ibid., pp. 218–19.

Chapter 7

1. *Within-group* here refers to the four groups of independent variables: group structure, context, substance, and decision process.

2. These assumptions, although not met per se, can be approximated at a nominal level of measurement if the dependent variable is dichotomous. However, a simple extension to the polytomous case (where the number of groups is greater than two) does not hold. See, for example, John Aldrich and Charles F. Cnudde, "Probing the Bounds of Conventional Wisdom"; Lawrence S. Mayer and Philip M. Burgess, "Contrasting Regression and Correlation Analysis with Discriminant Analysis for Investigating Nominal Measures of Behavior."

3. For just such a formal derivation, see Robert H. Dorff, "Employing Simulation Analysis in Decision-Making Theory," chap. 9.

4. The more general multivariate case holds for any p-dimensional space defined by p independent variables.

5. This assumption is central to the derivation and application of discriminant analysis and implicitly incorporates many other necessary assumptions, such as the presumed equality of covariance matrices across groups. It is also necessary to assume that within each group the observations are normally distributed across the independent variables. For a detailed treatment of these critical assumptions and their general implications for a multivariate discriminant analysis, see Dorff, "Employing Simulation Analysis," pp. 223–48.

6. For a discussion of the OLS model, particularly its geometric characteristics, see Ronald S. Wonnacott and Thomas H. Wonnacott, *Econometrics*.

7. It would be meaningless, of course, to speak of "explained variance" when dealing with a purely categorical dependent variable.

8. Two very useful articles that highlight the central issues of this debate are David K. Hildebrand et al., "Prediction Analysis in Political Research," and Herbert F. Weisberg, "Evaluating Theories of Congressional Roll-Call Voting."

9. See Hildebrand et al., "Prediction Analysis," for a detailed treatment of the utility of the PRE measure in the assessment of a model's predictive capability. In addition, see the book by the same authors, *Prediction Analysis of Cross-Classifications*.

10. Weisberg, "Congressional Roll-Call Voting," p. 555.

11. $(.25) (.124) + (.25) (.206) + (.25) (.305) + (.25) (.365) = .25$. This baseline derives from Laplace's Rule of Insufficient Reason.

12. Hildebrand et al., "Prediction Analysis," p. 520.

13. Perhaps a more familiar alternative is one based on Goodman and Kruskal's Lambda and is discussed in Weisberg, "Congressional Roll-Call Voting," p. 562. The difference in this case lies in the denominator: rather than dividing by the number of correct predictions expected from chance, the complement of this figure is employed (that is, $1 -$ the number expected from chance). For a much more detailed and general derivation of this measure, see Hildebrand et al., "Prediction Analysis," pp. 519–21. Since Dorff originally employed the measure described in the text, we will use it in discussing our results. The selection of the measure is secondary to the comparison of results, however, so it hardly matters which formula one employs.

14. See Hildebrand et al., "Prediction Analysis," p. 509, for a further discussion of this point.

15. Weisberg has argued that one must employ both quantitative (statistical) and qualitative (verisimilitude) criteria in the evaluation of a substantive theory. Since statistical criteria alone are often indeterminate in the choice among competing models, the degree to which a model actually corresponds to the processes at work in the real world phenomenon being investigated (verisimilitude) may provide the relevant basis for deciding which model is best. See Weisberg, "Congressional Roll-Call Analysis." As we noted in chapter 5, this is one strong reason for employing simulation analysis: it allows us to incorporate much of the dynamic flow process that we believe characterizes many decision-making situations.

16. SAS contains an option for performing this test, whereas SPSS has not yet implemented this option. The test itself is a simple chi-square based on the treatment in M. G. Kendall and A. Stuart, *The Advanced Theory of Statistics*, vol. 3.

17. See Dorff, "Employing Simulation Analysis," pp. 242–48.

18. Ibid., pp. 129–41.

19. This highlights the difficulty in trying to press the analysis too far. Since this discriminant function serves primarily to distinguish amicable agreement from nondecision, we are not really able to break down our four decision modes and examine each of them in detail. For the most part we are better off trying to concentrate on the groups most clearly distinguished by the function.

20. For the original analyses, see Dorff, "Employing Simulation Analysis," pp. 116–24.

21. The important point to keep in mind is that with the second discriminant function we are distinguishing primarily between majority decision and nondecision, which is not precisely the same as the first function. And, as discussed in this section, the second function picks up information not picked up by the first, and so on. As a result, such seeming contradictions are quite likely to emerge, and we should not attach undue significance to them.

22. For the original analysis, see Dorff, "Employing Simulation Analysis," pp. 129–41.

23. Thirty cases are not included in the classification procedure because of missing values on some of the variables. In both classification procedures, prior probabilities were set equal.

24. Even when we employ the modal category (36.5) as the baseline, our improvement is still 52.1 percent.

25. For a discussion of this assumption and the implications of relaxing it for a discriminant analysis, see Dorff, "Employing Simulation Analysis," pp. 242–48.

26. Ibid., pp. 242–48.

27. To examine the degree to which this discriminant analysis overstates the true model's classificatory potential, we conducted a split half-sample analysis for both the pooled and unpooled versions. In the following table we report the overall classification results for the calibration subset on which the discriminant functions were calculated (A) and the test subset (B), the observations of which were classified according to the parameters estimated on A.

Split Half-Sample Discriminant Analysis

	Pooled	Unpooled
A	62.7%	93.6%
B	41.1%	43.5%

Both pairs of results indicate that to a certain extent the overall classification results are inflated as a consequence of being maximized to this specific set of data. This test indicates that, particularly for the unpooled version, we should not expect the true model to achieve the 77 percent classification rate discussed in the text. Although speculative, our suggestion is that the actual successful classification results for the discriminant analysis fall somewhere between 41.1 and 62.7 percent. Consequently, this reinforces our decision to use the pooled results in assessing the degree to which our simulation is successful.

28. This is also an indication that we should seriously reconsider the nature of the number of governmental functions variable. We will return to this in the next chapter when we outline the parameters of the simulation.

29. We were also able to verify that by reducing our total number of independent variables to twenty (the twenty most important ones), we were able to classify virtually the same 55 percent of the cases correctly. This reinforces our estimation of the stability of the structure tapped by discriminant analysis.

Chapter 8

1. See Robert H. Dorff, "Employing Simulation Analysis in Decision-Making Theory," pp. 127–29.

2. Ibid., p. 137.

3. Ibid., p. 138.

4. Because of the institutionalized system of amicable agreement, the sharing of power by the Swiss parties makes a distinction between party control and opposition control somewhat arbitrary. See, for example, Jürg Steiner, *Amicable Agreement versus Majority Rule*.

5. Dorff, "Employing Simulation Analysis," pp. 194–95.

6. We should note, however, that the number of proposals will be implicitly included in the simulation as a component of the origin of the proposals.

7. We were forced to combine the variables because of the high degree of collinearity between the two indicators. Otherwise, this collinearity would seriously confound the interpretation of the results.

8. Whereas this redundancy would make linear estimations potentially biased and unstable, we do not labor under the same mathematical constraints when we employ our simulation. Consequently, two variables that are highly correlated can nevertheless provide useful information: if both are present, this could be a sign of a potentially useful interaction effect.

9. Of course, it is always possible for people to leave once the meeting has begun, so that from a technical point of view even these variables will not remain perfectly constant. However, this should not detract from the argument we wish to make concerning the approximate hierarchy among our four sets of independent variables.

10. A complete discussion of the hypotheses and predictions can be found in Dorff, "Employing Simulation Analysis," pp. 306–34.

11. David K. Hildebrand et al., "Prediction Analysis in Political Research," p. 516.

12. See, for example, Herbert F. Weisberg, "Evaluating Theories of Congressional Roll-Call Voting," and Hildebrand et al., "Prediction Analysis."

13. A close examination of the flow chart will reveal that certain logically possible paths do not appear in it. Because the chart was so large and complicated, we decided to exclude those combinations for which we had no observed cases in order to make the chart more comprehensible. For a more general simulation these possibilities would have to be reincorporated.

14. "Predominantly" is operationalized as "greater than 50 percent." See Dorff, "Employing Simulation Analysis," p. 111, and the earlier treatment in chapter 6 of this book.

15. We noted in chapter 6 that decision by interpretation may become more frequent in large groups in which high-status participants occupy leadership positions.

16. These indeterminate cases posed an additional problem for the evaluation of results. The question was how to treat them in calculating an overall rate of successful prediction, that is, as successes or as failures. Although one might argue that we successfully predicted their unpredictability, we felt that this interpretation of success was too loose and unstructured. At the same time we felt that counting these cases as incorrect predictions would inappropriately penalize our prediction rate. Therefore, we decided to treat them as a distinct category and simply to exclude them from the calculation of the success rate.

17. Dorff, "Employing Simulation Analysis," pp. 306–34.

18. For these 25 indeterminate cases it is interesting to note the observed distribution of the decision modes:

majority decision   = 8
amicable agreement   = 1
nondecision   = 8
decision by interpretation = 8

Obviously, there is a strong tendency for amicable agreement not to occur. At the same time, the observed frequencies for the three remaining modes of decision-making are the same. Indeterminate seems a wholly appropriate label for this category of decision-making situations.

Chapter 9

1. For this and other distinctions among political parties see James Q. Wilson, *Political Organizations*, pp. 95–118.
2. Arend Lijphart, *Democracy in Plural Societies*.
3. Ibid., pp. 118–19.
4. Ibid., p. 129.
5. Ibid., p. 134.
6. Ibid., pp. 152–53.

Chapter 10

1. For an interesting approach to developing a system of values, see Duncan MacRae, Jr., *The Social Function of Social Science*. For a critique of the book, see Jürg Steiner, "Die soziale Funktion der Sozialwissenschaften."
2. Ralf Dahrendorf, *Class and Class Conflict in Industrial Society*; Lewis Coser, *The Functions of Social Conflict*.
3. Johan Galtung, "Violence, Peace and Peace Research," pp. 167–92.
4. See Charles Lewis Taylor and Michael C. Hudson, *World Handbook of Political and Social Indicators*.
5. Karl Popper, *The Open Society and Its Enemies*.
6. Raimund Germann, *Politische Innovation und Verfassungsreform*.
7. Samuel A. Kirkpatrick et al., "The Process of Political Decision-Making in Groups," p. 50.
8. Arend Lijphart, *Democracy in Plural Societies*, p. 51.
9. Lester G. Seligman, "Political Elites Reconsidered," pp. 299–314.
10. Murray Edelman, *Politics as Symbolic Action*.

11. Lijphart, *Democracy*, p. 51.

12. Some interaction effect might also occur between the levels of innovation and participation, but it is controversial what this effect might be. Huntington, for example, argues against the common wisdom when he hypothesizes that "innovation is easier when substantial portions of the population are indifferent" (Samuel P. Huntington, "Postindustrial Politics," p. 177).

13. Max Imboden, *Helvetisches Malaise*.

14. Albert O. Hirschman, *Exit, Voice and Loyalty*.

15. Lijphart, *Democracy*, p. 165.

16. Karl W. Deutsch, *Die Schweiz als ein paradigmatischer Fall politischer Integration*.

17. Karl W. Deutsch, *The Nerves of Government*.

Appendix Notes

1. Peter Bachrach and Morton S. Baratz, "Two Faces of Power," pp. 947–52.

2. Peter Bachrach and Morton S. Baratz, "Power and Its Two Faces Revisited," pp. 900–901.

3. Ibid., p. 900.

4. A good summary of this discussion can be found in Door C. van der Eijk and W. J. P. Kok, "Nondecisions Reconsidered," pp. 277–301.

5. Similar distinctions are made by Eijk and Kok, "Nondecisions Reconsidered."

6. Bachrach and Baratz, "Power and Its Two Faces Revisited," p. 901.

7. For these informal gatherings the same method of observation was used as was used for the small formal meetings (see chapter 3).

Bibliography

Aldrich, John, and Cnudde, Charles F. "Probing the Bounds of Conventional Wisdom: A Comparison of Regression, Probit, and Discriminant Analysis." *American Journal of Political Science* 19 (August 1975): 571–608.

Almond, Gabriel A.; Flanagan, Scott C.; and Mundt, Robert J., eds. *Crisis, Choice and Change: Historical Studies of Political Development*. Boston: Little, Brown and Company, 1973.

Bachrach, Peter, and Baratz, Morton S. "Power and Its Two Faces Revisited: Reply to Geoffrey Debnam." *American Political Science Review* 69 (September 1975): 900–901.

——. "Two Faces of Power." *American Political Science Review* 56 (December 1962): 947–52.

Barry, Brian. "Political Accommodation and Consociational Democracy." *British Journal of Political Science* 5 (October 1975): 477–505.

——, ed. *Power and Political Theory: Some European Perspectives*. New York: John Wiley and Sons, 1976.

Bluhm, William T. *Building an Austrian Nation: The Political Integration of a Western State*. New Haven: Yale University Press, 1973.

Bodzenta, Erich, ed. *Die österreichische Gesellschaft*. Vienna: Springer Verlag, 1972.

Bodzenta, Erich, and Freytag, Norbert. "Soziale Ungleichheit." In *Die österreichische Gesellschaft*, edited by Erich Bodzenta. Vienna: Springer Verlag, 1972.

Brams, Steven J. *Game Theory and Politics*. New York: The Free Press, 1975.

Budge, Ian. "Consensus Hypotheses and Conflict of Interest: An Attempt at Theory Integration." *British Journal of Political Science* 3 (January 1973): 73–98.

Butler, David, and Stokes, Donald. *Political Change in Britain*. College Edition. New York: St. Martin's Press, 1971.

227

Coser, Lewis. *The Functions of Social Conflict*. New York: The Free Press, 1956.

Crossman, Richard. *Inside View*. London: Jonathan Cape, 1972.

Daalder, Hans. "The Consociational Democracy Theme." *World Politics* 26 (July 1974): 604–21.

Dahl, Robert A. "Power." *International Encyclopedia of the Social Sciences*. Edited by David L. Sills. Vol. 12. New York: Macmillan and The Free Press, 1968.

Dahrendorf, Ralf. *Class and Class Conflict in Industrial Society*. Stanford: Stanford University Press, 1959.

Deutsch, Karl W. *Die Schweiz als ein paradigmatischer Fall politischer Integration*. Bern: Paul Haupt, 1976.

———. *The Nerves of Government*. Glencoe, Ill.: Free Press, 1963.

Dorff, Robert H. "Employing Simulation Analysis in Decision-Making Theory." Ph.D. dissertation, University of North Carolina, Chapel Hill, 1978.

Dorff, Robert H., and Steiner, Jürg. "Political Decision-Making in Face-to-Face Groups." Unpublished manuscript, 1979.

Dunn, James A., Jr. "Consociational Democracy and Language Conflict: A Comparison of the Belgian and Swiss Experiences." *Comparative Political Studies* 5 (April 1974): 9–16.

Edelman, Murray. *Politics as Symbolic Action*. Chicago: Markham Publishing Company, 1971.

Eijk, Door C. van der, and Kok, W. J. P. "Nondecisions Reconsidered." *Acta Politica* 10 (1975): 277–301.

El-Hakim, Sherif. "The Structure and Dynamics of Consensus Decision-Making." *Man* 13 (March 1978): 55–71.

Fischer, Heinz. "Empirisches zur Arbeit des Nationalrates in der XIII. Gesetzgebungsperiode." *Österreichische Zeitschrift für Politikwissenschaft* 2 (1973): 77–94.

Fox, John, and Guyer, Melvin. "Group Size and Others' Strategy in an N-Person Game." *Journal of Conflict Resolution* 21 (June 1977): 323–39.

Galtung, Johan. "Violence, Peace and Peace Research." *Journal of Peace Research* 6 (1969): 167–92.

Germann, Raimund. *Politische Innovation und Verfassungsreform: Ein Beitrag zur schweizerischen Diskussion über die Totalrevision der Bundesverfassung*. Bern: Verlag Paul Haupt, 1975.

Gilg, Peter. "Parteien und eidgenössische Finanzpolitik." *Schweizerisches Jahrbuch für Politische Wissenschaft* 9 (1969): 41–74.

Glass, Harold E. "Subcultural Segmentation and Consensual Politics:

The Swiss Experience." Ph.D. dissertation, University of North Carolina, Chapel Hill, 1975.

Greenberg, George D.; Miller, Jeffrey A.; Mohr, Lawrence B.; and Valdeck, Bruce C. "Developing Public Policy Theory: Perspectives from Empirical Research." *American Political Science Review* 71 (December 1977): 1532–43.

Gruner, Erich. *Die Parteien in der Schweiz*. Bern: Francke Verlag, 1969.

Gudinas, Ruth A. "Wisconsin Winnebago Political Organization: Structure/Culture Incompatibility and Organizational Effectiveness." Ph.D. dissertation, University of Chicago, 1974.

Heisler, Martin O. "Patterns of European Politics: The European Polity Model." In *Politics in Europe: Structures and Processes in Some Postindustrial Democracies*, edited by Martin O. Heisler. New York: David McKay, 1974.

————, ed. *Politics in Europe: Structures and Processes in Some Postindustrial Democracies*. New York: David McKay, 1974.

Hildebrand, David K.; Laing, James D.; and Rosenthal, Howard. "Prediction Analysis in Political Research." *American Political Science Review* 70 (June 1976): 509–35.

————. *Prediction Analysis of Cross-Classifications*. New York: John Wiley and Sons, 1977.

Hinckley, Barbara. "Introduction to Special Issue on Coalitions and Time." *Behavioral Scientist* 20 (April 1975): 444–50.

Hirschman, Albert O. *Exit, Voice and Loyalty*. Cambridge, Mass.: Harvard University Press, 1970.

Homans, George. *Social Behavior: Its Elementary Forms*. Revised edition. New York: Harcourt, Brace and Jovanovich, 1974.

Hughes, Christopher. *The Parliament of Switzerland*. London: Cassell, 1962.

Huntington, Samuel P. "Postindustrial Politics: How Benign Will It Be?" *Comparative Politics* 6 (January 1974): 163–91.

Imboden, Max. *Helvetisches Malaise*. Zurich: EVZ Verlag, 1964.

Inglehart, Ronald, and Sidjanski, Dusan. "Dimension gauche-droite chez les dirigeants et électeurs suisses." *Revue Française de Science Politique* 24 (October 1974): 944–1025.

Jenny, Beat Alexander. *Interessenpolitik und Demokratie in der Schweiz*. Zurich: Polygraphischer Verlag, 1966.

Johnston, J. *Econometric Methods*. New York: McGraw-Hill, 1963.

Kendall, M. G., and Stuart, A. *The Advanced Theory of Statistics*. Vol. 3. London: Griffen, 1966.

Kerr, Henry H. *Switzerland: Social Cleavages and Partisan Conflict.*
Beverly Hills: Sage Professional Papers, 1974.
Kirkpatrick, Samuel A.; Davis, Dwight F.; and Robertson, Roby D.
"The Process of Political Decision-Making in Groups: Search Behavior
and Choice Shifts." *American Behavioral Scientist* 20 (October 1976):
33–64.
Kneucker, Raoul F. "Austria: An Administrative State. The Role of
Austrian Bureaucracy." *Österreichische Zeitschrift für Politikwissen-
schaft* 2 (1973): 95–127.
Kocher, Gerhard. *Verbandseinfluss auf die Gesetzgebung.* Bern: Francke
Verlag, 1967.
Lasswell, Harold D. *On Political Sociology.* Edited by Dwaine Marvick.
Chicago: University of Chicago Press, 1977.
Lawler, Edward J., and Youngs, George A., Jr. "Coalition Formation:
An Integrative Model." *Sociometry* 38 (March 1975): 1–17.
Lehmbruch, Gerhard. "Das politische System Österreichs in vergleich-
ender Perspektive." *Österreichische Zeitschrift für öffentliches Recht*
22 (1971): 35–56.
———. "Liberal Corporatism and Party Government." *Comparative
Political Studies* 10 (April 1977): 91–126.
———. "A Noncompetitive Pattern of Conflict Management in Liberal
Democracies: The Case of Switzerland, Austria, and Lebanon." In
*Consociational Democracy: Political Accommodation in Segmented So-
cieties*, edited by Kenneth McRae. Toronto: McClelland and Stewart,
Carleton Library, No. 79, 1974.
Lehner, Franz, and Schütte, Hans Gerd. "The Economic Theory of
Politics: Suggestions for Reconsideration." In *Power and Political
Theory: Some European Perspectives*, edited by Brian Barry. New
York: John Wiley and Sons, 1976.
Lijphart, Arend. "Consociational Democracy." *World Politics* 21 (January
1969): 207–25.
———. *Democracy in Plural Societies: A Comparative Exploration.* New
Haven: Yale University Press, 1977.
———. *The Politics of Accommodation: Pluralism and Democracy in the
Netherlands.* 2nd edition. Berkeley: University of California Press,
1975.
Lowi, Theodore. "American Business, Public Policy, Case-Studies and
Political Theory." *World Politics* 16 (July 1964): 677–715.
———. "Decision Making vs. Policy Making: Toward an Antidote for
Technocracy." *Public Administration Review* 30 (May–June 1970):
314–25.

————. "Four Systems of Policy, Politics, and Choice." *Public Adminis-tration Review* 32 (July–August 1972): 298–310.

MacCrimmon, Kenneth R., and Messick, David M. "A Framework for Social Motives." *Behavioral Science* 21 (March 1976): 86–100.

MacRae, Duncan, Jr. *The Social Function of Social Science*. New Haven: Yale University Press, 1976.

Mayer, Lawrence S., and Burgess, Philip M. "Contrasting Regression and Correlation Analysis with Discriminant Analysis for Investigating Nominal Measures of Behavior." *BSL Research Report* 14 (July 1970).

Nash, Gary B. *Quakers and Politics: Pennsylvania, 1681–1726*. Princeton: Princeton University Press, 1968.

Neidhart, Leonhard. *Plebiszit und pluralitäre Demokratie: Eine Analyse der Funktion des schweizerischen Gesetzesreferendums*. Bern: Francke Verlag, 1970.

Nordlinger, Eric A. *Conflict Regulation in Divided Societies*. Harvard University Occasional Papers in International Affairs, No. 29. Cambridge, Mass.: Harvard University Press, 1972.

Oberreuter, Heinrich, ed. *Parlamentarische Opposition: Ein Internationaler Vergleich*. Hamburg: Hoffmann und Campe, 1975.

Obler, Jeffrey; Steiner, Jürg; and Diericks, Guido. *Decision-Making in Smaller Democracies: The Consociational "Burden."* Beverly Hills: Sage Professional Papers in Comparative Politics, 1977.

Olson, Mancur, Jr. *The Logic of Collective Action: Public Goods and the Theory of Groups*. Cambridge, Mass.: Harvard University Press, 1965.

Orbell, John M., and Fougere, Geoffrey. "Intra-Party Conflict and the Decay of Ideology." *Journal of Politics* 35 (May 1973): 439–58.

Panitch, Leo. "The Development of Corporatism in Liberal Democracies." *Comparative Political Studies* 10 (April 1977): 61–90.

Pelinka, Anton. "Repräsentative und plebiszitäre Elemente im österreichischen Regierungssystem." *Österreichische Zeitschrift für Politikwissenschaft* 2 (1973): 33–47.

Popper, Karl. *The Open Society and Its Enemies*. Princeton: Princeton University Press, 1963.

Powell, G. Bingham, Jr. *Social Fragmentation and Political Hostility: An Austrian Case Study*. Stanford: Stanford University Press, 1970.

Rabinowitz, George B. "Popular Perception of Public Figures and Their Implications for Candidate Strategies." Paper presented at the Southern Political Science Association meeting, Atlanta, Georgia, November 1976.

Rae, Douglas W., and Taylor, Michael. *The Analysis of Political Cleavages*. New Haven: Yale University Press, 1970.

Riker, William H. *The Theory of Political Coalitions*. New Haven: Yale University Press, 1962.

Schmitter, Phillippe C. "Modes of Interest Intermediation and Models of Societal Change in Western Europe." *Comparative Political Studies* 10 (April 1977): 7–38.

Seligman, Lester G. "Political Elites Reconsidered." *Comparative Politics* 6 (January 1974): 299–314.

Sidjanski, Dusan; Roig, Charles; Kerr, Henry H.; Inglehart, Ronald; and Nicolas, Jacques. *Les Suisses et la politique*. Bern: Herbert Lang, 1975.

Steiner, Jürg. *Amicable Agreement versus Majority Rule: Conflict Resolution in Switzerland*. Chapel Hill: University of North Carolina Press, 1974.

———. "Die soziale Funktion der Sozialwissenschaften." *Neue Zürcher Zeitung*, 17 February 1977.

———. "Why So Few Minimal Winning Coalitions?" Kleine Studien zur Politischen Wissenschaft, Universität Zürich, No. 56, 1975.

Steiner, Kurt. *Politics in Austria*. Boston: Little, Brown and Company, 1972.

Stiefbold, Rodney P. "Segmented Pluralism and Consociational Democracy: Problems of Political Stability and Change." In *Politics in Europe: Structures and Processes in Some Postindustrial Societies*, edited by Martin O. Heisler. New York: David McKay, 1974.

Stodgill, Ralph M., ed. *The Process of Model-Building in the Behavioral Sciences*. Columbus: Ohio State University Press, 1970.

Sullivan, Terry. "Voter's Paradox and Logrolling: An Initial Framework for Committee Behavior on Appropriations and Ways and Means." *Public Choice* 25 (Spring 1976): 31–44.

Taylor, Charles Lewis, and Hudson, Michael C. *World Handbook of Political and Social Indicators*. 2nd ed. New Haven: Yale University Press, 1972.

Urio, Paolo. *L'Affaire des Mirages: décision administrative et contrôle parlementaire*. Geneva: Editions médecine et hygiène, 1974.

Walker, Patrick Gordon. *The Cabinet*. London: Jonathan Cape, 1970.

Weilenmann, Hermann. *Pax Helvetica oder die Demokratie der kleinen Gruppen*. Erlenbach: Rentsch Verlag, 1951.

Weisberg, Herbert F. "Evaluating Theories of Congressional Roll-Call Voting." *American Journal of Political Science* 32 (August 1978): 554–77.

Welan, Manfried. "Vom Proporz- zum Konkurrenzmodell: Wandlungen der Opposition in Österreich." In *Parlamentarische Opposition: Ein internationaler Vergleich*, edited by Heinrich Oberreuter. Hamburg: Hoffmann und Campe, 1975.

Wilson, James Q. *Political Organizations*. New York: Basic Books, 1973.

Wonnacott, Ronald S., and Wonnacott, Thomas H. *Econometrics*. New York: John Wiley and Sons, 1970.

Zapotoczky, Klaus. "Religion als Grundwert." In *Die österreichische Gesellschaft*, edited by Erich Bodzenta. Vienna: Springer Verlag, 1972.

Index

Age of group members. *See* Structure of decision group

Almond, Gabriel A., 3

Amicable agreement. *See* Modes of decision making

Ausgleich, 5

Austrian great coalition, 12–13

Bachrach, Peter, 23, 56, 203, 204, 206, 207

Baratz, Morton S., 23, 56, 203, 204, 206, 207

Barry, Brian, 4, 9, 177

Bereichskoalition, 13

Bereichsopposition, 13

Bern: characteristics of canton, 43–44; distribution of cabinet seats, 219 (n. 26)

Bivariate contingency tables, 76–77, 79–121

Bluhm, William, 17

Brams, Steven J., 27, 31

Butler, David, 93, 94

Competitive decision making: defined, 4; and consociational decision making, 9–15

Conflict: defined, 51; dimensions of, 51

Conflict dimensions. *See* Conflict

Consociational decision making, 4; facilitating conditions of, 4; preconditions of, 4–5; and immobilism, 5; and the historical context, 5; and competitive decision making, 9–15; and grand coalition, 9; in Switzerland, 9–12; in Austria, 12–13; in the Netherlands, 14; in Belgium, 14; in Northern Ireland, 14, 199; in Cyprus, 14; and innovation, 19–20; and political participation, 19

Consociational democracy, 4

Consociationalism, 4; in Switzerland, 16–17; in Austria, 17–18; in the Netherlands, 18–19. *See also* Consociational theory

Consociational theory, 3–6, 176–78; key features of, 3–5; and subculture, 4; ambiguities of, 5–20; theoretical universe of, 6–8; patterns of decision making, 9–15; problems of causality, 15–20; and hostility, 16; in Italy, 176–77; in Canada, 177; in Israel, 177; in Malaysia, 177

Context of conflict, 36, 148–49, 156–57; and decision modes, 38

—Parliamentary elections, 102–6, 148–49, 153, 156–57; and modes of decision making, 103–6

10; allocation of seats, 10; and
  the "magic formula," 195
Fischer, Heinz, 13
Focus of decision process. *See*
  Decision process
Formality of decision process. *See*
  Decision process
Fox, John, 81
Free Democratic party. *See* Parties
Frequency of interactions. *See*
  Structure of decision group

Germann, Raimund, 19, 20
Greenberg, George D., 93
Guyer, Melvin, 81

Hildebrand, David K., 127, 158
Hinckley, Barbara, 89–90
Hirschman, Albert O., 33, 193
Homans, George, 80, 89
Homogeneity of decision group.
  See Structure of decision group
Hostility: and consociational theory, 16; and modes of decision
  making, 189–93

Imboden, Max, 19
Importance of conflict. *See* Substance of conflict
Informal gatherings, 204–6
Information basis of discussion.
  See Decision process
Inglehart, Ronald, 19
Innovation. *See* Substance of conflict
Interaction effects: defined, 73

Junktim, 5
Jura problem, 45

Kerr, Henry H., 7
Kirkpatrick, Samuel A., 187

Lasswell, Harold D., 28
Latent conflicts, 22, 203; and nondecisions, 203
Lawler, Edward J., 28
Lehmbruch, Gerhard, 4, 5, 13, 15
Lehner, Franz, 26
Lijphart, Arend, 4, 5, 9, 14, 15, 18,
  176, 177, 180, 187
LOGIT, 73, 75
Lowi, Theodore, 93

MacCrimmon, Kenneth R., 26
Majority decision. *See* Modes of
  decision making
Malaise Helvetique, 19, 192
Manifest conflicts, 22
Messick, David M., 26
Methods of data analysis, 69–78;
  general approach, 70; nature of
  problem, 71–74; OLS regression,
  71, 74; PROBIT, 72, 74; LOGIT,
  73, 75; nominal measures of
  association, 75; bivariate contingency tables, 76–77, 79–121;
  multivariate discriminant analysis, 77–78, 122–43; simulation,
  78, 144–70
Methods of data collection, 46–50;
  participant observation, 46–49;
  analysis of documents, 49, 179–
  80; interviews, 50, 180; reliability and validity, 178–81
Modes of decision making: typology of, 23, 55–64; nondecision,
  23, 56, 203–7; formalization of,
  23–24; decision by interpretation, 24, 56–64; majority deci-